THE COMPLETE RAINBOW GUIDE TO OS-9 LEVEL II

Volume I: A Beginners Guide to Windows

By Dale L. Puckett and Peter Dibble

Falsoft, Inc.
Prospect, Kentucky

THE COMPLETE RAINBOW GUIDE TO OS-9 LEVEL II

Volume I: A Beginners Guide to Windows

Editor: Jo Anna Wittman Arnott
Technical Editor: Cray Augsburg
Art Director: Rita Lawrence
Cover Illustration: Tracey Jones

The Rainbow Bookshelf™ books are published by Falsoft, Inc., Lawrence C. Falk, President; James E. Reed, Executive Editor.

First published in 1987.

ISBN: 0-932471-09-9
Library of Congress Catalog Card Number: 85-70113

Printed in the United States of America
1 2 3 4 5 6 7 8 9 10

ACKNOWLEDGMENTS

Sandra Blackthorn
Jody Doyle
Jody Gilbert
Jill Hopkins
Judi Hutchinson
Cynthia L. Jones
Tracey Jones
Angela Kapfhammer
Jutta Kapfhammer
Heidi Maxedon
T. Kevin Nickols
Denise Webb

table of contents

FOREWORD

We at Falsoft are pleased to present *The Complete Rainbow Guide to OS-9 Level II — Volume I: A Beginners Guide to Windows*. We're sure you'll find this book to be quite helpful in your study of the new windowing capabilities of OS-9 Level II on the Color Computer. Dale Puckett and Peter Dibble offer easy-to-understand tutorials and examples for beginner and old pro alike.

The world of the Color Computer is expanding by leaps and bounds, and we're pleased that so many of you turn to Falsoft for your information source. We're pleased because long ago we made a commitment to the CoCo Community to broaden the base of knowledge about our computer and its vast potential. Your response has let us know that we're keeping that promise.

Dale and Peter, authors of *The Complete Rainbow Guide to OS-9* (published in 1985), have repeated their earlier success at making the OS-9 operating system understandable to everyone. This volume focuses on windowing abilities and the incredible power they bring to the Color Computer, and gives some helpful applications, too. Maxwell Mouse and CoCo Cat will be looking over your shoulder throughout the book; we hope you enjoy their antics.

Dale and Peter have included many sample programs that are instructional and useful, too. They will help ease the learning process.

I hope you enjoy this first volume of our two-volume set on OS-9 Level II. It's a pleasure serving the CoCo Community.

Lawrence C. Falk
Publisher

PREFACE

welcome to our second rainbow guide to os-9!

In *The Complete Rainbow Guide to OS-9*, we explained how OS-9 works — inside, as well as on the command line. We gave you the foundation and structure needed to build a stable of OS-9 programming skills. We hope you will continue to learn from it as you use this book to move up to the fascinating windowing environment made possible by Tandy's Color Computer 3 and OS-9 Level II.

A HANDS-ON APPROACH

In this book, *The Complete Rainbow Guide to OS-9 Level II, Volume I: A Beginners Guide to Windows*, we're taking a more relaxed approach. You'll get your hands on the keyboard early. We'll watch over your shoulder as you read some of your first error messages and try to help you understand what they mean. The best way to use this book is with your manual open in front of you for easy reference.

We'll suggest a task you might want to accomplish and then set about finding a way to do it with your OS-9 tool kit. But, we'll also take time out to play in an early chapter. As a matter of fact, we don't plan to let the material get too heavy at all. CoCo Cat and Maxwell Mouse will be looking over your shoulder, too!

We'll be showing you how to do the same job several different ways as we introduce OS-9's versatility. Since BASIC09 is part of the OS-9 Level II package, we'll also introduce you to it! In fact, by the time you reach the end of the book, you will have learned how to program several of the key parts of a *Sidekick*-type desk accessory package using BASIC09.

WHAT DO I HAVE AT MY FINGERTIPS?

If we had to answer that question with only one word, we would scream "power!" But, let's use a few more.

OS-9 is the key you need to unlock the treasure waiting inside your new Color Computer 3. It's the gateway to an ever growing list of application programs that can increase both your productivity at work and your pleasure at play. OS-9 brings you applications that let you crunch numbers in a spreadsheet, build effective databases, draw impressive pictures and communicate with other computers, online databases or bulletin board systems. As you progress through this new OS-9 Level II guide, we'll show you how to set up your system to run several of these applications.

Think of OS-9 as a toolbox full of tools. Just as an apprentice carpenter learns how and when to use a hammer while building a house, you'll learn how and when to use filters and other OS-9 utilities to get your work done.

DO I NEED ADDITIONAL HARDWARE?

We recommend you install 512K of memory soon. Some of the high resolution graphics windows you may be using can take up to 32K bytes each. Since the OS-9 system workspace alone uses 64K of memory, you can see how easy it is to quickly run out of memory on a 128K machine.

We also recommend that you use double-sided disk drives while running OS-9. As we have already noted, the OS-9 toolbox is quite full. It takes two single-sided disks just to hold the system and utility programs. If you only have two drives, that doesn't leave any room for your data files or your own programs. If you can swing it, a hard disk will increase your enjoyment of OS-9 many times.

PROLOG

Microware Systems Corporation's 6809-based OS-9 operating system was first exposed to the consumer market on the Radio Shack Color Computer in October 1983. It created quite a stir. Power-packed and efficient, OS-9 brought a UNIX-like environment to an inexpensive microcomputer for the first time.

In 1987, history repeated itself. The selection of Microware's OS-9 Level II as the operating system for the new Color Computer 3 has already introduced thousands of new users to this powerful operating system.

ABOUT THE AUTHORS

Dale L. Puckett is a free-lance writer and programmer who first learned about bits, bytes and BASIC when he built a "television typewriter" — an SWTPC CT-1024 — in 1975. When the keyboard didn't arrive with his kit, he wired a set of nine slide switches together and put his first message on the screen one byte at a time.

A month later he built an SWTPC 6800 microprocessor with 12K of memory and has been programming ever since. A cassette storage unit wasn't available then, so he often left his computer on for weeks at a time after finishing a long program.

His programs include *DynaSpell, Esther, Help, Lk* and *Readtest*. He also designed and is co-author of *The Speller*, which runs on the IBM PC and Apple II, and *Hayden Speller* on the Macintosh.

Dale is a contributing editor to THE RAINBOW and author of that magazine's monthly column "KISSable OS-9." He serves as the director at large and is a former president of the OS-9 Users Group, an Iowa corporation with members worldwide. He has previously written for *HOT CoCo, InfoWorld, Micro* and *'68 Micro Journal*.

An amateur radio operator (K0HYD) since 1956, Dale has held a first-class radiotelephone operator's license since 1962. He has worked at several radio and television stations in Kansas and New Jersey.

Puckett received a bachelor of science degree from the William Allen White School of Journalism at the University of Kansas in 1966. He also earned a master of arts in management from Webster College at St. Louis, Missouri.

Dale is a lieutenant in the United States Coast Guard and presently serves as the Chief, Internal Information Branch at Coast Guard Headquarters in Washington, D.C. He lives in Rockville, Maryland, with his wife, Esther.

Peter Dibble was born in Waterbury, Connecticut, and received a bachelor of science in chemistry from the University of Connecticut. He has held jobs as an applications programmer, a systems programmer and the assistant director in charge of the University of Rochester Computing Center's user services department. He is presently a graduate student in the University of Rochester computer science department. He has had several OS-9 articles published in THE RAINBOW and, until recently, wrote a monthly column called "OS-9 User Notes" for *'68 Micro Journal*. He also recently served two terms as vice president of the OS-9 Users Group. Peter and his wife, Catherine, live in Honeoye Falls, New York.

ACKNOWLEDGMENTS

We thank Lonnie Falk at Falsoft who first published *The Complete Rainbow Guide to OS-9*; Jo Anna Arnott, our editor, and the entire staff at THE RAINBOW. Without their encouragement and support, this book would have never been published. They demonstrated the faith and patience that let it work.

Dale thanks his wife, Esther Puckett, who patiently watched while he searched for words that wouldn't come, edited those that didn't work and tried every example in the book. She deserves much of the credit for his success.

Special thanks go to Brian Lantz who contributed the `Alarm` procedure in Chapter 8.

CHAPTER 1

let's get started

Welcome to the exciting world of computing. The Color Computer 3 and OS-9 Level II will let you do many jobs today that, a dozen years ago, required a mainframe computer.

We hope that when you finish this book, you will be able to use your Color Computer to automate a number of the nasty tasks that eat up your free time. We also hope you pick up enough confidence with OS-9 that you will start to use it to find solutions to a wide range of problems.

First, put your mind at ease. Forget that OS-9 is an operating system! That term sounds too scary. Rather, think of OS-9 as a giant toolbox full of interesting gadgets that can help you get your work done. If you would rather, think of it as a giant toy box full of toys that just happen to be tools too.

Think of yourself as the producer. You set the stage (bought the computer) and hired the actors (the applications programs). This makes you the boss. Think of OS-9 as the director. As you read this book, you will learn to take charge of OS-9. It will then direct your applications programs to make sure they run in the right windows at the right time. Working together, you should be able to stage quite a show. You may even make beautiful music together.

Enough commercial — let's dive in!

WHAT DO I NEED TO START OS-9?

You can run OS-9 Level II on any Color Computer 3 equipped with one disk drive and 128K of memory. You'll only be able to open one graphics window in a 128K Color Computer 3.

Ideally, then, you will find smoother sailing if you start your OS-9 experience with a Color Computer 3 loaded with 512K of memory and two disk drives. You'll also want a printer to capture a hard copy of your work, and you will most likely want to connect a hardware serial port to your Color Computer eventually. This will let you use it to communicate with other computers. A serial port can also be used to connect your computer to a modem, which will let you reach large commercial database systems where you can make airline reservations, read the latest news or find just about any fact you can imagine.

To connect this external hardware, you need to use the Color Computer Multi-Pak Interface. It has four slots that let you plug in a disk controller and three other hardware devices — a serial communications port, Modem Pak and hard disk controller perhaps.

Let's talk about disk drives for a moment. Since OS-9 is essentially a disk-based operating system — don't worry, we won't mention that scary phrase too many times — you will find that it stores most of its tools on a floppy disk. You'll know this soon because, when you are running OS-9, your disk drives will seem like they are running all the time.

If you haven't already purchased your disk drives, you should stop now and consider two things. Because OS-9 needs to get information from your disks frequently, you'll want them to be fast. And since OS-9 itself fills two single-sided floppy disks, you will most likely want to use double-sided or maybe even double-sided, quad-density drives. Remember, you also need to have room to store your data.

FIRST, TURN EVERYTHING ON

We can't put it off any longer. It's time to get your feet wet. Hook up your Color Computer, Multi-Pak Interface, disk drives and any other hardware you want to use.

Follow the directions that came with your Color Computer and Multi-Pak Interface. Additionally, you'll want to make sure that the floppy disk controller cartridge is plugged into Slot 4 of the Multi-Pak Interface. It will not work in the other three slots.

Most veteran OS-9 users plug their RS-232 Pak into Slot 1 and their Modem Pak in Slot 2. A hard disk controller or RAM disk cartridge often fills Slot 3.

IT'S TIME TO BOOT OS-9

No, don't kick your CoCo! The word "boot" is short for bootstrap — a buzzword that describes a process where a very short and stupid program loads another program that's a little smarter. That program then loads another program that's even more intelligent. The process continues until the desired program is completely loaded in your computer's memory. That program then runs and takes control of the computer. So when we say we are going to "boot" OS-9, we mean we are going to load it and get it running on your Color Computer.

If you have finished hooking up all of your hardware, go ahead and turn it on. Follow the order suggested in the manuals that came with your hardware. We usually turn on our monitor first. Then, our disk drives, Multi-Pak Interface and Color Computer in that order.

THE BIG MOMENT IS HERE

When you turn on your Color Computer, it should print an OK message on your screen, most likely in black letters on a green screen. If so, take the disk labeled "OS-9 Level Two Operating System — System Master" out of its sleeve. Check to make sure that a write-protect tab covers the square notch along the side of the disk. If so, insert the disk in Drive 0. Close the door to your disk drive, turn to your keyboard, type `DOS` and press ENTER.

If you have hooked up everything properly, your disk drives should begin to spin and you'll soon see the message `OS9 BOOT` in the middle of your Color Computer's screen. The drives will continue to spin, and you'll hear the heads move back and forth along the surface of the floppy disk.

A few seconds later, you'll see a new message on your screen:

```
OS-9 LEVEL TWO VR. 02.00.01
COPYRIGHT 1986 BY
MICROWARE SYSTEMS CORP.
LICENSED TO TANDY CORP.
ALL RIGHTS RESERVED

* Welcome to OS-9 LEVEL 2 *
* on the Color Computer 3 *
```

```
  yy/mm/dd hh:mm:ss
Time?
```

OS-9 is asking you to tell it the time and date. You can type it like this:

```
87/04/15 23:59:59
```

Did you make it to the post office in time to get your income tax in the mail? Next year you will know how to set up your Color Computer to use an OS-9 database or spreadsheet program. Tax preparation will go much easier, and you may even have your refund check by the time the deadline rolls around.

If you didn't make it on time, you probably aren't in the mood to fool around typing the slashes and the colons. Those keys are a pain to touch-type. OS-9 lets you do it the easy way:

```
87 04 16 00 01 15
```

Better late than never! And, it's easier this way. Your disk drive should spin again and, in a second or two, more information will appear on your screen.

```
April 16, 1987          00:01:15
Shell
OS9:
```

The `OS9:` message is a prompt that means your Color Computer is waiting for you to give it a command. It will be quite happy to sit there and wait until you are ready for your next step, so take your time. Take a deep breath and enjoy your accomplishment.

BUT, I DON'T CARE ABOUT THE TIME

You can skip typing the two-digit number representing the seconds field if you like. That field is optional. In fact, the system will even let you answer the `Time ?` prompt by simply pressing ENTER. You'll see something like:

```
          ??? 00, 1900 00:00:00
Shell
OS9:
```

Don't be tempted. You may not care what time it is, but your computer needs to know. Besides, all those zeros are certainly not aesthetically pleasing.

After you learn the basics, you'll start running a lot of applications programs that create data files for you. When OS-9 saves these files, it enters the date and time the file was created into the directory. It also keeps track of the date and time when the file was last modified. If you give your system a bogus time, you could confuse one of your applications programs that depends on the date and time to make a delete/not delete decision. You could be sorry. Or, you could easily become confused yourself and delete the wrong file. It's not worth skipping a few keystrokes.

Many modern software developers are acutely aware of this need. They use a program named *Make* that looks at the date and time stamp on a file to determine which source code files need to be recompiled to build an applications program. Many times only one module in a program needs to be recompiled. This means *Make* needs only recompile one module. It merely links the rest of the modules with the new module. This saves the programmer a lot of time.

HOW TO PREPARE A WORKING SYSTEM DISK

When you started OS-9 Level II this time, you used your original system master disk. This disk is precious and must be saved from accidental damage. It's the only one you have. From now on you will want to work with a copy of the system master disk when you boot OS-9. Working with a copy is a cheap price to pay for insurance.

But you say you don't have a working system disk. Let's see if we can solve that problem.

Before you can store OS-9 programs or data on a new disk, you must format that disk. Formatting is a process that writes a fixed pattern of information on every sector of a disk. The OS-9 tool or utility that does this job for you is named `Format`.

While `Format` works, it checks your disk to verify that every sector on the disk is good. If it finds a bad sector, it simply removes that sector from an allocation map on the disk. If a sector is not recorded in this map, OS-9 does not know that it exists.

You need to know this for two reasons. First, this verification process protects you from the bad data you might read from that bad sector. If you don't write to the bad sector, you won't have to worry about reading bad data from it. And OS-9 won't write anything on it if it doesn't know the sector exists.

The second reason you need to know that `Format` checks the integrity of your disks is related to `Backup`, the next OS-9 tool or utility you will run in the process of making a copy of your OS-9 system master disk.

`Backup` can only make a copy of a disk on another disk that is formatted in exactly the same way. This means that if `Format` finds three bad sectors while it's preparing your disk and writes them out of the allocation map, the two disks will not be identical.

One will be formatted with $276 sectors. The other will have only $273 sectors. Backup will not let you make a copy on this $273-sector disk. But don't fret, you wouldn't want it to anyway.

However, you may feel free to go ahead and store your data on this new $273 sector disk. The $273 sectors that Format verified and placed in the map are fine. Only the three sectors that are now forgotten are bad.

Our formatting sequence here assumes that you have two disk drives. Your original system master disk is still mounted in Drive /d0. Notice that, when we are running OS-9, we call disk Drive 0 /d0. That's the name OS-9 knows that drive by, and if we tell it to do something to a disk on /d0, OS-9 will go straight to Drive 0. It won't even stop to collect $200.

It's time now to take a new disk from the box and place it in Drive /d1. Shut the door on the drive and we'll begin. Type:

```
format /d1
```

and press ENTER. You will see:

```
COLOR COMPUTER FORMATTER
Formatting drive /d1
y (yes) or n (no)
Ready?
```

Go ahead and answer OS-9's prompt with a 'Y' and in a few seconds you'll hear disk drive /d1 start to spin. You'll also hear a distinct clicking sound as your drive steps from track to track. If you count the clicks, you'll hear exactly 35 — the number of tracks you are formatting. In a few seconds the drive will stop and you'll see a new message on your screen:

```
Disk name:
```

Answer with:

```
OS-9 System Disk
```

and press ENTER. OS-9 will immediately begin to verify the data on each track. It will count the tracks and print the number of each sector in Hex (hexadecimal notation) on your screen as it goes. It should look something like this:

```
000  001  002  003  004  005  006  007
008  009  00A  00B  00C  00D  00E  00F

010  011  012  013  014  015  016  017
018  019  01A  01B  01C  01D  01E  01F

020  021  022

Number of good sectors: $000276
```

Did you know that $022 in Hex notation is the same as 34 in decimal notation? The `Format` tool set up tracks 0 through 22 in Hex, or 0 through 34 in decimal. This means the system formatted the disk for 35 tracks. If you divide 276 Hex — which is 630 decimal — by 35, you will know how many sectors OS-9 formats on each track. It had better be 18.

We'll trust you to do your homework. If you don't believe that 276 Hex is the same as 630 decimal, type:

```
free /d1
```

and press ENTER. You should get an answer that looks like this:

```
"OS-9 System Disk" created on: 8
7/04/16
Capacity: 630 sectors (1-sector
clusters)
620 Free sectors, largest block
620 sectors
```

You're moving right along! You have successfully run two OS-9 tools, `Format` and `Free`. And you have a freshly formatted OS-9 disk to prove it. You ran one tool because you needed it to help you make a new system disk. You ran the other for fun. Let's go for number three.

NOW, TO FINISH THE JOB

If your success is contagious and you feel like formatting the rest of the disks in the box, let us show you a trick. If not, stand by to make that copy of your system master disk.

If you decide to format the rest of the disks, you will be running the OS-9 `Format` utility command (remember, that's just two long words that take the place of a four-letter word: tool) nine more times.

Each time you run `Format`, OS-9 will need to go to your system master disk in Drive /d0, load it into memory and then run it. Since it takes quite a bit of time to load a tool from a floppy disk, you might want to try this. Type:

```
load format
```

and press ENTER.

Now, when you place your new disk in Drive /d1 and type `format /d1`, you'll notice that `Format` goes to work instantly. However, if you take this course of action, we have a "gotcha" for you.

Remember the old saying, "what goes up must come down"? Well, it works the same way here. Everything that is loaded must eventually be unloaded. After you have finished formatting the remaining nine disks (gee, you're ambitious), type:

```
unlink format
```

and press ENTER.

That should do the job nicely. If you're wondering why you must unlink a tool after you use it, consider this. Each time you load a tool, you are using at least 8,000 bytes of memory in your Color Computer. That's not much, but if you get sloppy and leave a dozen of these programs laying fallow in memory, you will be wasting 8 x 12 or 96K of memory. You couldn't be that slothful in a 128K machine if you wanted to. There wouldn't be enough memory to go around. Trust us; unlinking your tools after you're through with them is simply a very good habit to get into. Just think of it as putting your tools back into the tool box.

ON TO THE BACKUP

Now, let's back up that disk. Leave your original OS-9 system master disk in Drive /d0. Take the freshly formatted OS-9 disk you made and place it in Drive /d1. Close the door and type:

```
backup #56K
```

and press ENTER. You'll see the following messages. (We typed the Ys and you should too.)

```
Ready to backup from /d0 to /d1?: y
OS-9 System Disk is being scratched
Ok ?: y
Sectors copied: $0276
Verify pass
Sectors verified: $0276
OS9:
```

Notice that since you didn't tell it which drive you wanted to back up, OS-9 decided that you wanted to back up the floppy disk in Drive /d0 onto the floppy disk in Drive /d1. This is one of the many defaults that makes OS-9 easy to use. By the way, "scratched," as used above, means "written to."

Notice also that since we knew we were using a 512K Color Computer and knew that OS-9 lets each tool use up to 64K of memory while it's running, we decided to let Backup use 56K of memory to do its job. If you subtract 8K (the amount of memory required to load the Backup module) from 64K, the maximum space OS-9 allows you to use, you get 56K. We used every last drop.

Many new users of OS-9 will be using only one disk drive. Since OS-9 is much easier to work with on a system that has two drives, this book will assume that the reader is using such a system. However, to make things easier for those with only one drive, we will show you how to format a disk and back it up on a one-drive system.

In general, you will follow the directions for a two-drive system, but there will be some important differences. When you booted OS-9, several commands (tools) were loaded into memory. Some were not, however. Two important examples of commands that are not loaded into memory are the `Format` and `Backup` tools. Now, if you were to place a blank disk in your disk drive and enter the `Format` command, OS-9 would give you an error message. This is because OS-9 tried to load the `Format` command from the system disk which was mounted in the drive. Since the disk in the drive is blank, OS-9 will be unable to find the `Format` tool and will, therefore, return an error. So what do we do?

The best thing to do is manually load the tools we need into memory. Before replacing the system disk in the drive with the blank disk to be formatted, enter:

```
load format
```

This will load the `Format` tool into memory and eliminate the need for OS-9 to load it from the disk during the formatting process. Now, place the blank disk in the drive and enter:

```
format /d0
```

The output you see on the screen will be almost the same as described earlier in the text. The only difference is that you are formatting a disk in Drive 0 instead of Drive 1. You will also answer the prompts in the same manner.

When OS-9 has finished formatting your disk, remove it from the drive and replace it with the System Master again. Since we will start the backup process with this disk in the drive, we will not need to load the `Backup` tool into memory first. Just enter:

```
backup s /d0 /d0 #48K
```

This line tells OS-9 you want it to perform a single-drive backup of the disk mounted in Drive 0 to another disk you will put in Drive 0. It also tells OS-9 to reserve 48K of memory for the backup process. This is important since you will be alternately switching the System Master Disk in Drive 0 for the disk we just formatted. The more memory we can reserve for this process, the fewer times we will have to "swap" these two disks.

Before answering 'Y' to the

```
Ready to backup from /d0 to /d0?:
```

prompt, remove the System Master Disk and place your freshly formatted disk in Drive 0. After you answer with a 'Y', you will see:

```
Ready Destination, hit a key:
```

As OS-9 proceeds with the disk backup, you will be prompted like this to alternately place the source and destination disks in the drive. Just remember that, in this case, the source disk is your OS-9 System Master and the destination disk is our freshly formatted disk. When you have inserted your formatted disk and pressed a key, you will see:

```
OS-9 System Disk
is being scratched
OK?:
```

"Scratched" means written to. Answer 'Y' and follow the prompts. When the backup is completed, you will see:

```
Sectors copied: $0276
Verify pass
Sectors verified: $ 276
```

WHY USE 56K?

If you're wondering why you would want to use the maximum amount of memory when you copy data from one disk to another, consider this. Backup is 1,202 bytes long. If you do not ask it to use a large amount of memory to transfer your data, it will use only 4,688 bytes.

How do we know this? We read it off the screen of our monitor. We used another OS-9 tool to find out. You can too. With your system master disk still mounted in Drive /d0, type:

```
ident  -x  backup
```

and press ENTER. You'll see:

```
Header for:         Backup
Module Size:        $04B2          #1202
Module CRC:         $129C2B        (Good)
Hdr parity:         $9E
Exec. off:          $0176          #374
Data size:          $1250          #4688
Edition:            $08            #8
Ty/La At/Rv:        $11     $81
Prog mod, 6809 obj, re-en R/O
```

This report tells us that Backup will read slightly more than 4,000 bytes of data from the floppy disk in Drive /d0 into memory and then stop and write those bytes from memory onto the disk in /d1. It will repeat this sequence until it copies the entire 161,000 bytes stored on the disk in /d0. When you watch your drives running during an operation like this, you'll notice that the red lights on the two drives go on and off, back and forth, continuously. All of this disk action takes time.

On the other hand, when you tell OS-9 that you want Backup to use 56K of memory, you'll notice that the red lights only go on and off three times each. The Backup operation takes a lot less time.

WHEN YOU MAKE A MISTAKE

Every once in a while you'll make a mistake and receive an error message. When you do, OS-9 lets you know with an error message. Let's make a few mistakes together now so we can show you how to tell what went wrong.

Now that you have a working system disk, take out your original system master disk and store it somewhere a long distance from your computer. Put the working system disk in Drive /d0. Always use your working system disk when you boot and run OS-9. Type:

```
dir
```

and press ENTER. You'll see a list of the directories and files stored on your system disk. Now type:

```
di
```

and press ENTER. You'll see:

```
ERROR #216
```

Our mistake is obvious. We must have been in a hurry and we pressed the ENTER key before we typed the 'r' in dir. You probably noticed that after you typed the first command, your drives quietly went to the directory track on the disk and you received your report rather quickly. However, the second time, when you typed di, your drives most likely came on and ran awhile, making a bit of noise as they searched the directory for a file that didn't exist on the disk.

As you may have already guessed, Error #216 is Pathname Not Found. Let's let OS-9 show you. Type:

```
error 216
```

OS-9 should return with:

```
216 - Path Name Not Found
```

Now you know how to get an English-language error message from OS-9. After a few hours you will have memorized a handful of the common error messages. You may never remember the rest. But it doesn't matter. OS-9 always reports an error number when something goes wrong. And you can always use the "error" tool above to find out what happened. Just change the error to match the number OS-9 reports each time you receive an error report.

If you're wondering where OS-9 finds the English-language error messages it prints, type:

```
dir sys
```

You'll see a listing of all the files stored in the SYS directory of your working system disk. In that listing — in fact it's the first file — you'll see a file named errmsg. Therein lie the magic answers.

In our example, the reason the pathname was not found is obvious. We typed the name of a file that didn't exist. Sometimes, however, your error may transcend the common typo.

For example, if you had typed dir properly, but had put the wrong disk in the drive, you would have received the same error message (if that disk did not contain a file named dir). Likewise, the same error message would have been printed on your screen if you had accidentally set your current execution directory to a directory that did not contain a file named dir — even though there was a copy somewhere else on the disk.

Sometimes finding out what caused an error can be like solving a good mystery. It's a challenge but it can also be fun. Especially when you start to understand what makes OS-9 tick. Hopefully, you'll have that edge when you finish this book. If not, we invite you to consult *The Complete Rainbow Guide to OS-9* and *The Basic09 Tour Guide* for additional help.

WHAT IF I CHANGE MY MIND WHILE TYPING?

The best place to notice a typo is before you press ENTER. If you are lucky enough to notice your mistake then, OS-9 gives you a way to fix your mistakes quickly.

If you press the back arrow key while typing a command line, you will notice that OS-9 backs up the cursor and deletes the character behind it. It does the same thing if you hold down the key marked CTRL and press the H key at the same time. Using one of these two methods, you can easily back up to your mistake and retype the rest of the line. It sure beats retyping the whole thing.

Every once in a while, you'll mess up the line beyond repair. If this happens, hold down the SHIFT and press the back arrow. You'll see the entire line disappear in front of your eyes. If you prefer to use the CTRL key, hold it down and press the X key. You'll get the same result. Try both of these editing keys several times until you get the hang of it. It will save you a lot of time in the long run.

If you can't seem to make the connection between CTRL-X and deleting a line, try to think in terms of crossing, or "X-ing," something out on a piece of paper. It will help you remember the key combination.

ARE THERE ANY SHORTCUTS?

Glad you asked! OS-9 has many special keys that can help you get your work done faster. For example, there are keys that will repeat your last command line, interrupt a program, quit a program and another key that causes your Color Computer to wait on you.

The "wait" key does just what its name implies. It stops the text from scrolling on your screen until you tell it to start again by pressing any other key. This gives you a way to stop and study several sentences in the middle of a long text file while you are listing it to your screen.

To tell your Color Computer 3 to wait, hold down the CTRL key on your keyboard and press the W key. When you are ready to list the rest of your file, press any key to tell OS-9 to continue.

If you have used OS-9's `Tmode` tool to tell OS-9 to pause, it will automatically stop scrolling when it has sent out enough lines to fill the window you are using. As long as the lines in your file are shorter than the width of your window, this automatic pause feature works perfectly. However, if you have extra long lines in your file, you may need to stop the text from scrolling with the CTRL-W key combination.

THE REPEAT KEY

You can use the OS-9 "repeat" key to increase your productivity and save your finger tips. You'll love it. To give it a try, hold down the CTRL key and press the letter A.

Every time you press CTRL-A, your last command line will magically reappear. You'll find the CTRL-A key combination is really handy when you need to run the same command line several times. To run the command again, you need only press ENTER. Let's give it a try! Type `dir` and press ENTER. You should see a listing of the contents of your current data directory. Now press CTRL-A and ENTER. Your trusty Color Computer 3 should list the directory again. If you think the repeat key is neat with a three-letter command, wait until you use it with a pathlist 72 characters long!

You'll find that using the CTRL-A combination sure beats typing a long command line over and over. Use it every time you get the chance.

PUSHING A JOB INTO THE BACKGROUND

If you ever need to interrupt a program while it is running, you can use the OS-9 "interrupt" key. Just hold down the SHIFT key and press the BREAK key. Or, hold down the CTRL key and press C.

Here's what happens when you send an interrupt signal to a program. As soon as you press the SHIFT-BREAK keys, an Error #003/and the `OS9:` prompt appear on your terminal screen. But, that's only half the magic. Give it a try. Type:

`list` *filename* `>/p`

Substitute `window.glr4` for *filename*. As soon as the printer starts running, press the SHIFT-BREAK combination. Watch what happens. Did the `OS9:` prompt reappear on the screen? Isn't something strange going on? Why is your printer still printing? What's going on?

Would you believe that when you pressed SHIFT-BREAK, you told OS-9 to run the printing job as a background task? That's what happened.

To prove it, type the `List` command again. This time leave off the `>/p`. Your window should fill with the same listing that is being printed. The printer should continue to print until it finishes the job.

Here's another handy key. Sometimes you need to redisplay the command line you are typing. To do this, press CTRL-D. D for display, maybe? Programmers working on older teletype terminals, which produced hard copy output but couldn't erase deleted characters, used this key a lot.

THE GREAT ESCAPE

OS-9 has one more special key. It lets you escape. The CTRL-ESC key combination on your Color Computer 3 sends an end-of-file signal to OS-9. This gives you a way to send an end-of-file signal to any process that receives its data from the keyboard. To use it, hold down the CTRL key and press the ESC key at the same time.

There's only one catch to the great keyboard escape. When you use the CTRL-ESC combination, you must type it as the first character on the line.

OTHER OS-9 MAGIC

Are you impatient? Do you hate to sit and wait for a computer to finish one job so you can command it to do another? Wait no more! OS-9 lets you type ahead.

While OS-9 is running one program, you can type another command line or answer the next prompt if you know what it is going to be. Sometimes you may be able to stay several command lines ahead of your Color Computer.

Unfortunately, there is a gotcha with type ahead — you will be typing blind. This is only a minor slow down, however, and it is much better than sitting around twiddling your thumbs. Also, you may have trouble with missing characters if you type ahead while the Color Computer's disk drives are running.

THE "I QUIT" KEY

When you get tired of a program and want to abort the process, never fret. OS-9 gives you a way to do it. Just press the BREAK key. You can also hold down the CTRL key while you press the E. The E must stand for "End it!"

THE "CTRL-NOTHING" KEY

We almost forgot something, control-nothing, that is. The CTRL-0 (zero) key combination lets you toggle the shift lock on the keyboard. If your keyboard is only sending out uppercase letters, you can get it to send lowercase letters by holding down the CTRL key and pressing 0.

To change back to all uppercase letters, you simply press the CTRL-0 combination again. That's why we call it a "toggle." By the way, when the keyboard is sending out lowercase letters, you can demand that it give you an uppercase letter by holding down the SHIFT key.

Here's an interesting problem to ponder. It is possible to type lowercase letters on the keyboard but only see uppercase letters on the screen. Why?

This happens when you set the Tmode uppercase lock mode to UPC. To make this change, type:

```
tmode upc
```

To see the lowercase letters again, use this command line:

```
tmode -upc
```

Remember, the shift lock function — the CTRL-0 key combination — only works visibly when you have used the Tmode tool to tell your window device to recognize both upper- and lowercase characters.

TURNING THE KEYBOARD MOUSE ON AND OFF

Since the Color Computer 3 and OS-9 Level II are very graphics oriented, you will find that many third-party software applications programs you can run will use a mouse. If you don't own a mouse or just don't feel like mousing around at the time, you may want to use the keyboard mouse. We won't be using this feature in this book, but you can use the four arrow keys and the two function keys marked F1 and F2 to simulate a mouse if you tell OS-9 what you are doing. To tell OS-9 you want the keyboard mouse, hold down the CTRL key and press the CLEAR key at the same time.

When you get tired of the keyboard mouse and want to go back to the real mouse, just press the same two keys again. You'll wind up back on the real mouse. By the way, when you are using the arrow keys as a mouse, you will not be able to use them as arrow keys. Don't even try.

REBOOTING

Occasionally your Color Computer may lock up and refuse to accept any commands from the keyboard. If it does this, you may have to reboot your computer. You can do this by pressing the (square-shaped) reset button located at the right-rear of your Color Computer 3.

At other times you may want to reboot OS-9 for another reason. For example, it is possible to have several disks that will boot up and use different hardware attached to your computer. To change hardware, you usually only need to reboot with the proper boot disk. You do this by pressing the reset button after you swap the disks.

I QUIT

Most actors like to make a graceful exit when they leave the stage. It's also a good habit to get into when you are working with a computer. If you want to exit from OS-9 gracefully, follow these simple rules. Never turn your computer off while a program is running. Turn it off only when you can see the OS-9 prompt.

Before you turn off your computer, make sure you remove your floppy disks from your drives. Once they are safely stored in their sleeves, you can safely turn off the power. Start by turning off your disk drives and printer. Your monitor should be turned off next, followed by your computer and Multi-Pak Interface.

You've learned a lot in this chapter, so you may want to make a quick review and practice using some of your new tools again before we move on.

CHAPTER 2

playing around

We put you through a lot in Chapter 1. It's time to have some fun! Now that you have a brand new OS-9 Level II working system disk, we can move ahead full speed.

When you booted OS-9 the first time, you probably noticed the familiar 16-line, 32-column green screen with black letters. The original master system disk that comes out of the package is set up to use a terminal device descriptor named `/term` that is set up to talk to the VDG (Video Display Graphics) in your Color Computer.

Let's take a quick look and see what other devices are available for us to use now. Type:

```
mdir
```

and press ENTER. Your Color Computer will fill the green screen with a listing of the modules, or programs, presently loaded in memory. Notice that it stopped with the cursor in the lower-right corner. It's almost as if there were more. Press the space bar or any other key and see what happens.

Now the listing of modules has grown by another five lines. The OS-9 `Mdir` tool paused and waited for you to read the information on the screen before it finished your listing. It did this because the /term device descriptor you are using was set to pause on the System Master Disk. If you would rather it scroll nonstop, type:

```
tmode -pause
```

and press ENTER.

Repeat the Mdir command you ran earlier and watch what happens. OS-9 is versatile. The change you just made is one of many ways you can customize your OS-9 Level II based Color Computer. If you want to see some of the other characteristics programmed into your /term device, type:

```
tmode
```

and press ENTER.

For a descriptive listing of the many Tmode parameters shown on your screen, consult your OS-9 Level II operating system manual (see "System Command Descriptions" in the OS-9 Commands section). For a detailed explanation of this and other OS-9 subjects, pick up *The Complete Rainbow Guide to OS-9*. For now, we need to get back on track. Run the Mdir tool again and we'll look at the listing together.

Look at the three rows of names beginning six lines from the top of the list.

```
TERM          W          W1
W2            W3         W4
W5            W6         W7
```

All of the modules listed here are OS-9 device descriptors. Each one of them tells a device driver how the device named is configured. Will it pause after you fill the screen? How many columns wide is the window? How many rows will fit in the window?

LET'S OPEN THE BUILT-IN WINDOWS

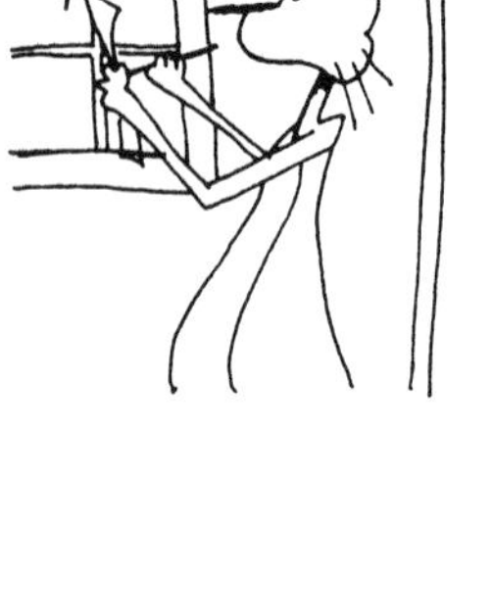

We'll start our tour of the windowing system by taking a look at the windows built into OS-9 when we turn it on. To switch from one window to another from the Color Computer keyboard, press the CLEAR key. Press that key now and see what happens.

If your system disk was set up like ours, nothing happened. When you first start OS-9, only the /term device descriptor has been initialized. You'll notice that following TERM, there are eight window device descriptors named W and W1 through W7. These device descriptors correspond to window devices named /w and /w1 through /w7.

Notice that in the Mdir output listing they are named W and W1 through W7. As you look at this list, you are looking at a list of module names. We will initialize them by using their module name. When we start talking to them later, we will need to use their device name — the module name with a slash in front of it.

You've stumbled into one of OS-9's secrets. You can tell you are communicating with a device if there is a slash in front of the pathname. File this information away for now; it's going to come in handy later on. Type the following two lines:

```
iniz w1
date t >/w1
```

Now, press the CLEAR key and see what happens. You're looking at your first homemade OS-9 Level II window. You should see the date and time displayed on the top line of the new window.

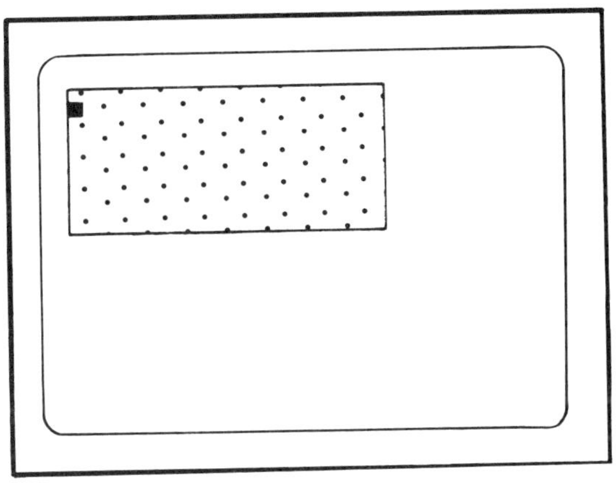

After you initialized the window named /w1, you ran the OS-9 Date tool. You told Date to send its output, the date and time, to a device named /w1, the window you just initialized. In "OS-9 speak," you have redirected the output of the Date utility command to the window device, /w1.

If you're looking at your new window on an RGB color monitor such as the Tandy CM-8, you're probably wondering if something is wrong. The colors don't look quite right.

Press the CLEAR key again and you'll find yourself staring at the green screen again. Type:

```
montype r
```

and press ENTER. Now, press the CLEAR key again. That looks much better, doesn't it? The black letters on the white screen with the red border wake you right up!

Let's initialize the rest of the numbered windows so we can take a look at them. First, press the CLEAR key again. Then, type:

```
iniz w2 w3 w4 w5 w6 w7
```

and press ENTER. Press the CLEAR key. There's the window with the date and time. Press it again! That's the green screen! What happened to the other windows we just initialized?

You're right, we have initialized the windows numbered W2 through W7. However, we have not written anything to them. Let's give one of them a try!

```
date  t >/w2
```

This time press the CLEAR key twice. If we're together, you should be looking at white letters printed on the blue background of a small window in the upper-right corner of the same screen that holds the window with the black letters on a white background. Notice the white block cursor under the date in the small screen. Press the ENTER key and see what happens.

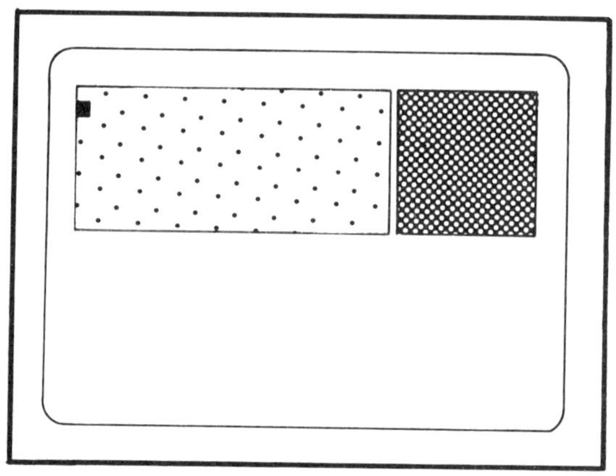

Whoops! Nothing happened because the window the cursor is located in is presently only an output device. We'll show you how to make your windows act like independent terminals a bit later. For now, let's continue to explore. Press the CLEAR key to get back to the green screen and type:

```
dir >/w3
```

Press the CLEAR key three times and take a look. That's nice! A listing of the files on your working system disk has been displayed in black letters on a cyan window that's 40 columns wide and 12 lines deep. Since you pressed the CLEAR key three times after typing the command in the green screen, the cursor should have moved to the same screen. Do you see it under the listing of filenames? Right on!

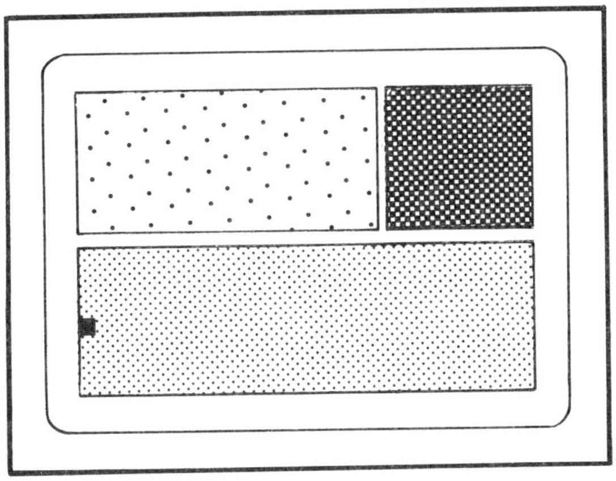

Let's try it again! Press the CLEAR key once to get back to the green screen and we'll go for another surprise.

```
dir sys >/w4
```

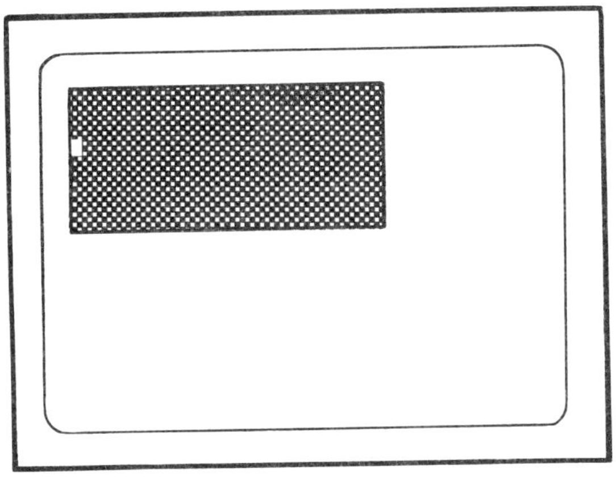

That's right, you're getting the idea! Press the CLEAR key four times. Notice how the cursor moves from window to window each time you press the CLEAR key? This is getting to be window heaven. This time you'll see a nicely formatted listing of the files in the SYS directory of your System Master Disk. Do you remember the `Error` tool we used in Chapter 1? There's the name of the file — `errmsg` — the answers came from. Hey! I'll bet the `helpmsg` file contains online help messages for the many OS-9 tools. Let's try it in the next window. Press the CLEAR key to move the cursor back to the green screen, then type:

```
help dir >/w5
```

Let's take a look. This time, press the CLEAR key five times. Yep! That looks like part of a help message. But, it's not all there. Window `/w5` is much too small to list help messages. Let's try something else. Back to the green screen, most honorable CLEAR key.

```
date >/w5
help dir >/w6
```

Let's take another peek. Six presses of the CLEAR key should do it this time. Much better! So that's the format of the output from the OS-9 `Help` tool. When you type `Help` followed by the name of a valid OS-9 utility command, `Help` will show you the proper syntax for the tool you named, tell you what you would use it for, and describe any options you may want to use on your command line. In the command line above, we told `Help` to display its output in a window device named `/w6`. In black letters on `/w6`'s white background, that's exactly what it did.

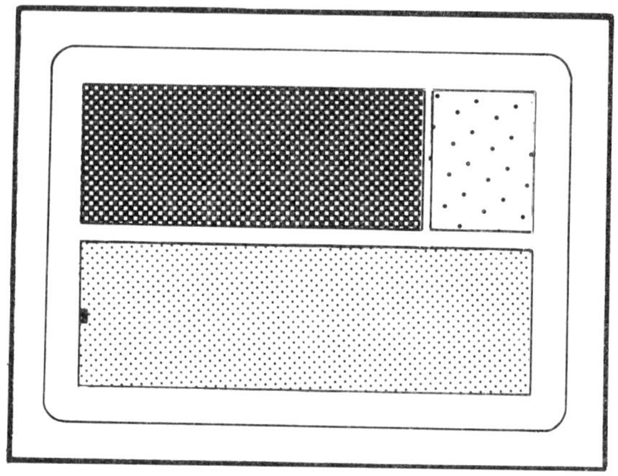

Well, if memory serves us right, we have one window left. Press the CLEAR key again. You should be back to the green screen. Let's go for it.

```
dir x >/w7
```

Don't worry, you won't wear the CLEAR key out. Press it seven times! In front of you, in white letters on a blue background, you should see a list of the commands available in the `CMDS` directory of your OS-9 Level II working system disk. You are looking at window device `/w7`. This window lets you write to 24 lines, which can contain up to 80 columns of text.

HOW CAN WE USE THESE WINDOWS?

You've completed a tour of the seven predefined windows that were programmed into your System Master Disk by Microware and Tandy. We'll see if we can put them to work for you now. In later chapters we'll be discussing setting up your Color Computer to run a few major applications programs. For now, we'll try to keep it simple. At the same time, we hope this chapter will spark your imagination enough that you'll jump right in and discover how the OS-9 Level II windowing environment can help you solve many common problems.

YOU CAN PRINT MANY THINGS IN WINDOWS

Many new computer users share a common problem. They find it hard to remember the names of the dozens of computer commands they must use to operate a sophisticated computer. Then, when they finally master the names, they can't remember the syntax for all those commands. We think the OS-9 Level II windowing environment can really help you with this problem.

So far, you have given OS-9 all your commands from the green screen named /term. It would be handy if you could work on a screen where you could see two or three windows at the same time. To do that you must tell one of the windows on the screen that you want it to be a terminal. You do that by starting a shell in the target window. Use the CLEAR key to go back to the green screen one more time and we'll give it a try!

```
shell i=/w5&
```

and press ENTER. Now press the CLEAR key until the cursor comes to rest following the OS9: prompt in the small, light blue window. Type:

```
display c
```

How about that! It's a small terminal, but it's a terminal and you were able to clear your screen. Since the window you are operating from is located on the same screen as two other windows, you will want to take advantage of the situation. For example, from your miniature window you could list a help message for a command in the second window and leave it displayed there while you try out that command in the third window.

However, before you can start, you need to know what commands are available. Type:

```
dir x >/w6
```

This command lists the names of the files in your current execution directory in black letters on the white 80-column window at the bottom of our screen.

WHAT ARE EXECUTION AND DATA DIRECTORIES?

As you have probably surmised, OS-9 allows several different directories on a disk. When you boot OS-9, two directories are selected for immediate use. These directories are referred to as your execution and data, or working, directories.

An execution directory is one that contains executable programs or commands. A data directory is generally one that holds procedure files, source code for high-level languages, such as BASIC09, and text files. When you first boot OS-9, your execution and data directories are automatically set to /d0/CMDS and /d0 respectively. This means that the executable programs you are running, such as Format and Backup, actually reside in the CMDS directory on your system disk. Also, unless you specify otherwise, any files you create with the Build tool will be saved in the root directory of Drive 0. The "root" directory is simply the "main"

directory of a disk. When we use /d0 or /d1 by itself, we are referring to a root directory.

In the previous examples, when we type `dir`, we are asking for a listing of all files in the current data directory, or `/d0`. When we issued the command, `dir SYS`, we were asking for a listing of all files in the `SYS` directory. To see what commands are in the `CMDS` directory, we use `dir x`. We could, however, have used `dir CMDS` instead since the `CMDS` directory is our current execution directory (this is what the little `x` stands for).

It is possible, and quite easy, to change your current execution and data directories to something other than `CMDS` and `/d0`. This is done with the `chx` and `chd` commands that will be covered a little later.

USING DEINIZ

Ever wonder what `Deiniz` could do for you? Type:

```
help deiniz >/w4
```

So `Deiniz` is used to detach a device, huh? If you `Deiniz` a window, it will probably disappear. What's your guess? Why not find out firsthand? Let's do it together.

```
deiniz w6
```

All gone! Do you suppose you can bring good old `/W6` back to life? Can't hurt to try!

```
iniz w6 ; dir x >/w6
```

Magic!

Microware and Tandy did you a big favor when they set up the OS-9 Level II `Shell` file. Remember, each file you load takes up at least 8K of memory, whether it needs it or not. Since the shell is only 1,532 decimal bytes long, there is plenty of room left in the shell's 8K memory block for a few more of the OS-9 tools you use most often. To find out which OS-9 tools are loaded with the `Shell` file when you start your Color Computer, type:

```
ident -x -s shell >/w6
```

The tools are: `Copy`, `Date`, `Deiniz`, `Del`, `Dir`, `Display`, `Echo`, `Iniz`, `Link`, `List`, `Load`, `Mdir`, `Merge`, `Mfree`, `Procs`, `Rename`, `Setime`, `Tmode` and `Unlink`. Now that's a bargain!

OK, you're from Missouri. You want to confirm that those tools are actually in memory. Type:

```
mdir >/w6
```

There they are at the bottom of the listing. You can thank the sharp programmers at Microware and Tandy for that trick. Since those tools are in memory all the time, you can run them almost instantly. OS-9 doesn't need to go out to your floppy disk drives, find them and load them into memory every time you want to run them. The speed with which the `Mdir` tool responded just a moment ago is a perfect example.

RUNNING PROGRAMS IN WINDOWS

Now that you are getting used to the idea of working with three windows at the same time, let us show you that OS-9 really can do more than one thing at the same time. Start by typing:

```
dir x>/w4 ; dir x>/w6
```

What happened? On our screen, OS-9 listed the names of the files in our current execution directory to the window in the upper-left corner of our screen. When it was finished, it immediately listed the same filenames in the white 80-column window in the bottom half of our screen. When you typed the line above, you told OS-9 to run two commands sequentially, or one after the other. However, life was a little easier because you were able to type both commands at the same time on the same command line.

The magic in that command line lies in the semicolon (;) between the `>/w4` and the second `dir`. When you type a semicolon in an OS-9 command line, you are telling your Color Computer that you want it to run the two commands on either side of that semicolon sequentially. Essentially, the command line you typed works the same as the following set of OS-9 command lines.

```
dir x>/w4
dir x>/w6
```

There is a difference, however. If you had decided to type the two command lines above individually, you would have needed to wait for the first command line to finish its job before you could type the second. You could have tried to type it blind into OS-9's type-ahead buffer, but because the command you were running was reading the disk drive to find the list of filenames in your current execution directory, you probably would have lost a few characters.

This happens because the hardware disk controller that plugs into your Multi-Pak Interface and acts as a link between your Color Computer and your disk drives pulls the "halt" line up on the 6809 microprocessor and will not let it do anything else while it is reading or writing a sector from a disk. If you type something while this halt line is high, it will be destined to go to that big bit bucket in the sky.

We still want to show you that OS-9 can do more than one job at the same time, so let's take another tack. We can't use the type-ahead buffer, but we can put our two command lines in a short procedure file and let OS-9 do the typing for us. When we type the procedure file, we will type an extra character at the end of each command line. Type:

```
build ConTask
```

Enter the following lines at the ? prompts:

```
dir x >/w4&
dir x >/w6&
```

Press ENTER twice after the last line.

You have just used the OS-9 Build tool to type your first OS-9 procedure file. The Build command in the first line above creates a new file in your current data directory (unless you changed it with chd, it should still be /d0) named ConTask. We thought about naming the file in our example ConJob, but we didn't want you to get the wrong idea.

After Build created the file ConTask, it wrote the next two lines you typed into that file. When you pressed the ENTER key without anything else on the line, you were signaling the Build tool that you were ready to quit. Let's take a look at your new file. Type:

```
display c >/w4 ; list contask >/w4
```

In white letters on that freshly cleared blue screen, you can concentrate on your handiwork. Notice the ampersand (&) character. That character is very special to OS-9 users because they use it almost every day. In fact, they use it every time they need to tell OS-9 to do more than one thing at a time.

When you type the ampersand character, you are telling OS-9 that you want it to run the task you just started in the background. Can you predict the scenario of events that will take place when you run your first procedure file? Give up? That's OK; your Color Computer should be doing the work for you anyway. Type:

```
display c ; contask
```

What happened? What are those two numbers at the top of your control window in the upper-right corner of your screen? Why did the OS9: prompt pop up so soon? Glad you asked. Let's see if together we can figure out what happened.

The moment you pressed ENTER, OS-9 went to work for you. It cleared the command window you were working in because you used the OS-9 Display tool in the first part of your command line. Display sends the hexadecimal characters following it to the standard output path. When you are set up to type command lines in window /w5, the shell interpreting those commands sends its standard output to window /w5. The c in your command line tells OS-9 to clear a window or screen. Since the shell sent the c to window /w5, OS-9 cleared that window for you.

That's enough window washing for the moment! Let's move

on. The &005 on the top line of your command window is trying to tell you something. In English, it's saying, "I have just started background task number five." A moment after OS-9 started task number five, it started task number six. It also ran task six in the background. You know that because of the &006 message and because a second after you see that message the OS-9 command line prompt, OS9: , appears.

Shortly after the &005 appeared, you should have noticed a listing of filenames begin to scroll in the window located near the upper-left corner of your screen. That was process number five in action. We should briefly pause here to tell you that in OS-9 parlance, a process is simply a program that happens to be running.

Likewise, a moment after the &006 message appeared in your control window, another listing of filenames started to scroll through the 80-column window along the bottom of your screen. At the same time, the listing action continued in the window at the upper-left corner of your screen and the command line prompt, OS9:, appeared in your control window. At least three things were happening at the same time.

With OS-9 Level II, you do not have to stop after running only two processes. In fact, you will be able to run several major programs at the same time without running out of memory on a 512K Color Computer. So you can prove to yourself that OS-9 can do more, repeat the last command and, as soon as the command line prompt appears in your control window, type:

```
list window.glr4
```

Were you fast enough? Probably not, but if so, OS-9 began to list a procedure file named window.glr4, which is stored in the root directory, or your current data directory into your small control window, while it continued to list the filenames in the other two windows. More magic!

Just in case it was hard for you to notice that OS-9 was doing two different tasks while running your procedure file ConTask because the two windows were both receiving listings from the same directory, we'll change one of the jobs in ConTask and add a third in another procedure file named ConTask2. Type:

```
build ConTask2
display c >/w4
display c >/w5
display c >/w6
dir x >/w4&
list sys/errmsg >/w6&
dir e
```

Be sure to press ENTER twice after the last line.

Let's get brave and go for the action right away! Type:

```
Display c ; ConTask2
```

How did it work? Hopefully, you saw a listing of the files in your current execution directory in the upper-left window, a listing of the file containing OS-9's English language error messages in the bottom window and an extended directory listing of `/d0`, your current data directory, in the small control window. Did you notice that a single copy of your OS-9 `Dir` tool was actually running in two windows at the same time?

BUT THERE'S ONE THING YOU CAN'T DO!

We need to make a very important point about window devices before we go any further. You cannot send the output from a program to a window you are already using as a terminal.

Let's say the same thing in OS-9 speak. If you have started a shell in a window, you cannot send output from another process to that window. You can tell if you have started a shell in an OS-9 Level II window because you will see the `OS9:` prompt in that window. Go ahead and confirm it for yourself so you can see what may happen.

You are presently using window `/w5` as a terminal. You have a shell running in that window. On that same screen you can see window number four, `/w4`, and window number six, `/w6`. All three windows in this screen are device windows, but `/w5` is the only one that is presently running a shell.

From your command window, `/w5`, type:

```
dir x >/w4
```

The light on your disk drive should light up and you'll see the filenames of utility programs stored in the `CMDS` directory. Everything should work as it did earlier.

Now, we'll start a shell in window `/w4` and repeat our command line above, so you can see what will happen when you try to send output to a window that already has a shell running in it. Type:

```
shell i=/w4&
dir x >/w4
```

Almost immediately you'll notice the word shell, followed by the prompt `OS9:` printed on window `/w4`. Then, attempting to obey your second command line, OS-9 tries to send a listing of your current execution directory to the same window, `/w4`. What happened?

In our terminal window, /w5, the black cursor went to the line following our short command line and sat there. Nothing happened on the blue window named /w4.

Now, press the CLEAR key until the cursor comes to rest in window /w4. Tap the ENTER key once. Although the drive motor runs briefly, nothing else happens. Tap it again! This time you will most likely see the first line of the output of the OS-9 Dir tool, something like: Directory of . 18:26:09.

If you keep pressing ENTER, you will eventually see all of the output from the Dir tool. Before you reach the end, you will need to press ENTER once for every line of output from Dir. This mode of operation will drive you nuts. So, always avoid redirecting output to a window with a shell in it.

"OK," you say. "But what do I do about the shell that is running in window /w4? How do I get rid of it?" Try executing it. If your cursor is still in window /w4, and is located in the first column following the last OS9 prompt, type:

```
ex
```

Now, use the CLEAR key to move the cursor over to window /w5 and use OS-9's Display tool to clear window /w4. Like this:

```
display  c >/w4
```

If it worked and you have a clear blue screen, you have successfully removed the shell from window /w4. To recap, if you want to remove a shell that is running in a window, type ex in the first column after the OS9 prompt. You can then clean the window from another command window using the Display tool. To remove the window altogether, you must then use OS-9's Deiniz tool.

```
deiniz /w4
```

Did the upper left-hand corner of your screen turn red with anger? If so, window /w4 is gone. Things can get complicated if you want to start window /w4 up again in the same place. We'll deal with these complications in the next chapter. To start another device window named /w4 on another screen, you can position the CLEAR key in window /w5 and type:

```
iniz w4
echo Hello World  >/w4
```

Press CLEAR seven times to see your new screen.

If you want to learn more about OS-9 theory and find out how the magic that lets windows work is created, we hope you will read *The Complete Rainbow Guide to OS-9*. For now, relax — you're on your way!

SETTING UP FOR SOME REAL WORK

Are you beginning to see the possibilities hiding beneath the surface of OS-9 Level II's powerful windowing environment? We'll stop here and encourage you to take a few moments to play around with OS-9 Level II's predefined windows. Then, we'll share a few ideas that may inspire you. In the next chapter we'll show you how to define your own windows so you can set them up to fit your jobs.

IF YOU'RE A WRITER

Perhaps you fancy yourself as the next Danielle Steele, Tom Clancy, or maybe even the next Ernest Hemingway. If so, you probably bought your Color Computer to write with and you want your writing tools to always be only a second away.

With the Color Computer loaded with 512K of memory and OS-9 Level II windows, you can do just that. Let's assume that when you bought your Color Computer you also purchased a word processing program with a companion outliner and spelling checker. For want of a better name, we'll call them *Magic Word*, *Magic Spell* and *Magic Line*.

The secret to having these word processing tools a second away is to have them in memory at all times. We could load them all at one time if we used the OS-9 `Build` tool to create a procedure file that would load our word processing files into memory for us. For example:

```
build LoadWP
load MagicWord
load MagicSpell
load MagicLine
```

You would need to press ENTER twice after the last line.

After you had created the file `LoadWP` and safely stored it in the root directory of the disk in Drive `/d0`, you could run it any time you wanted to by simply typing:

```
loadWP
```

If you are a serious writer, you will want to enter `LoadWP` as one of the lines in your OS-9 `StartUp` file so that you will have these writing tools in memory each time you start your Color Computer. We'll show you how to build a customized `StartUp` file in a later chapter.

After you do this, *Magic Word*, *Magic Spell* and *Magic Line* will be loaded for you automatically every time you boot Color

Computer OS-9 Level II. You will be able to start writing immediately. Now if someone would just write a program that could write a book!

If you are a C programmer, you could build a similar procedure file named `LoadC` to load each of the programs needed by your C compiler. If you are in this for entertainment, you could build a similar procedure file to load all of your game programs. After your most-used applications programs or programming tools are loaded, they will be ready for you to use at a second's notice.

In the next chapter we'll show you how to create windows that look the way you want them to look, show you how to make them the size you want them and place them exactly where you want them. We'll also show you how to make them the color you want and let you play around with the border, background and foreground colors on the fly.

CHAPTER 3

let's define our own windows

Once you've exercised the windows we showed you in Chapter 2 for a while, you'll most likely be ready to move on. It's sort of like moving into a new house. Shortly after the moving van leaves, you feel like you have to put up your own curtains and window shades. When you get a house, you want it to reflect your personality. The same goes for its windows.

After you have read this chapter, you'll no longer need to peek into a Color Computer window that doesn't reflect your personality. You'll be able to roll your own.

We'll start by creating a text window or two in the same screen. We'll pick our own size and color. We may even come up with a more useful configuration than the standard windows pre-defined in the device descriptors. However, the important thing to remember as you begin to follow our examples is that by emulating them, you will be able to define your own windows to suit your needs.

You'll be using two OS-9 tools to build most of your windows. `Wcreate` is a tool that lets you define a window and display it on a screen. `Display` is a standard OS-9 tool that lets you send any number of non-printing codes to a window or other device attached to your Color Computer.

`Wcreate` has several advantages that caused us to pick it to create our new device windows. This OS-9 windowing tool lets you give it the size and location of the window you are creating by typing decimal numbers. `Display`, on the other hand, requires you to type hexadecimal numbers. Unless you think in hexadecimal, `Wcreate` will save you a lot of translation.

OUR FIRST HAND-CRAFTED SCREEN

In our first experiment, we'll create one screen with five windows. Four of these windows will be device windows, and the fifth will be an overlay window. All but the overlay window will be 80 characters wide. All will be text-only windows. We'll create each of these windows from the `OS9:` prompt by typing individual command lines.

Our first window will be located two lines down from the top of the screen. It will be two lines deep. We'll set it up to be a command window, or terminal, by starting a shell in it. Immediately after we create this window, we'll move into it by pressing the CLEAR key. Once there, we'll stay there and create all of our new windows from this control window.

We will create our command window first because to create a window on the same screen as another, you must be operating in that screen. For example, if you create two customized windows from `/term` (the green screen) you will wind up with two windows, but they will appear on different screens. You won't be able to see them at the same time.

Next, we'll create a window on the top two lines of the screen and put a title in it. After the title is in place, we'll create an overlay window at the right end of the title window and display the date in it. Two additional 80-column by 10-line windows will round out our first screen. The first will be located four lines from the top of the screen, the latter, 14 lines from the top. When we are finished, all 24 lines in the 80-column by 25-line screen will be full.

Once you have created these windows, you can use them in many different ways. For example, you could follow the same course we charted in Chapter 2 and use one of the 10-line windows to display a listing of the tools available in your OS-9 `CMDS` directory while you run them from the command window and display their output in the second 10-line window.

Or perhaps you have memorized the names of your OS-9 tools by now and are more interested in looking at a listing of the files you have stored in one of your data directories. Once these filenames are displayed in one 80-column, 10-line window, you can work on them using the OS-9 tools, or utility commands, which you can call to action from your command window. You can send the results of your work — the output of the OS-9 tools — to the second 80-column, 10-line window.

Later you might want to take advantage of OS-9's ability to send its error messages and data output to a different path. By using the OS-9 redirection operators on the command line, you'll be able to send error messages to the first 10-line screen, the data output to the second. Or, maybe you'll want to change the size of those two screens and create a four-line window to capture the error messages and a 16-line window to display the data.

Additionally, since four of the windows on your screen are device windows, there will be nothing to stop you from starting a shell in each one of them and running an applications program from within each window. In the future, many applications programs will automatically configure themselves to the size of the window they are running in. This opens up many additional opportunities.

You could start a shell and turn the two 10-line windows into command windows. After you have the shells running, you can use the CLEAR key to move to each window. You'll know the new shells are running because you'll see the OS-9 prompts. Once your cursor has come to rest next to the OS-9 prompt in a window, you can use any OS-9 tool or run any applications program in that window.

The screen editor that comes with the OS-9 Developers Package is a perfect example. If you need to rewrite a document, you could move to each of the new command windows and run the screen editor by typing its name on the command line. You can then open the document you need to rewrite using the copy of the screen editor running in the top window and display it 10 lines at a time while you do the actual rewrite with the copy of the screen editor that is running in the bottom window.

This is a perfect place to pass along an important point about OS-9. Because applications programs like the screen editor are re-entrant, OS-9 only needs to keep one copy of the program in memory. The two screen editing windows in our example are actually taking their time sharing the one piece of code that is loaded into your Color Computer's memory. However, each window is working with data in two distinct data memory areas.

In the future, you'll be able to run OS-9 applications from a visual desktop that lets you point to an application and then click a button on your Color Computer mouse to run it. When this new visual interface named *Multi-Vue* arrives, a clipboard will allow you to transfer data between two different applications.

In our screen editing example, this means you could use the CLEAR key to move into the top editing window, mark a block of text and copy it to the clipboard. Once the desired text is on the clipboard, you can use CLEAR to move back to the bottom editing window. Once you are back in this window, you can move your insertion point to the desired location in your new text file and paste the material from the clipboard into the new document.

A FEW ADDITIONAL POINTS ABOUT WINDOWS

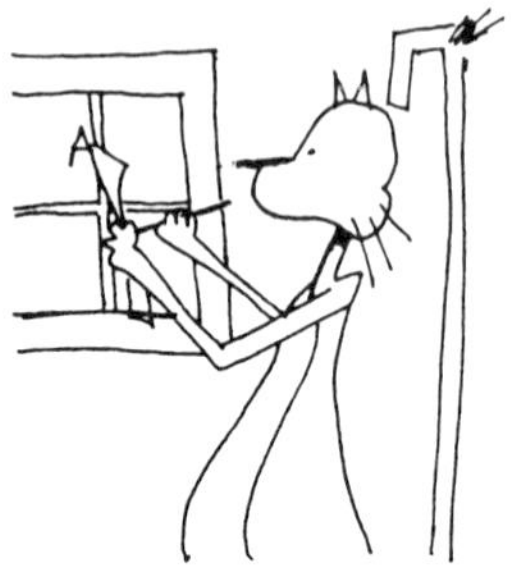

The windowing system is actually built into OS-9. That's why you are able to create a window from the command line prompt. There are two types of built-in windows, device and overlay.

You can cause a device window to act like an independent terminal by starting an OS-9 shell in it. Once you have started this shell, you can run any OS-9 tool or applications program in that window. With many of the older OS-9 tools and applications programs, you'll run into a "Gotcha!"

For the most part, these programs assume you are running OS-9 on a computer terminal or in a fixed-size screen on your Color Computer. They have never heard of windows. Newer applications and tools will take care of the screen-size problem for you automatically, however, and you won't have too much to worry about.

As you start to design your own screens, remember this: Device windows may not overlay each other. You cannot put one device window on top of another and then move back and forth between them. If the area filled by two windows occupies the same space on the screen, you will need to create these windows on two separate screens. If you create them on two separate screens, you won't be able to see both device windows at the same time.

All is not lost, however, because on many occasions an OS-9 overlay window will do the job. An overlay window can be placed on top of all or any part of a device window — or on top of another overlay window for that matter. Any number of overlay windows may be stacked like this. But, remember: There must always be a device window on the bottom of the stack.

If you are a programmer, you'll find yourself using overlay windows when you want to send the person using your applications program a message. On some computers, overlay windows are known as dialog boxes. One more thing. You cannot open up a graphics overlay window and draw a picture — a stop sign perhaps — if the device window underneath that overlay window is a text window. In OS-9 speak, overlay windows assume the screen type of the device windows they overlay.

MAKING TEXT WINDOWS

It's almost time to dive in and create your first customized screen. But first, we must give you a quick overview of the choices you have when you get ready to create your own screens.

Before you create a window, you must determine how big you want it to be, its color and its type. Let's look at the size first.

Your windows can be any size as long as they are smaller than the screen on which you plan to place them. The size of the screen is determined by the type of screen you create. There are six basic screens you can generate with OS-9 Level II. Two of them are text-only screens; the others are designed to handle graphics at varying resolutions. In addition to the six basic screen types, there are two other types that let you control the location of the next window you generate.

THE BASIC WINDOW TYPES

OS-9 Level II can generate two screens that will accept text data only. If you create a Type 01 screen, you will be able to display 24 lines holding 40 characters each. The Type 02 screen gives you 24 lines that will hold up to 80 characters each. If you are short on memory, or need larger characters because you are using a television set for a monitor, you will want to generate Type 01 screens. Each Type 01 screen uses 2K bytes of memory. You can use eight colors with both Type 01 and Type 02 screens.

When we switch from text windows to graphics windows, we start to use more memory. And we start defining our windows in terms of pixels instead of characters. OS-9 uses two sets of standard fonts that let you display text in your graphics windows. One of them is six pixels wide; the other is eight wide. This is to give you an idea of the size of a pixel.

The Type 05 and 06 graphics screens use less memory than any other. They require 16K. The Type 05 screen lets you display 640 pixels horizontally across the screen. This equals approximately 80 characters of text if you are using the eight-by-eight pixel character font — approximately 106 characters if you choose the font that uses six-pixel-wide characters. A Type 05 screen is 192 pixels, or approximately 24 characters, deep. If you create a Type 05 window, you are limited to two colors.

A Type 06 screen supports 40 characters of text on 24 lines. This screen allows a graphics resolution of 320 pixels by 192 pixels in any of four colors.

The two remaining screen types require 32K of memory. One of them, Type 08, generates screens 320 pixels wide by 192 pixels deep. Again, that's approximately 40 characters on each of 24 lines. If you use the six-pixel-wide font, you can expect to see approximately 53 characters on each line. A Type 08 screen lets you use 16 colors.

The other basic screen is Type 07. With this screen you can display your words and pictures on a screen 640 pixels wide by 192 pixels deep. You can use four colors with this screen.

The two default screen types that you use are Type 00 and Type FF. If you tell OS-9 Level II to generate a Type 00 window, it places that window on the screen where it is displaying the current process. Remember, in OS-9 speak, a process is a program running. You generate a Type FF window from within one of your programs when you want that window to appear on the currently displayed screen.

Perhaps a table is in order.

TABLE 3-A: Window Sizes

Type	Size	Number of Colors	Memory Needed
01	40 X 24 characters	eight	2K
02	80 X 24 characters	eight	4K
05	640 X 192 pixels	two	16K
06	320 X 192 pixels	four	16K
07	640 X 192 pixels	four	32K
08	320 X 192 pixels	sixteen	32K

THE BASIC WINDOW COLORS

There are eight basic colors you can choose from when you are displaying text or graphics material in a window. Each of these basic colors has a number assigned to it. To pick a color, you display the proper number in your command line. We'll show you how to select the color of your foreground, background and border when you create a new window. Later we'll show you how you can change any of these values on the fly.

Since you are going to be "painting by number" so to speak, we suggest you make several copies of the table below and post it all around in your computer room.

TABLE 3-B: Available Colors

Screen Color	Decimal Number	Hex Number
White	00	00
Blue	01	01
Black	02	02
Green	03	03
Red	04	04
Yellow	05	05
Magenta	06	06
Cyan	07	07
White	08	08
Blue	09	09
Black	10	0A
Green	11	0B
Red	12	0C
Yellow	13	0D
Magenta	14	0E
Cyan	15	0F

We show you the hexadecimal numbers in this color chart because these are the ones you will need to type when using the OS-9 `Display` tool to create windows or change the color in an existing window.

MAKING A DEVICE WINDOW

We're ready now to move ahead and make our first customized screen. However, before we can type a single character, we must decide what we want our first window to look like. Earlier we said we needed to make our new command window first, start an OS-9 shell in it and and then generate the other windows on our screen. Before we enter our command line, we need to answer some questions. We will jot the answers down in OS-9 speak — numerical form — and then type our command.

- What type of screen do you want?
- What is horizontal coordinate of upper left-hand corner?
- What is vertical coordinate of upper left-hand corner?
- How wide is the window?
- How tall is the window?
- What color do you want your characters?
- What color do you want your background?
- What color do you want your border?

We'll use the OS-9 `Display` tool to generate this first window to show you how it works. This means you'll need to answer the questions for the first window in hexadecimal.

Earlier we said this window will be a text-only window, which will start two lines down from the top of the screen. It will be 80 characters wide, two lines deep. Further, it will generate black letters on a white background. The screen's border will be blue. The answers to our questions in decimal and hexadecimal are printed below.

Characteristic	Decimal Value	Hex Value
Window type	2	2
Upper left horizontal	0	0
Upper left vertical	2	2
Horizontal size	80	50
Vertical size	2	2
Color of characters	2	2
Color of background	0	0
Color of border	1	1

Now that you have answered these questions, you are ready to create your first custom window. Use the CLEAR key to move the cursor to the green screen with the black letters and enter each of these lines:

```
iniz w1
merge  sys/stdfonts  >/w1
display 1b 20 2 0 2 50 2 2 0 1 >/w1
shell i=/w1&
```

Press the CLEAR key to arrive in the window you just created. You should be looking at a blue screen with a small white window located two lines below the top of the screen. If not, remember to type `montype r` from the green screen. You should see the `OS9:` prompt displayed in black type. Let's review the steps above and point out a few areas where it is easy to make a mistake.

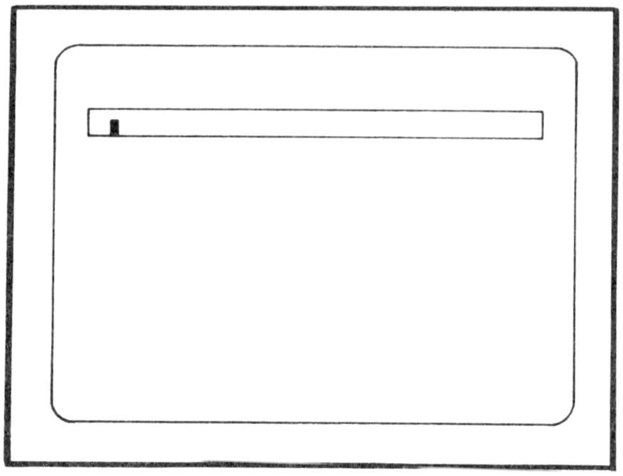

It is a good idea to reserve a block of memory for the first window on a screen by using the OS-9 `Iniz` tool. OS-9 often takes care of it for you automatically, but it is always better to be safe than sorry. Strange things can happen in a windowing environment unless everything is just right.

MERGING IN THE FONTS

You must merge the file `sys/stdfonts` into a buffer before you create a graphics screen. If you don't, you won't be able to see the characters you send to a graphics window. All characters will appear as dots. However, you only have to use this command line once during a session. That makes it a good candidate for your startup file. If you put it there, it will be run for you automatically every time you start OS-9 on your Color Computer.

Here's an important point you must remember about merging the `stdfonts` file into your system. Your fonts can only be merged into a window device. They cannot be merged into the VDG device. Remember! The device named `/term` with its black letters on a green background is a VDG device. You cannot merge the `stdfonts` file to it. It won't know what to do with them. Always merge your `stdfonts` file to a window device. You can tell a device is a window device because its name starts with a `w`. Always merge your `stdfonts` file to one of these window devices.

Now let's talk about the line that was hard to type. `Display` is an OS-9 tool that sends a list of hexadecimal characters to the standard output device. These characters are usually non-printable control characters — they cause your Color Computer to do something, but they do not show up on the screen.

The first two characters, `1b 20`, have a name. When they are sent together, they are known as `DWSet` — or device window set — in OS-9 speak. If you look closely, you'll notice that the numbers following these two characters are the hexadecimal answers you gave to the list of questions earlier.

After you typed the number that answered the last question, you typed `>/w1`. The right caret tells the OS-9 shell to redirect the standard output path used by `Display` to the device named `/w1`. If you had not typed the re-direction operator, those characters would have been sent to the green VDG screen where they wouldn't have met anything and nothing would have happened. However, when the window device named `/w1` receives your characters, it takes them for action and creates the window you ordered.

CREATING OVERLAY WINDOWS

Press CLEAR until the cursor follows the `OS9:` prompt in your new window. Now, let's create the title window and an overlay window where we'll display the date. Enter the following:

```
wcreate /w2 -s=0 0 0 80 2 0 2 1
echo Color Computer Window Classroom >/w2
display 1b 22 1 30 0 20 2 6 5 >/w2
date t  >/w2
```

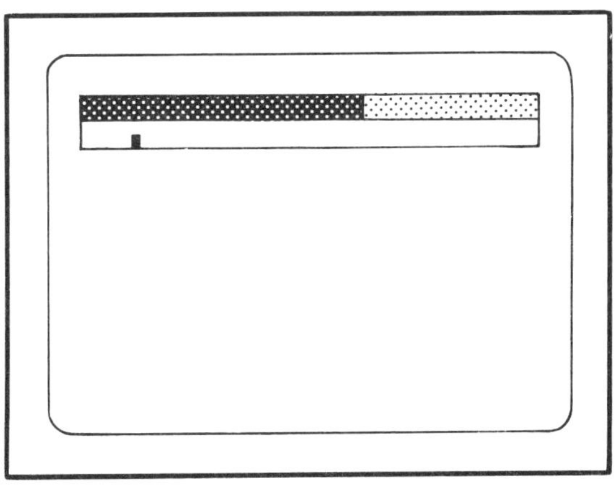

`WCreate` seems to be a little easier to use than `Display` when it comes to creating new windows. Let's take a look at our latest sequence of OS-9 command lines.

The statement `Wcreate /w2` tells the OS-9 windowing code that we want to create a new window named `/w2`. The `-s=0` means that we want the window we are creating to be displayed on the same screen as the current process. If we do this, it will automatically adopt the characteristics of that screen. In our case, the new screen will be a Type 02 text-only window, which can display 24 lines of 80 characters each.

After typing the `-s=0` to define the window type, we entered the answers to the rest of the questions in our list. However, notice that this time we answered the questions with decimal numbers rather than hexadecimal numbers. That's a big improvement over the `Display` command we first showed you. The `0 2 1` at the end of the list tells OS-9 that we want it to display white letters on a black background with a blue border. Guess what!

A moment after you typed that command line, a black window popped into the first two lines on the screen. Our next command line uses the OS-9 `Echo` tool to display a title on our new window. In white letters against the black background, it reads "Color Computer Window Classroom." Did you notice how similar the OS-9 `Echo` tool is to the `PRINT` statement of BASIC?

After we displayed the title in our new window, we moved on to create an overlay window in that same screen. Once again, we called on the trusty OS-9 `Display` tool. Following `Display` we see `1b 22`. In OS-9 speak, these two hexadecimal characters mean `OWSet` — for overlay window set.

The number `1` tells OS-9 that we want it to save the information displayed on the device window before it creates the overlay window. If we hadn't wanted OS-9 to save the information displayed, we would have typed the number `0` when we created the overlay window.

If you save the information displayed on a device window while creating an overlay window, that information will immediately pop back on the screen when the overlay window is closed. You close an overlay window by displaying the sequence `1b 23` on it. Like this:

```
display 1b 23 >/w2
```

If you have opened the overlay window from within a high level programming language like BASIC09, you simply close the path to the overlay window. When you close the path, the window disappears immediately.

Notice that the numbers used in the command line that create the overlay window are all typed as hexadecimal numbers. We typed the `30` to tell OS-9 that we wanted the window to start 30 Hex characters — or 48 decimal characters — from the left edge of the screen. The `0` that follows places the top of the overlay window along the top edge of the screen, and the next two hexadecimal characters tell OS-9 that we want this overlay window to be 20 Hex — or 32 decimal — characters wide and two lines deep.

And finally, the last two characters in the command line tell OS-9 that we want it to print magenta letters on a yellow background. Notice also that we redirected the output of the `Display` tool to the window where we wanted to create the overlay window, `/w2`.

As a rule of thumb, you almost always display the window codes to the window where you want the action to take place. You always do this with the OS-9 standard output path redirection operator, the right caret, >.

Finally, after we created the overlay window, we ran the OS-9 `Date` tool with the time option enabled to display the date and time in our new overlay window. Notice that we also redirected its output to `/w2`. If we had not done this, the date and time would have been printed in window `/w1`.

Next, we move on to create two windows where we can display the output of our OS-9 tools and applications programs.

```
wcreate /w3 -s=0 0 4 80 10 2 4 1
echo Hello Window Three >/w3
wcreate /w4 -s=0 0 14 80 10 2 7 1
echo Hello Window Four >/w4
```

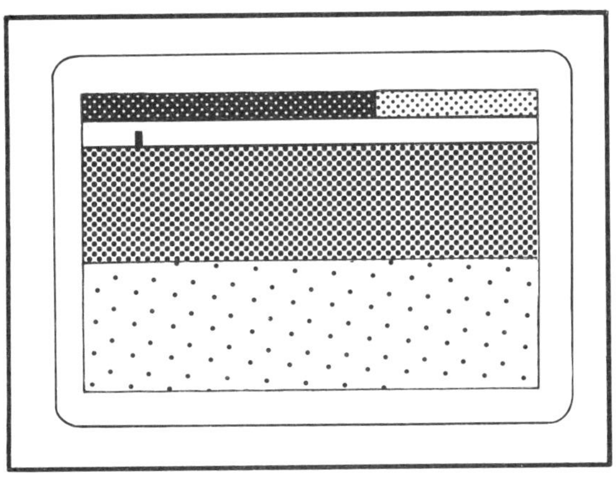

Take time here to notice another difference between the `Wcreate` command and the `DWSet` display sequence. The latter is always redirected to the window where we want the action to take place. The `Wcreate` output is not redirected. Rather, the window device it is creating is named as part of the actual command.

WHAT IF I CHANGE MY MIND?

You have just taken a look at your finished screen, but you don't quite like what you see. You think the entire screen would look a little better if the command window `/w1` was cyan like the bottom window. No problem, go ahead and change it. Type:

```
display 1b 33 7
```

Not bad! Notice that we did not need to redirect the output of the OS-9 `Display` tool here because we wanted the action to take place in window `/w1` — where we typed the command. Now, how do you suppose it would look if we made the border magenta? Try it:

```
display 1b 34 6
```

Doesn't look too great! How about red? Type:

```
display 1b 34 4
```

It just might work if we make window device `/w3` green. Again, notice that we did not need to redirect the output of these commands since the border is global to the entire screen. Let's check out a green screen!

```
display 1b 33 3 >/w3
```

Notice that we did need to type the redirection operator here to make sure OS-9 changed the background color of the right window. But, what's wrong? The background color of our window is still red. Or is it? Let's clear that window and find out.

```
display c >/w3
```

Looks a little loud. Let's give blue a try!

```
display 1b 33 1 >/w3
display c >/w3
```

Looks like a winner! Now, let's make a billboard out of the window at the bottom of the screen by creating two overlay windows. We'll print our message on the second overlay window. But first we'll display some information on the screen so we can show you that it's still there when we close the overlay windows.

```
dir x >/w4
display 1b 22 1 2 2 4c 6 0 2 >/w4
echo Hello Overlay One >/w4
display 1b 22 1 2 2 46 2 1 5 >/w4
echo For The Best OS-9 Theory Read The Complete Rainbow
Guide To OS-9 >/w4
```

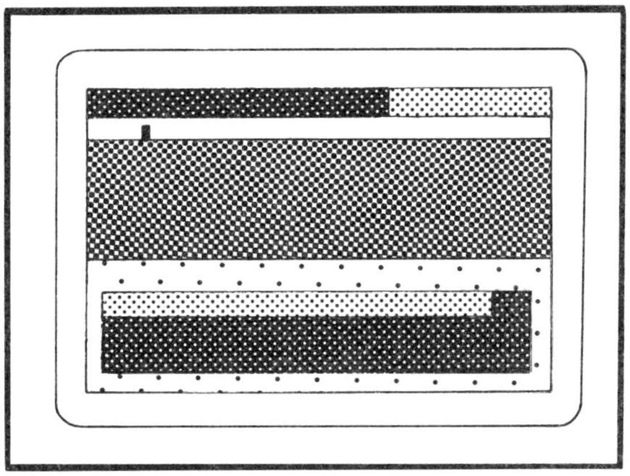

Let's close the overlay windows and see if our directory listing is still intact on window device /w4.

```
display 1b 23 >/w4 ; display 1b 23 >/w4
```

These windows are really amazing! There's the directory listing. Just the way we left it.

MAKE A GRAPHICS WINDOW TO DRAW

You use the same techniques to create a graphics window that you used to create text windows. Just answer the type question with a different number in your command line.

Since the screen we are working on is a text screen, we cannot create a graphics window on it. This means the window we are about to create will appear on another screen.

```
wcreate /w5 -s=7 0 0 80 12 0 2 4
```

BREAKING WINDOWS

One of the things we haven't shown you about windows in this chapter is how to get rid of them. We did show you how to close the overlay windows, but you also need to be able to remove your device windows to free the memory they use. Don't worry, the command is almost the same. To get rid of a window, you merely type:

```
display 1b 24 >/w2
```

That command line should have wiped out your customized window device /w2. Now wipe out window device /w1 — the one you're typing in.

```
display 1b 24 >/w1
```

Did you notice what happened? Since you were running a

shell, OS-9 closed your customized window as you requested. But, it fell back into the pre-defined window `/w1`. Window `/w1` is described in the device descriptor `/w1` that is loaded into memory when you boot OS-9. The moral of the story? To get rid of a window that is running a shell, you must first get rid of the shell in that window. To do that, move to the window in question and type:

```
ex
```

After you press ENTER, you'll notice that you can no longer type in this window. You can, however, press CLEAR until you return to another OS-9 shell where you can remove the window you were operating in using the `display 1b 24` sequence.

That's it for creating windows! In the next chapter we'll fire up a graphics window or two and show you several ways to use OS-9's built-in drawing tools.

CHAPTER 4

automating the window game

When you work with a computer, you must pay attention to detail. These modern machines almost make you think you are back in your fourth grade English class where the teacher made you dot every 'i' and cross every 't'.

Probably about the fifth time you received an error message after slowly typing in an OS-9 command line using the hunt-and-peck method, you were very frustrated. And all you wanted to do was make your Color Computer print, "Hello World!"

Your predicament calls for an OS-9 hero known as the procedure file. We showed you how to use the OS-9 `Build` tool to put together a procedure file in an earlier chapter. Those first procedure files helped us get a few small jobs done, but now it's time to get serious. So serious, in fact, that we need to show you how to work with the OS-9 text editor.

Why would you want to edit a file? Let's use the OS-9 techniques we practiced in the last chapter to explain. After you got comfortable with the idea of filling a screen with custom windows designed to solve your problems, you most likely had an urge to experiment.

"I wonder how it would work if I change the size of that window from two rows to four? If I do that, I'll need to make the other display window 12 rows deep instead of 16. I sure am going to have to type a lot of these silly commands before I can start doing my real job."

While you were using the OS-9 `Build` tool, you wound up in serious trouble if you made a mistake just before you pressed ENTER. Your mistake was entered in the procedure file. To change it, you had to delete the entire file and start over. Then, the next time you tried, you made a mistake on another line. It seemed like you just couldn't win.

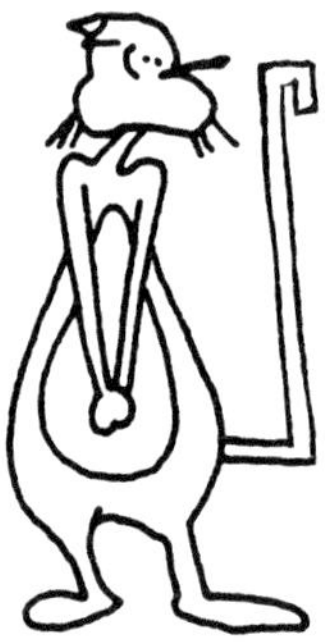

With an editor you can enter OS-9 command lines directly into a procedure file like you did with the `Build` tool. After you run the procedure file the first time and find a few mistakes you want to correct, you can then reopen the procedure file with your text editor and change it. Usually, you just need to change one or two characters. This done, you can quickly close the file and run the procedure file again. If you like what you see, you can keep it. It you want to change another thing or two, you only need to start up the editor again and make the additional changes.

We'll start you off with the editor, and a file containing English language text, which is easier to understand. Then, we'll move on and show you a few tricks you can use when you enter the command lines needed to create and manipulate OS-9 windows. In fact, we'll automate all those steps you slowly typed in by hand in the last chapter.

When you were using the OS-9 `Build` tool to enter those procedure files early in the book, you may not have realized that you can also use `Build` to save real information. For example, a short list of names and addresses is a very handy thing to have at your finger tips. It's much easier to tell your Color Computer to find a name for you than it is to search through several hundred business cards scattered all over your desk.

Here's how you might build a list of names and numbers. Type:

```
build address_list
Rainbow, Prospect, KY 40059
Puckett, Dale L.; Rockville, MD 20852
Internal Information Branch, USCG Headquarters 20593
```

When you are finished, press ENTER. As long as your list of names and addresses is short, you can use the OS-9 `List` utility command to find a name. Just type:

```
list address_list
```

Later, when the list grows and your OS-9 utility program library expands, you can use a more powerful OS-9 pattern-matching utility command like Grep to find a single entry in your file.

CHANGING A FILE

But what happens when someone in your name and address file moves? Then, you'll need to find a way to change the address. For starters, you can use the OS-9 Edit application. It comes with OS-9 Level II for the Color Computer.

Edit is an extremely powerful text editor that you can use to both prepare and change text files. You can use its macro capability to automate many tasks. For now, we'll stick with a few basic techniques to help you get started entering and editing your own files.

Here's how you can edit the address file you created with the Build tool earlier. Type:

```
edit address_list
```

The OS-9 Edit program will load and in a few seconds your screen should look something like this.

```
OS9: Edit address_list
*END OF FILE*
E:
```

The E: prompt tells you that Edit is waiting for you to give it a command. Let's start by making sure we have the right file. To list the entire file, at the E: prompt type:

```
l*
```

Now let's insert a new name at the beginning of the file. At the E: prompt, press the space bar and type:

```
Pimental, Bruce A.; Seattle, WA. 98118
```

The space tells Edit that you want it to insert the text that follows in front of the line you just listed. Let's see if our new edition is in place. Type:

```
-*l*
```

You should see:

```
Pimental, Bruce A.; Seattle, WA. 98118
Pimental, Bruce A.; Seattle, WA. 98118
Rainbow, Prospect, KY 40059
Puckett, Dale L.; Rockville, MD 20852
Internal Information Branch, USCG Headquarters 20593
```

Good! `Edit` moved its pointer to the very top of your file. The `-*` told it to do this. When it arrived at that point in your file, it listed the line at which it was pointing to your Color Computer screen — the line you just added.

After it listed that line, it read the `l*`, which told it to list your entire file. That's why the line you added appears twice in the listing above. The main thing to remember while you are using `Edit` is that when the program prompts you with an `E:` after it lists a line to the screen, it is pointing to the first character in that line. If you insert something at this point, it will show up in front of that line.

Likewise, if you issue `Edit`'s `Delete` command by typing a single 'd' at this point, it deletes the line that was just printed.

Let's show you how to add a new name and address at the bottom of the file. Type:

```
+*
Midgett, Randy, Governors Is., NY 10004
```

Notice that we always type our `Edit` commands as the very first character after the prompt. Press the space bar once before making the next *text* entry, but if you accidentally press the space bar before you type a *command*, you will wind up inserting the command you type into your text file. Let's see if we managed to insert that name in the right place. Type:

```
-*l*
```

You should see:

```
Pimental, Bruce A.; Seattle, WA. 98118
Pimental, Bruce A.; Seattle, WA. 98118
Rainbow, Prospect, KY 40059
Puckett, Dale L.; Rockville, MD 20852
Internal Information Branch, USCG Headquarters 20593
Midgett, Randy; Governors Is., NY 10004
```

Now let's imagine that Bruce Pimental moves to the Silicon Valley. We'll need to change his address. Type:

```
-*
C*/Seattle, WA. 98118/Sunnyvale, CA 94087/
```

Now check your file by typing `-*l*`. You should see:

```
Pimental, Bruce A.; Sunnyvale, CA 94087
Pimental, Bruce A.; Sunnyvale, CA 94087
Rainbow, Prospect, KY 40059
Puckett, Dale L.; Rockville, MD 20852
Internal Information Branch, USCG Headquarters 20593
Midgett, Randy; Governors Is., NY 10004
```

This sample editing session should give you a feel for the OS-9 `Edit` application. Practice by adding a number of names and addresses from your personal telephone book.

As you practice, try some of the commands listed below. Our table gives you an overview of the editing commands that you'll need to get started. After you master these, study the operating system manual you received with OS-9 Level II. You'll have the `Edit` tool aced in no time.

TABLE 4-A: Beginning Editing Commands

Keys	Action
space bar	Inserts text following the space at the position of the edit pointer.
ENTER	Moves edit pointer forward one line.
+	Moves edit pointer forward one line.
+6	Moves edit pointer forward six lines.
+*	Moves edit pointer to bottom of file.
/	Moves edit pointer to bottom of file.
-	Moves edit pointer back one line.
-4	Moves edit pointer back four lines.
-*	Moves edit pointer to top of file.
`C/old string/new string/`	Changes first "old string" to "new string."
`C3/old /new /`	Changes next three occurrences of "old" to "new."
`C*/bad word/good word/`	Changes every "bad word" to "good word."

`Edit` has many other commands that can make your editing easy. After you master these, dig in and we'll go to work on a long procedure file.

Here's the one thing you must always remember. When you give one of the commands above to `Edit`, you must start typing it at the first character position in the line. If you press the space bar first, `Edit` will insert the line you type.

Finally, when you are satisfied with your data file and are ready to stop editing, don't forget to type:

```
q
```

This causes `Edit` to save your file in your current data directory and returns you to the shell.

EDITING PROCEDURE FILES

Practice editing some English language files first. When you're ready to move on, join us here and we'll give you a few tips to help you edit your procedure files.

First, consider the color chart we discussed in the last chapter. Red, white and blue make sense. The numbers '4', '0' and '1' somehow just don't seem to make it in the real world.

Why don't you type the real name for the colors you want when you define your windows? After you have entered the complete procedure file, you can go back and use Edit's global change function to change each occurrence of "red" to "04," each "white" to "0," etc. At least you'll feel like you understand what you are trying to create.

In fact, there are some things you will be typing while creating customized window devices that won't mean much in English. For example, how on earth would you ever guess that `display 1b 20` means "Make a Device Window"? Why don't we call it `MakeDW` when we type our long procedure file? You can use Edit's global editing feature to translate it into a form OS-9 can digest.

If we play our cards right, we may even be able to put the global change commands needed to convert our English language procedure files back to OS-9 usable procedure files in a special edit command file we can redirect into Edit. If we do this, you'll be able to sit back and watch while Edit does the work automatically.

We'll take a look at an English language version of our procedure first. Then, we'll convert it to a valid OS-9 procedure file and test it on our Color Computer.

THE LISTING: EnglishScreen

```
echo Create four text windows and
echo several overlay windows
echo on the same screen.
display a
echo New window devices will be
echo named W1 W2 W3 and W4.
*
* Notice that we could not type /W1
* in the Echo command line above
* We could do this by typing double quotes
* around the entire line ... like this:
*
display a
echo "New window names: /W1, /W2, /W3 and /W4!"
*
* First, create four windows on the same screen
* Make it an 8Ø X 24 text screen

* The "-z" tells wcreate to take its input
* from the standard input path, which is the
* Notice that we
* put the information it needed on the next
* four lines.  Normally, a blank line would have
* followed our four lines of window definitions
* but we put an asterisk because it causes OS-9
* to show you what it is doing "live" while you are
```

```
* running the procedure file.
* You should run this procedure file from a window
* device, ie, /W1, /W2, etc.  Do not run it from a VDG
* device like /TERM.
*
wcreate -z
/w1 -s=2 Ø 2 8Ø 2 black white blue
/w2 Ø Ø 8Ø 2 white black blue
/w3 Ø 4 8Ø 1Ø black red blue
/w4 Ø 14 8Ø 1Ø black cyan blue
*
*
* Print a Banner in Window /W2
*
clearscreen >/w2
echo Color Computer Window Classroom >/w2
*
* Create an Overlay on the right end of window /W2
*
makeoverLay 3Ø Ø 2Ø black magenta yellow>/w2
*
* Now Print the Date and Time in that window
*
date t >/w2
*
* Identify windows /W3 and /W4
*
Echo Welcome to Window /W3 >/w3
Echo Welcome to Window /W4 >/w4
*
* Now change the Color of the command window to Cyan
*
background cyan >/w1
*
* And change the border color to red
*
border red >/w1
*
* Make the background of window /W3 blue
*
background blue >/w3
clearscreen >/w3
echo I'm still Window Three >/w3
*
* Display a directory listing in window /W4
*
dir x >/w4
*
* Create an overlay window covering your file names
* But, tell OS-9 to save your directory listing
*
makeoverlay 2 2 4C 6 white black >/w4
*
```

```
* Display a message in the overlay window
*
echo Hello from Overlay Window Number One >/w4
*
* Two overlay windows are better
* Notice that the coordinates of the second window
* are relative to the device window, not the first
* overlay window as you might suspect.
*
makeoverlay 4 4 46 2 blue yellow >/w4
*
* Make sure we know the Overlay Window Works
*
* Note that the following line must all be typed on one line.
echo For the BEST OS-9 Theory READ The Complete Rainbow Guide to OS-9 >/
*
* To display text on an open overlay window, we send
* the text to the device window it overlays.
*
* Start an OS-9 Shell in window /W1
*
selectwindow >/w1
shell i=/w1&
```

Create the file above using `Edit`. To do this, type:

```
load edit
edit EnglishScreen
```

After you see `Edit`'s `E:` prompt, type the procedure file, just like you typed the names when you were working with the address file earlier in this chapter. Don't forget to press the space bar before you enter each line.

You may skip typing the comment lines if you want. They are the lines that begin with an asterisk (*). However, by adding comment lines to your procedure files when you first type them, you will be able to tell what you were trying to do when you pull the listing out of a file folder and try to run it six months later.

TRANSLATING YOUR COMMANDS MANUALLY

After you have typed in the procedure file, exit `Edit` by typing a `q` in the first position following the `E:` prompt. This saves the procedure file you typed in an OS-9 file named `EnglishScreen`. That file will be stored in your current data directory.

Since you loaded the `Edit` module into your Color Computer's memory before you began to enter the procedure file, you will be able to re-enter `Edit` and go right back to work quickly. But first, you will want to save a copy of the English language version of your file, EnglishScreen. Type:

```
copy EnglishScreen MakeScreens
```

You can now keep the English language version of your file intact. This will help you translate the actual procedure file, MakeScreen, when you look at it months from now. But now, it's time to translate MakeScreen into a format OS-9 can understand. We'll make the first change manually. Then, we'll show you how to do the job automatically. In fact, you'll be able to use the Translate file we describe over and over again if you like this technique. First, type:

```
edit MakeScreens
```

At Edit's E: prompt, type:

```
E: c.black.2.
```

Edit will echo the line that you just changed and you will notice that the number 2 has been substituted for the word black. OS-9 understands 2 when you display it in a windowing command. It would not have understood the word black.

Now exit Edit temporarily by typing a q immediately following the E: prompt. Edit will save a new copy of MakeScreen that contains the single change you made.

Making a dozen changes manually could become quite tedious. Once again, however, the magic of OS-9's redirection saves the day. By redirecting the input or output of an OS-9 application we can often perform miracles. The problem at hand is a perfect example.

Run OS-9's Edit tool again and type in the following lines. Remember while working within the editor that you must press the space bar before you begin typing each line.

```
edit Translate
```

When the E: prompt appears, type:

THE LISTING: Translate

```
c* .white.Ø.
-*
c* .blue.1.
-*
c* .black.2.
-*
c* .green.3.
-*
c* .red.4.
-*
c* .yellow.5.
```

```
-*
c* .magenta.6.
-*
c* .cyan.7.
-*
c* .makeoverlay.display 1b 22 1.
-*
c* .background.display 1b 33.
-*
c* .border.display 1b 34.
-*
c* .clearscreen.display c.
-*
c* .selectwindow.display 1b 21.
-*
q
```

After you have typed these lines, you can exit the editor to save your new file. It will be stored in your current data directory. Its name will be Translate.

After you try this method, you'll probably want to add many additional lines to the file Translate. You could use names like TextWin80, TextWin40, HiResWin2Color, HiResWin4Color, MedResWin4Color and MedResWin16Color.

These names would translate to "display 1b 20 02," "display 1b 20 01," "display 1b 20 05," "display 1b 20 07," "display 1b 20 06" and "display 1b 20 08." If you feel other names would make more sense, the ball's in your court. Name that window!

Time out for a warning! Before you begin, decide how you are going to type these names. MedResWin4Color is easy to read and understand. But, medreswin4color is much easier to type. Unfortunately, we have a "gotcha!" If you have typed medreswin4color in your English language procedure file and MedResWin4Color in your Translate file, Edit won't be able to find medreswin4color and your procedure file will not be translated. If this happens and you try to run it with OS-9, it will not work. OS-9 won't recognize medreswin4color either. In computer speak, Edit's change function is "case sensitive."

Back to work. You have typed in an English language procedure file and a special command file for the OS-9 Edit tool. Translate will let you automatically translate your English language procedure file to OS-9 window talk. To perform this magic feat, type:

```
edit #44K MakeScreens <translate
```

That's all there is to it. The OS-9 Edit tool will do the rest. Before you type the command line above make sure that you have turned off the pause feature in the window you are running Edit in. In case you need a gentle reminder, you can do that by typing:

```
tmode -pause
```

The result of your translation is shown in the listing of the file MakeScreens that follows.

The power in the Edit command file Translate comes from the fact that you only need to type it in once. After you have done that, you can use it to translate your English language procedure files to OS-9 window talk forever. You will probably want to enter more English language definitions into Translate so that all of the OS-9 features you use regularly will be available in English.

You'll also most likely want to create another translate command file for the many OS-9 high resolution drawing commands. Most of them can be generated from the OS9: prompt using the Display tool.

In the future, you may wind up purchasing one of the more advanced OS-9 tool kits. There are several of these utility packages on the market and almost all of them are full of filters that you can use in an OS-9 pipeline. The TR — for Transliterate — tool is one of the most popular and can be found in most of the packages.

Most versions of TR let you translate a file on a character per character basis. However, at least one TR we know of lets you translate entire English language words. This one would come in handy here and you could do the same job you did with your Edit-based Translate file. Your command line would look like this:

```
tr "clearscreen"display c" EnglishScreens > MakeScreens
```

If you plan on using this TR to translate your English language procedure files to OS-9 window talk, you will most likely want to build a procedure file that loads TR and then runs it a number of times — once for each translation you need to make.

When TR finishes, your procedure file will unlink TR and return you to the OS9: prompt. This is the type of job that is made to be done in the background while you are using your Color Computer to do other work, or play. Remember, to tell OS-9 that you want it to run these TR processes in the background, you will need to put an ampersand (&) at the end of each command line in your procedure file. This character tells OS-9 to run the process it is starting in the background.

While you're still learning about computing, Edit — a tool that comes with OS-9 Level II on the Color Computer — does the translation job quite nicely. Here are the results after we used "translate" to get from English to OS-9 window talk.

THE LISTING: MakeScreens

```
echo Create four text windows and
echo several overlay windows
echo on the same screen.
display a
echo New window devices will be
echo named W1 W2 W3 and W4.
*
* Notice that we could not type /W1
* in the Echo command line above
* We could do this by typing double quotes
* around the entire line ... like this:
*
display a
echo "New window names: /W1, /W2, /W3 and /W4!"
*
* First, create four windows on the same screen
* Make it an 8Ø X 24 text screen

* The "-z" tells wcreate to take its input
* from the standard input path, which is the
* Notice that we
* put the information it needed on the next
* four lines.  Normally, a blank line would have
* followed our four lines of window definitions
* but we put an asterisk because it causes OS-9
* to show you what it is doing "live" while you are
* running the procedure file.
* You should run this procedure file from a window
* device, ie, /W1, /W2, etc.  Do not run it from a VDG
* device like /TERM.
*
wcreate -z
/w1 -s=2 Ø 2 8Ø 2 2 Ø 1
/w2 Ø Ø 8Ø 2 Ø 2 1
/w3 Ø 4 8Ø 1Ø 2 4 1
/w4 Ø 14 8Ø 1Ø 2 7 1
*
*
* Print a Banner in Window /W2
*
display c >/w2
echo Color Computer Window Classroom >/w2
*
* Create an Overlay on the right end of window /W2
*
display 1b 22 1 3Ø Ø 2Ø 2 6 5>/w2
*
* Now Print the Date and Time in that window
*
date t >/w2
```

```
*
* Identify windows /W3 and /W4
*
Echo Welcome to Window /W3 >/w3
Echo Welcome to Window /W4 >/w4
*
* Now change the Color of the command window to Cyan
*
display 1b 33 7 >/w1
*
* And change the display 1b 34 color to 4
*
display 1b 34 4 >/w1
*
* Make the display 1b 33 of window /W3 1
*
display 1b 33 1 >/w3
display c >/w3
echo I'm still Window Three >/w3
*
* Display a directory listing in window /W4
*
dir x >/w4
*
* Create an overlay window covering your file names
* But, tell OS-9 to save your directory listing
*
display 1b 22 1 2 2 4C 6 Ø 2 >/w4
*
* Display a message in the overlay window
*
echo Hello from Overlay Window Number One >/w4
*
* Two overlay windows are better
* Notice that the coordinates of the second window
* are relative to the device window, not the first
* overlay window as you might suspect.
*
display 1b 22 1 4 4 46 2 1 5 >/w4
*
* Make sure we know the Overlay Window Works
*
* Note that the following line must all be typed on one line.
echo For the BEST OS-9 Theory READ The Complete Rainbow Guide to OS-9
>/w4
*
* To display text on an open overlay window, we send
* the text to the device window it overlays.
*
* Start an OS-9 Shell in window /W1
*
display 1b 21 >/w1
shell i=/w1&
```

Compare the listing of MakeScreen above to the individual OS-9 command lines you typed in Chapter 3. They are almost identical.

The Wcreate command line is the major exception. You need to use a different syntax when you use Wcreate in an OS-9 procedure file. The secret to that syntax lies in the -z option at the end of the command line.

Essentially the -z lets Wcreate tell the OS-9 shell, "Hey, get my input from the standard input path. I don't want to wait all day for some jerk to type my commands."

Since Wcreate is being run from within an OS-9 procedure file, the standard input path is already feeding the characters from the file into the shell. After Wcreate issues the -z option, it also will get its characters from the procedure file. The next four lines contain our input to Wcreate.

We made one off-the-wall change in the procedure file MakeScreen. Normally, you must follow the list of windows you are defining with Wcreate with a blank line in your procedure file. If you do this, however, Wcreate sends you back to the window that you used to start the procedure file and you will not be able to watch the magic.

We wanted you to see everything pop on the screen live while the procedure was running. In the process, we discovered that if we failed to terminate Wcreate's window list with a blank line, Wcreate would simply send its "usage" or help message to the window that started the procedure file. But, it leaves the screen receiving your new windows active and you can sit back and watch the show.

We only used a handful of the windowing commands available in OS-9 Level II in this chapter. Generally, the OS-9 windowing tools work in the same manner and are generated with the Display tool. An excellent description of all available windowing commands is listed in alphabetical order in the Windows section of the OS-9 Level II manual.

PROCEDURES CAN HELP REMOVE WINDOWS

While you are perfecting a procedure file like MakeScreen, you will find you need to debug your instructions several times before you get the windows to look just the way you want them to look. To survive this process, you must find a way to remove the inferior windows before you make another attempt.

Every time you run MakeScreen or a similar procedure file, you will generate four new windows. If you merely edit your procedure file and run it again, you will run into all kinds of problems and you'll find yourself memorizing the definition of Error Number 184 — Window Already Defined.

You'll remember from Chapter 3 that you can close a shell running in your windows by typing:

```
ex
```

But, the window the shell was running in will remain open. You must then remove the window with the OS-9 "device window end" command, 1b24. You do that like this:

```
display 1b 24 >/w4
```

That command line will remove window /w4. But, what about the other four windows? You got it. You'll need to type that command line three more times. The next time you can redirect the output to window /w3, etc. That could be a real pain. But OS-9 has several tools that can speed us along.

USE THE SHELL'S EDITING KEYS

After we enter the command line above and the OS9: prompt returns, we can simply hold down the CTRL key and press the A key. In a split second our previous command line will pop back on the screen. The cursor will be sitting immediately after the 4 in /w4.

Press the back arrow on your Color Computer keyboard until the cursor backs over the 4. Then, type a 3 in place of the 4 and press ENTER again. Next time, use the same technique to change the 3 to a 2, and then the 2 to a 1. Almost painless. But, there's a better way.

You guessed it. Since you're going to be debugging for an hour or more, you may want to use the OS-9 Build tool or Edit to enter a short procedure file. We called ours Kill4W. It looked like this.

```
display 1b 24 >/w4
display 1b 24 >/w3
display 1b 24 >/w2
display 1b 24 >/w1
```

You must be careful when you remove windows, especially those that are being used by copies of the shell. If you don't, it is possible to create pure pandemonium. For example, if you reverse the list in the procedure file above to remove /w1, /w2, /w3 and /w4 in that order, it will not work. It will remove all four windows. But after you kill window /w4, the system will get lost because it doesn't know where to go and your Color Computer will hang up.

The best way to avoid this problem is to keep one window device or the /term device open and running a shell at all times.

Think of it as the home window. When you open and close windows, do it from the home window. Following this protocol should keep you out of trouble.

If you understand how OS-9 works, you will know what is happening when you open a window and start a shell and can feel at ease when you open and close windows, and start and kill shells. You'll know which windows you can kill and which you can't kill because you understand the hierarchy of OS-9 processes. This is a good place for an explanation.

IT'S EASY TO CREATE PROCESSES

You'll find that it is very easy to start a new process with OS-9. In fact, the shell and kernel do most of the work for you.

To create a new process, type the name of the module — or the file that contains the module that contains the program — at the OS9 prompt. When you do this, you are passing a request for a particular action to the OS-9 shell. When you make this request, you must also give the shell the names of any files or other information the new process will need.

The shell first tries to find a module with the name you gave it in the module directory. Remember, this directory contains the name of all modules that are present in memory. If it finds the name of your program in the module directory, the shell will link to the module and run it for you.

If the shell cannot find the name of your program in the module directory, it looks for a file by the same name in your current execution directory. If it finds the file, it will load it into memory, link to it and run your program.

The kernel sets aside an area of memory that your program can use for data storage. It finds out how much memory your program needs by reading the storage size value from the module header.

When the kernel starts a new process, it assigns a unique ID number to it. These ID numbers can range from one to 65,535.

If any of the steps above are unsuccessful, the shell does not create your process. Yet, it won't leave you hanging. It lets you know what happened by printing a message that contains a special error number that tells you what went wrong.

PROCESSES, LIKE PEOPLE, HAVE MANY CHARACTERISTICS

OS-9 processes are a lot like people. In fact, if you think of OS-9 as a family of processes, you will find it much easier to understand. Let's look at the genealogy of a family of OS-9 processes.

When a process creates another process, it becomes a parent. The new process is called a child. Further, if the child creates another process, it also becomes a parent. A process can create any number of children.

This whole discussion may seem absurd. Yet, the family concept makes OS-9 much easier to understand. If you apply it when you look at the output of the OS-9 `Procs` utility, you can almost visualize a family tree.

CHILDREN INHERIT THEIR PARENTS' PROPERTIES

Just as human children inherit characteristics from their parents, OS-9 child processes inherit a number of properties from their parent process.

For example, each person using a computer running OS-9 has been assigned a user number. If a person starts a process, that process belongs to him — it carries his user number. If that process then starts another process, the child process inherits his user number and belongs to him also.

Other properties that are inherited by a child process include the standard input and output paths, the process priority, and the current execution and data directories.

For example, if the standard input and output path used by a parent process is sending data to a window device named `/w7`, any children created by that process will also send their output to `/w7`.

Likewise, if you start a process with a low priority, any children created by that process will also have a low priority. This is important because the process priority tells the 6809 microprocessor how important a job is to you. If you give a process a low priority, the 6809 will give it a very small share of its time.

The bottom line — you cannot remove a shell that has created other shells (a parent) until the shells it created (its children) are terminated. To do so is to create chaos within your Color Computer.

OTHER WINDOW CAUTIONS

First, be careful when you type on your Color Computer keyboard. You will have to be extra careful if you cut your teeth on the Color Computer 1 or 2. Remember when you needed to hold down the CLEAR key to emulate the CTRL key? On the Color Computer 3, it is very easy to accidentally press the CLEAR key while you are holding down the CTRL key — especially if you are reaching for the ESC key to send an end of file signal.

If you do press the CTRL-CLEAR combination, you are going to be in for an interesting surprise the next time you attempt to back space to correct a typing error. The left arrow flat out doesn't work. Actually, it is working — but as one part of a keyboard mouse instead of as a backspace key. Be careful.

Two more quick window notes and we'll let you practice until you wear out the keyboard. First, if you plan to create graphics windows with the `Wcreate` tool, you must make sure you have merged the `sys/stdfonts` file into a graphics window — any graphics window will do — before you run `Wcreate`. If you run `Wcreate` and then merge in the `sys/stdfonts` file, you will not be able to see any text on your new window. You will see dots instead.

The easy way to solve this problem is to add a line in your OS-9 start-up file to merge `sys/stdfonts`. Since the window descriptor `/w4` has been predefined to be a graphics window, we use the following line.

```
merge sys/stdfonts >/w4
```

Remember that the `sys/stdfonts` file only needs to be merged into the system once. Once it is there, all windows you create can use it.

Finally, if you have quite a bit of Color Computer 2 software that ran on Level I, Version 2.00.00 of OS-9, you may want to run more than one VDG window. The VDG window is the 32-by-16 green screen that comes alive when you first boot OS-9. Since it emulates OS-9 Level II, most software written for Level I OS-9 on the Color Computer 2 can also run on the Color Computer 3. But, what if you want to run one Level I program in one window while you are running another in `/term`? Remember, `/term` is the only Level I compatible window.

First, pick a window. Make sure that it is not active, and run the OS-9 `Deiniz` tool on it. Then, run the OS-9 `Xmode` tool to set the number of lines on the screen to 16 and the type to 1. After you do this, you can `Iniz` the window and open a path to it. When you see it, you'll be back in green screen heaven. Here's what the command sequence looks like:

```
deiniz /w3
xmode /w3 type=1 pag=16
shell i=/w3&
```

That's it for windowing. In the next chapter we'll create a small command window and a large graphics window. We'll help you get the artist in you out of the closet as we explore the many OS-9 drawing commands.

CHAPTER 5

getting ready to draw

Our goal in this chapter is to show you how you can set up your system to work on several major projects at the same time. When you are through, you'll know how to write a procedure file that will automatically prepare your Color Computer for the day's work. You'll also pick up a few more tricks and OS-9 subtleties along the way.

Your Color Computer will automatically open four windows, starting a screen editor in one window and BASIC09 in another. It will leave a shell you can use to run scores of additional OS-9 tools in a third window and create a display-only screen where you can print messages or study the output of your programs. You will be able to switch from testing a BASIC09 procedure to writing a paragraph of documentation about it with a single keystroke. The VDG green screen will also be available for additional tasks.

By using our procedure file as a model, you can set up a similar environment to do the work most dear to your heart. For example, you could start a screen editor in one window, a spreadsheet program in another, a database program in a third and a professional drawing application in a fourth. With a single keystroke, you could then take a look at the latest financial data, prepare an illustration or ponder the mailing list for the sales pitch you are writing.

After setting up a model work environment, we'll start your introduction to the powerful graphics primitives you can use directly from the OS-9 Level II command line. We'll show you how to write a procedure file that will set you up with a two-window screen where you can experiment with OS-9's graphics cursors.

In this chapter you'll learn how to use the graphics cursors by typing short commands at the OS-9 prompt. Learning how things work at this low level will help you understand what is happening when you use the same commands from BASIC09. In the next chapter we'll give you a brief introduction to BASIC09, the high level language that comes with OS-9 Level II on your Color Computer. Then, we'll move back to the drawing board and help you draw a few pictures from the OS-9 command line and BASIC09.

While we're drawing with the OS-9 `Display` tool, we'll show you how you can put several drawing commands into a procedure file to create an impressive graphics presentation. Once you've completed a dress rehearsal and are satisfied with the pictures you've created, we'll show you how to redirect the output of your procedure file into another file. This file will contain only the actual codes the OS-9 `Display` tool sends to your windows to perform drawing magic. Finally, we'll show you how you can merge this new file to the window of your choice for automated, high-speed drawing.

Since we're starting to tackle more ambitious assignments in each chapter, we thought this would be a good time to show you how to set up your system so you can work without stopping. After you emulate this procedure with your own applications programs, you will no longer need to wait for your applications tools to load into memory when you change from one to the other.

In fact, we'll show you how to work in a manner that won't require you to exit your applications programs. This means you won't even have to wait for them to start up. They'll be ready to work immediately. We created an OS-9 procedure file to do the job.

Actually, we set up two procedure files. The first is our standard `StartUp` file, which is always stored on the root directory of the working system disk. Our second procedure file is named `StartApps`.

We set up our `StartUp` file to do only those jobs that we need to do every time we start our computer. It is important that you remember the jobs you need to do might be different because you are using different peripheral hardware. But, you can use ours as a model.

After you experiment with `StartUp` and `StartApps` a few times and ponder the issues, you'll see how you can create a number of different `StartApps` files that let you do different types of work with your Color Computer.

THE LISTING: StartUp

```
*
* Lock shell and std utils into memory
*
link shell
*
echo *        DaleSoft
echo * Dale and Esther Puckett
echo *       Rockville, MD
*
display a a
*
* Note we did not run the setime
* tool because we are using a
* real time hardware clock.
*
date t
echo Setting monitor type
montype r
*
* You have to run montype every time
* you boot.  Just as well put it in
* StartUp.
*
dØoff
*
* Our customized hardware requires
* us to run dØoff.  OS-9 switches our
* current execution directory and
* current data directory to /HØ/CMDS
* and /HØ automatically when we boot OS-9.
* However, the motor in /DØ continues
* to run so we run "dØoff to shut it off.
*
echo Setting Printer lf's
xmode /p lf
*
* Our Epson printer requires this command.
*
iniz w7
Echo Merging Fonts to /W7
merge /dd/sys/stdfonts >/w7
shell i=/w7&
*
* Now we'll load the applications
* we know we'll need every time
*
Echo Loading Screen Editor
load ds
```

```
Echo Loading RunB
load runb
Echo Loading Basic09
load basic09
*
* You will want to substitute the
* name of the screen editor you
* purchased for "ds" in the command
* line above.  "ds" is the name of the
* file and module that contains our
* screen editor.
*
echo Type CLEAR for 80 Columns
*
* It's always a good idea to send
* messages to computer operators so
* you won't leave them wondering
* what to do next.
*
```

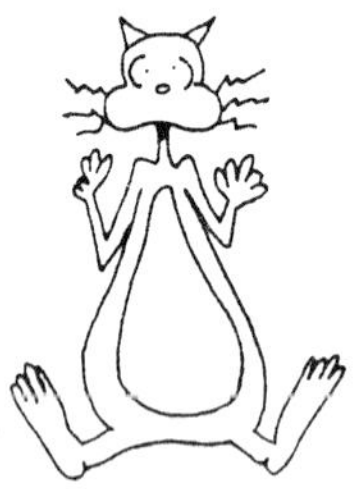

We have been extremely liberal with our comments in this StartUp procedure file. You should do the same thing when you create your customized version. The comments will help you determine what you were trying to do if something doesn't work. They will also help you remember what you did, months from now.

Remember, to put a comment line into an OS-9 procedure file, you type an asterisk (*) in the first column of that line.

Can you see how to display your own personalized sign-on messages by using the OS-9 Echo tool? Also, did you notice that we used the default device descriptor — /w7 — the one built into the OS9Boot file that came with the OS-9 Master System Disk when we created window /w7? This gave us a quick way to create an 80-by-24 text window where we could start a shell with a big screen to work in.

Toward the end of our StartUp file, we tell OS-9 to load the major applications programs needed every time we start up our Color Computer. The choice here is personal and you will find it easy to follow our model when you set up your own system.

Our screen editor gives us a convenient way to edit text files. BASIC09 gives a tool we can use to write quick utility programs or complicated applications. And we will need RunB, BASIC09's run time interpreter, every time we want to run a "packed" BASIC09 program.

Later in the book we'll show you how you can merge several needed modules into the Gfx2 file so they'll be in memory every time you need them — without using any additional memory. Also in a later chapter, we feature a simple screen editor written in BASIC09. If you haven't purchased a screen editor yet, this one will get you started. But, those are other chapters!

Notice also that we used the OS-9 Echo tool to send messages to our start-up window every time we told our Color Computer to perform a task that would take more than a second or two. This can relieve a lot of worry.

For example, if you see a message that says "Loading BASIC09," you know that the operation will take a while and you won't worry when nothing happens for a few seconds. These messages become especially important if you load five or six major applications programs at a time. Without a message, the operator could wind up staring at a static screen for more than a minute.

SETTING UP OUR SYSTEM TO DO A LOT OF WORK

Now take a long look at the OS-9 procedure file StartApps. After you run it — or a similar customized version — you will have BASIC09, a screen editor, two OS-9 shells and a display window ready to use instantly. Each will only be a CLEAR key away.

Each one of the applications you install with your own StartApps will have a full 80- by 24-column screen to work in. You will be able to flip from the middle of an editing assignment to the middle of a BASIC09 programming project with a minimum number of keystrokes. You will need to be working on a 512K Color Computer to use a procedure file like StartApps, however.

THE LISTING: StartApps

```
*
* First, we'll create our windows
*
* Notice that we have already created
* /W7, a 80 X 24 Text Window in the
* StartUp file so we won't need to
* repeat those steps here.  In fact, we
* couldn't create /W7 again here anyway.
*
* We would cause an "error 184" -- OS-9's
* window already defined error."
*
* We have also started a Shell in /W7.
* This gives us a place where we can run any
* OS-9 text-based tool on a large screen.
*
* Notice also that we have already merged the
* sys/stdfonts file into window /W7
* in our startup file.
*
* We'll almost always need these fonts
* when we're working with windows.
```

```
*
* Now we'll build an 80 x 24 graphics window in
* device /W6 and start Basic09 in it.
*
* We'll make /W6 a four color window that gives
* us 640 x 192 graphics pixels to work with.
*
* Note here that OS-9 Level II will give us a
* chance to break old habits.
*
* Instead of exiting Basic09 with
* "BYE" or a <CTRL><BREAK>
* we will now want to just strike the
* <CLEAR> key when we finish
* working with a Basic09 program.
*
* This will take us to another window where
* we can do another type of work.
*
* Basic09 will still be running when we
* return to this window.
*
* When we need to work with another
* Basic09 procedure, we will strike
* the <CLEAR> key until the cursor
* returns to the "B: " prompt.
*
* We can then go back to work in Basic09.
*
iniz w6
display 1b 20 7 0 0 50 18 2 0 2 >/w6
basic09 #20K <>>>/w6&
*
* Basic09 should be running now
* and we can go to it by striking the
* <CLEAR> key till we get to the
* white window with the black letters.
* Now we'll create window /W5
* and start our screen editor in it.
*
* We will want to follow the same
* procedures when we exit the editor.
*
* Instead of telling it to exit the file
* we are editing and return to the Shell,
* we want to simply have the editor write
* the file we are working on to a disk file
* and return to its own prompt.
*
* The bottom line:  We want to keep our editor
* running so we can move to it at
* a moments notice by striking the <CLEAR> key.
```

```
*
* We predict that you can now begin
* to see the time savings the OS-9
* windowing environment makes possible.
*
iniz w5
display 1b 2Ø 2 Ø Ø 5Ø 18 1 7 3 >/W5
ds <>>>/w5&
*
* Note here that you should substitute
* the name of the screen editor you purchased
* for the "ds" we typed above.  "ds" is the module
* and file name of the editor we are
* using as we prepare examples for
* The Complete Beginners Guide to OS-9 Level II.
*
* To start work on your own text, strike
* the <CLEAR> key until you see the cursor
* stop behind your editor's prompt.
*
* Notice that we created a text window for our screen
* editor because text windows operate faster.
*
* We created a four color graphics screen
* for BasicØ9 because we wanted to
* experiment with the graphics commands.
*
* Now, we'll create one more window which
* we can use to display the output of the
* many OS-9 tools.
*
* Notice that we will not start a Shell in this window.
*
* We want to keep it available for our use as a display.
*
* Remember!  You cannot send the output
* of an OS-9 tool to a window running a Shell
* without creating much visual confusion.
*
* We will also always leave the VDG --
* or hardware screen -- named /TERM
* active with a Shell running in it at
* all times.  This gives us a home
* to return to if everything goes haywire
* during a late night session.
*
iniz w4
display 1b 2Ø 2 Ø Ø 5Ø 18 2 Ø 1 >/w4
echo Display Window Number Four at your service >/w4
*
* Notice that sending a message to window /W4
* opens a path to it and makes it appear on
```

```
* our monitor when we move to it with the <CLEAR>
* key.  If we had not sent a message to it, that
* window would have remained invisible until we
* did.
*
```

We used an interesting OS-9 trick in the procedure file StartApps. Can you pinpoint it?

We started both BASIC09 and our text editor in a special way. We did not run them from an OS-9 shell. Rather, we started them directly from our procedure file and redirected their standard input, standard error and standard output paths to the window we wanted them to appear in.

You should be prepared for a surprise if you start BASIC09 or any application using this technique, however. You won't hurt anything, but if you accidentally — or even purposely — exit BASIC09 or your application, you will suddenly be looking at a dead screen. You'll see the cursor on the screen but when you press a key or type a command, nothing will happen.

Nothing is really lost, however, and if you want to restart the process you can return to your home window — the green VDG screen — and start your application again. Remember, an OS-9 process is nothing more than a program that happens to be running. Since you loaded your program into memory in your StartUp file, it will come alive quickly.

The secret of your ability to work quickly with OS-9 Level II is in the magic of the CLEAR key and the fact that you can leave several of your applications running at the same time — albeit in different windows. Every time you press this key, you will change windows.

This means you could be in the middle of writing a complicated paragraph for a user's manual you are preparing about a new program when you forget exactly how the routine you are describing works. No problem — if you are using OS-9 Level II.

Just press the CLEAR key until your cursor appears back in the window running your new BASIC09 program. List the procedure or make a test run. When you are satisfied that you understand what is happening, press CLEAR again until your cursor is back in the window running your screen editor. You'll find the cursor winds up back at the same exact position you left it in. Magic! (And very productive.)

MAKING A GRAPHICS SCREEN TO EXPERIMENT IN

When you start working with a powerful operating system like OS-9, you'll discover that there are many different ways to do the same job. First, we'll show you a procedure that will turn any window you happen to be working in (except the VDG hardware green screen) into a four-color, 640- by 192-pixel window instantly! You'll find this window colorful and useful for many tasks.

Then, we'll show you a procedure file that will create a four color, 640- by 192-pixel screen designed just for experimenting. The screen it creates will hold two windows. One will be a 20-line display window you can use to display your graphics output. The other will be a four-line command window where you can type your commands. Let's look at our instant graphics window procedure first.

THE LISTING: Makegw

```
* First we must terminate the
* window we are working in.
*
* OS-9 will not allow us to have
* more than one window with the
* same name.  We will send the code
* for the OS-9 Device Window End call.
*
display 1b 24
*
*Now we must create a new window in
* the same device.  Since we are already
* working there, we don't need to redirect
* the output from this procedure.  The output
* goes to the standard output path which is
* the window we are working in.  The next
* code we send is the OS-9 Device Window Set
* call.
*
display 1b 2Ø 5 Ø Ø 5Ø 18 1 Ø 4
*
* Now we must tell OS-9 which font
* we want to use in our new graphics
* window.  We do this with the OS-9
* Font Call.  The "c8" we see in the
* command line is hex for the number
* 2ØØ in decimal.  It is the group number
* that holds the fonts merged from the
* file sys/stdfonts.  The Ø1 which follows
* tells OS-9 to use buffer number one which
* contains the standard 8 x 8 pixel fonts.
*
display 1b 3a c8 Ø1
*
* Now we must select the window we just
* created.  We do it with the code for the
* OS-9 Window Select call.
*
```

```
display 1b 21
*
* And finally, we decide to change the foreground
* color of our new window to blue with the OS-9
* FColor system call.
*
display 1b 32 1
*
* That's all folks!  Go for it!
*
```

Remember: You must have merged the `sys/stdfonts` file into a window device before you run the procedure to make the graphics window above. We did this in our startup file. If you forget this, you will not be able to display any text in your new windows. If you display text to a graphics window when there are no fonts available in the system, you will see only periods on that window.

Run `Makegw` several times and watch it work. To run it, make sure it is stored in your current data directory, then type:

```
makegw
```

If the file `Makegw` had not been stored in your current data directory, you would have needed to type a complete pathlist to the file. It might have looked something like this:

```
/h0/my_experimental_procedures/makegw
```

Now let's speed up the operation. Run this OS-9 command line:

```
makegw >mgw
```

You have just sent the output of the OS-9 `Display` commands you typed in the procedure `Makegw` to a new file named `mgw`. If you were to look inside that file, you would see only the characters that display normally sends to the standard output path. It would look like this.

```
1b 24 1b 20 07 00 00 50 18 01 00 04 1b 3a c8 01 1b 21 1b
32 01
```

You can see those characters if you use the OS-9 `Dump` tool that comes with the OS-9 Software Developers Package. If you have run Level I OS-9 on a Color Computer 2, you own the `Dump` command from that package.

Caution: Do not get in the habit of running OS-9 Level I utility commands on an OS-9 Level II based Color Computer. Some of them will not work. The reason they won't work rests with the differences between the memory management techniques used in OS-9 Level I and OS-9 Level II. For an excellent explanation of OS-9 memory management, pick up a copy of *The Complete Rainbow Guide to OS-9*.

Now that you have created the file mgw, stand by for some fast action. Move to a text window — /w7 for example — and type:

```
merge mgw
```

That was quick service, wasn't it? If you want to turn another display window into an OS-9 high resolution graphics window, you can do it if you take advantage of OS-9's redirection feature. For example, if you are working from the VDG hardware green screen and you want to change window device /w7 from an 80-by-24, type-two text window to a type-seven, 640- by 192-pixel, high resolution window, type:

```
merge mgw >/w7
```

That should do the trick. Experiment with this technique when you get a chance and we'll use it some more when we start throwing pictures on your Color Computer screen. For now, let's look at a procedure file that will set you up to experiment with the OS-9 graphics primitives.

THE LISTING: ReadyDraw

```
*
* Merge all available fonts fonts into a window
* Notice we have two in our collection that do
* not come with OS-9 Level II.  In the near future
* you will likely see hundreds of fonts
* available for your Color Computer III.
*
merge /dd/sys/stdfonts >/w
merge /dd/sys/ibm      >/w
merge /dd/sys/future   >/w
*
* Now merge the graphics cursors
*
merge /dd/sys/stdptrs  >/w
*
* And the standard background patterns.
* for the four color -- type seven -- graphics window
*
* Other files are available in your SYS directory
* with background patterns for windows with
* both two and 16 colors.
*
merge /dd/sys/stdpats_4 >/w
*
* Notice that we merged everything into the
* window device named /W.  When you create
* a window on this device it uses the next
* available window number.  By using /W we
* didn't need to remember the names of the
* windows where we had already started Shells.
```

```
*
* Remember, if you try to send output to a
* window running a Shell, you create much
* visual confusion.
*
* After everything is merged, we create our
* two new windows using the wcreate tool.
*
wcreate -z
/w1 -s=7 Ø Ø  8Ø 2Ø 2 Ø 4
/w2      Ø 2Ø 8Ø  4 2 7

*
*Now start a Shell and prepare to move to it
*
display 1b 21 >/w2
shell i=/w2&
```

In ReadyDraw make sure to leave out the lines that merge the ibm and future fonts unless you have these fonts. Instead, you could make them "invisible" by putting an asterisk in the first column of each of the two lines.

Press the CLEAR key to move your cursor to the command window you just created with the procedure file ReadyDraw and we'll show you how you can put some basic drawings on your screen by issuing a series of display codes — or commands — to the graphics primitives built into OS-9.

PLANNING OUR ATTACK

The temptation is to sit down and wing it. Unfortunately, it doesn't work that way when you start using graphics primitives. If you wing it, you are certain to wind up with strange looking birds. If you want to create memorable images, you must take the time to plan your work before you begin.

The first thing you need to do is start thinking of your screen in a different manner. When computers first started to appear in homes, most of them displayed only text. Very few of them could draw pictures. None of them could do windows!

If you owned a Color Computer 2 before you purchased your Color Computer 3, you probably got used to thinking of your screen in terms of 16 rows of 32 text characters. On the Color Computer 3, I'll bet you're enjoying the 24 rows with 80 characters.

To draw pictures, however, you need to start thinking in terms of pixels — short for picture elements — rather than characters. For example, on the screen you just created with the procedure file above, you are looking at a 640-pixels-wide by 192-pixels-high screen. Each one of these pixels is represented by one tiny dot on the screen.

ReadyDraw created two windows on that screen. The drawing

window is 640 pixels wide and 160 pixels high. The command screen at the bottom is 640 pixels wide and 32 pixels high.

When you display text on a graphics window like the one you just created, your Color Computer actually draws the characters on the screen. Each character from the first buffer in the `stdfonts` file is eight pixels high and eight pixels wide.

When you type a character, the picture tube on your Color Computer must display eight individual lines before you can see the character. Each one of those lines is one pixel high. The individual dots that make up the character you typed are highlighted as the beam crosses them during its trip across the screen. After the beam makes eight trips, you see the character. Fortunately, your Color Computer works so fast that the entire character seems to appear all at one time.

We've created two tables that show the relationship between character position and pixel position. One deals with the horizontal position on your window or screen. The other compares vertical character positions to vertical pixel positions. Make a copy when you are ready to draw with the graphics primitives. Things will go a lot smoother.

TABLE 5-A: Horizontal Character/Pixel Positions

Character Position	Pixel Position	Hex High	Hex Low
0	0	0	0
5	40	0	28
10	80	0	50
20	160	0	A0
30	240	0	F0
40	320	1	40
50	400	1	90
60	480	1	E0
70	560	2	30
80	640	2	80

TABLE 5-B: Vertical Character/Pixel Positions

Character Position	Pixel Position	Hex High	Hex Low
0	0	0	0
2	16	0	10
5	40	0	28
7.5	60	0	3C
10	80	0	50
12.5	100	0	64
15	120	0	78
17.5	140	0	8C
20	160	0	A0
24	192	0	C0

We'll start our drawing exercise with some prefabricated characters. If you pressed the CLEAR key when we told you to earlier, your cursor should be sitting just behind the `OS9:` prompt — in a four-line green window with black letters. That's window `/w2`. You should see a clear white screen with a red border at the top of your screen. Its name is `/w1`. Now, type:

```
display 1b 39 ca 04 1b 4e 01 40 00 50
```

Where did that hourglass come from? It just popped up out of nowhere. Not really! If you were to translate the escape code sequence the `Display` tool sent to your screen into OS-9 speak, it would read:

```
display GCSet Hourglass PutGC 320 80
```

Let's try a read-through. Essentially, you want OS-9 to use its `Display` tool to "set," or name, the graphics cursor you want to use. Then, you want to actually put that graphics cursor on the screen at a position 320 pixels from the left edge of the screen and 80 pixels from the top. You want an hourglass to appear in the middle of the white screen.

Go ahead, ask! If you want the cursor to appear at a position 320 pixels in and 80 pixels from the top, why did you type `01 40 00 50`? That's an excellent question and a very relevant one. The answer lies with the OS-9 `Display` tool, which accepts only hexadecimal numbers as input. This means you must translate your pixel position into hexadecimal before typing your command line.

The coordinates 320 and 80 in decimal translate to 01 40 and 00 50. Because the high resolution screen is more than 256 characters wide — that's FF or the largest single byte value in Hex — you must give OS-9 both the most significant and least significant byte of your coordinates. You must do this for both the X and Y positions even though the Y position can never be greater than 00 C0.

In computer speak, the OS-9 drawing commands expect you give them 16-bit — or two-byte wide — coordinates. `Display` can only send one byte at a time so you must split them up yourself. For this reason you could probably get rich by writing and selling an OS-9 `Display` tool that can speak both decimal and Hex.

Since the abbreviations above still don't make a lot of sense, let's move them one step closer to English. We'll use two lines.

```
display Graphics Cursor Set
display Put Graphics Cursor
```

To issue the actual commands in two lines, you would type an OS-9 command line like this:

```
display 1b 39 ca 04
display 1b 4e 01 40 00 50
```

The Graphics Cursor Set is the official English description of `GCSet`. The display codes you must send to issue the command `GCSet` are `1b 39`. You must follow those codes with the group number and buffer number. Both must be typed in Hex.

Likewise, `PutGC` stands for Put Graphics Cursor. To send it, you display the codes `1b 4e`. Those codes are followed by the X and Y coordinates of the location where you want to display the cursor. Let's try something new. Type:

```
display 1b 39 ca 02 1b 4e 02 40 00 60
```

Did the hourglass on your screen turn into a pencil, drop down two lines and jump to a position near the right edge of your screen? What happened? Why did the hourglass turn into a pencil?

Look closely at the command line you typed. You changed the `04` following the `ca` to `02`. That must mean the `04` calls for an hourglass while the `02` summons a pencil! You're on track. We'll put the rest of the OS-9 graphics cursors in a table so you'll know what's available.

TABLE 5-C: OS-9 Graphics Cursors

Group #	Hex Value	Buffer #	Icon
202	CA	01	Arrow
202	CA	02	Pencil
202	CA	03	Large Cross Hair
202	CA	04	Hourglass
202	CA	05	"No"
202	CA	06	Text Insert
202	CA	07	Small Cross Hair

TABLE 5-D: OS-9 Four-Color (Type 07) Background Patterns

Group #	Hex Value	Buffer #	Pattern
204	CC	01	Dots
204	CC	02	Vertical Lines
204	CC	03	Horizontal Lines
204	CC	04	Crosshatch
204	CC	05	Left Slanted Lines
204	CC	06	Right Slanted Lines
204	CC	07	Small Dots
204	CC	08	Large Dots

To apply the information from these graphics cursor tables, simply substitute the buffer number that represents the style of cursor you want in your command line. For example, if you want to display the international icon that means "no," type:

```
display 1b 39 ca 05
display 1b 4e 02 40 00 60
```

Let's experiment some more! If you created window /w7 in your StartUp file, move to it with your CLEAR key and turn it into a graphics window. Do you remember how? Use the Makegw procedure file we showed you earlier or merge mgw, the fast version of Makegw. After you are sure that window /w7 is a graphics window, press the CLEAR key until you get back to your small green control window. Now type:

```
display 1b 39 ca 02 1b 4e 02 40 00 60 >/w7
```

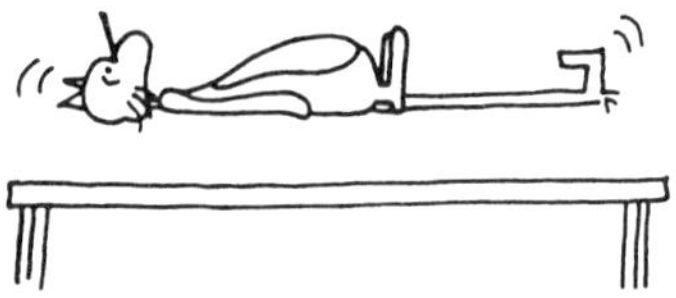

Move to window /w7 by pressing CLEAR. If the shell you started in /w7 from your StartUp procedure file is still running, you will need to press ENTER several times. This lets the characters you redirected to window device /w7 from your control window through, and a pencil should pop on the window in the same position it appeared in window /w1.

If you are running /w7 as a display window only — which means you haven't started a shell in it yet — you won't need to press ENTER. The pencil will appear on its own.

Now move back to /w2, your four-line green control window, and we'll try something different. Type:

```
display 1b 39 ca 02 1b 4e 02 40 00 60 >/w1
```

Nothing happened! OS-9 appears to be placing its graphics cursor at the coordinate specified on the selected screen. It pays no attention to window boundaries.

To prove this, type the command line above over again, but this time drop the redirection operator, >/w1.

```
display 1b 39 ca 02 1b 4e 02 40 00 60
```

It worked! The display command sent its output to the standard output path that was connected to window device /w2. Yet, the graphics cursor appeared in window /w1.

Now hold down the CTRL key while you press the A. Your most recent command line should pop back in the window. Press the left arrow twice and back over the 60. Replace it with B8 by typing those two characters. Now press ENTER.

Did the pencil pop into the green control window? Was it about one character position above the bottom of the screen? That's where you told it to go when you typed the B8. The decimal equivalent of B8 Hex is 184. Since the screen is 192 pixels deep, the point of your pencil should be located 192 minus 184, or eight pixels from the bottom of the screen.

Remember: OS-9 graphics cursors are global to the selected screen. They can be placed anywhere on the screen, inside or outside a window. The first time you use an applications program that lets you point to an icon on the screen with the mouse and click the firebutton to perform a task, you'll understand why the cursor must be able to move anywhere on the screen. The main reason the graphics cursors exist is to pinpoint the location of the mouse on your screen.

Use the tables above to experiment with the OS-9 graphics cursors. Notice two things. First, if you prefer to use the same cursor all the time, you do not need to run the OS-9 `GCSet` command each time you move the cursor. You only need to set the graphics cursor the first time you display a cursor on the screen. However, as you discovered, you can change the appearance of the cursor any time you want by running the OS-9 `GCSet` command.

Once you have told OS-9 which graphics cursor you want to use with the `GCSet` command, you can move that cursor anywhere on the screen by running the `PutGC` command. But, I'll bet you have one more question. How do you get rid of a graphics cursor once you have set it?

To remove a graphics cursor from your screen, you must run the `GCSet` command again. But this time you tell OS-9 that you want a group and buffer number of zero. It should look like this when you type it:

```
display 1b 39 00 00
```

Experiment with these graphics cursors until you understand what is happening. Then, join us in the next chapter for a brief introduction of BASIC09 followed by a few examples of OS-9 drawing.

CHAPTER 6

first steps with basic09

You can do so much with OS-9 without resorting to programming that you may happily forget that your computer is programmable. Most people who use computers don't program them, but someday you may want to write a program of your own. Whether you want to program or just understand programming, this chapter will help you get started.

We should start by warning you that programming can be addictive. Seemingly normal people with a few weeks' exposure to programming have been known to neglect everything else and program until they drop. They say that artists and scientists have the same problem: The problem at hand becomes so involving that the rest of the world is tuned out.

A computer program must be written in a computer language. Fortunately, computer languages are much easier than human languages. They have small vocabularies and simple grammar. Unfortunately, computers insist on precisely correct usage. The spelling, punctuation and grammar must be flawless.

A program is a set of instructions that solves some problem. A programmer invents the solution and writes the instructions. If a programming language is bricks and mortar, a program is a finished house. Like a house, a good program is functional, and, in a way, beautiful.

SETTING THE SCENE

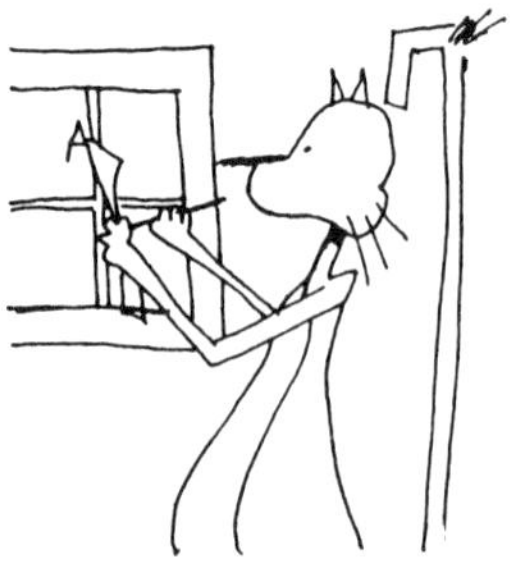

Imagine we are gathered around your computer. Most of the time we are sitting at the keyboard and you are beside us watching what happens and asking questions. You have read the BASIC09 manual, but you're not sure how to put it together and write a program. We'll create a few programs in front of your eyes, explaining as we go along.

We're going to be using BASIC09, the language that came with your copy of OS-9. It is enough like other versions of BASIC that you can run many BASIC programs under BASIC09. If BASIC is an old friend, BASIC09 will feel comfortable. Unlike most versions of BASIC, BASIC09 is a modern language. If you are a member of the Committee to Stamp Out BASIC, you'll want to forget BASIC09's name, but you'll love its elegant structure.

You will want a collection of books on hand while you are reading this. We will show you how to construct a program, but we'll skip lightly over the details of the BASIC09 language. You should definitely have the *Basic09 Manual* and *The Basic09 Tourguide*. The *Basic09 Manual* is the encyclopedia of BASIC09 with descriptions of every feature. *The Tourguide* explains things in more detail with plenty of examples.

THE FIRST STEP

You can easily get OS-9 to print `Hello World` on your screen by using the command:

```
echo Hello World
```

That's how you get OS-9 to print `Hello World` on the screen using the `Echo` utility program. BASIC09 is a general-purpose utility. We should be able to get it to print `Hello World`, too. Let's see if we can.

First, run BASIC09 by typing `Basic09` at the `OS9:` prompt. If OS-9 can start BASIC09, your screen will clear and you'll see a copyright notice at the top of the screen. Under the copyright you'll see:

```
Basic09
Ready
B:
```

Pay attention to the `B:`. It is the BASIC09 command mode prompt.

If you got an error message when you tried to start BASIC09, you should check two things before you go off on a major hunt for the problem. If you got

```
ERROR #216
```

it means OS-9 couldn't find BASIC09. Make sure BASIC09 is either loaded into memory or in the current execution directory by typing `chx /d0/CMDS` before you try to start it. (For more information on execution directories, see Chapter 2.) If you got:

```
ERROR #207
```

OS-9 couldn't find enough memory for BASIC09. You'll have to find something to take out of memory before BASIC09 will be able to squeeze in. Look into getting rid of a window or unlinking some modules.

When you have BASIC09 running, type:

```
e Hello
```

at the `B:` prompt. BASIC09 will respond with:

```
PROCEDURE Hello
*
E:
```

It is telling you that you are editing a procedure called `Hello`. The `E:` prompt indicates edit mode. `Hello` will start as a one-line program: a `print` statement. Type:

```
print "Hello World"
```

at the prompt. Be sure to press the space bar once before typing the statement. A space is the edit mode command for "insert the following line in the procedure." That's it — a complete, working program.

LISTING YOUR WORK

Type `l*` (that's l as in list) at the next BASIC09 `E:` prompt. The `l*` command tells BASIC09 to print out the procedure. You'll see:

```
PROCEDURE Hello
0000        PRINT "Hello World"
*
E:
```

BASIC09 always types important words like `PRINT` in capital letters. It will come out that way even if you typed everything in lowercase. Pay no attention.

You need to get out of edit mode to run your program. Type `q` at the `E:` prompt to quit the edit mode. BASIC09 will return to command mode and give you a `B:` prompt.

ENJOYING THE NEW PROGRAM

You can enjoy your program from the command prompt.

Every time you press the ENTER key, BASIC09 will print the directory of BASIC09 procedures it knows about. So far, all it has is Hello, but it will tell you that Hello uses 48 bytes of memory, plus another 22 bytes of data when it's running.

Run the program by typing run Hello at the B: prompt. You should end up with something like:

```
B:run Hello
Hello World
Ready
B:
```

at the bottom of your screen.

Try running the program a few more times. Make up another procedure that prints some other string, and play around until you feel comfortable. Now try putting two or more print statements into a program. Can you write a program that prints Hello World down the side of the screen like this?

```
H
e
l
l
o

W
o
r
l
d
```

You're probably getting annoyed with the clutter on the screen. Let's start using some screen control to clear the screen before writing on it. Start editing your Hello procedure. Remember how? Type:

```
e Hello
```

Now, type:

```
run gfx2("clear")
```

at the E: prompt. Be sure to put a space before run so BASIC09 will know that you mean to insert the line. If you list the program again, you will see that the new statement is inserted *before* your print statement. If you get back to command mode and run Hello, you will find that the screen is cleared and "Hello World" appears at the top. If, instead, you get an error message, you need to check and make sure the module gfx2 is in memory. If it isn't, you will need to load it from the BASIC09 disk.

There are two things still wrong. `Hello World` would look better in the middle of the screen and

```
Ready
B:
```

shouldn't be right under it. We'll use cursor positioning to fix both problems.

After the screen is cleared, we want to put the text cursor near the middle of the screen, and after printing `Hello World`, we want the cursor near the end of the screen. If you have a 32-by-16 screen, you'd like `Hello World` to start at column and row (10,7) and `ready` to appear at (0,14). Use the BASIC09 editor to put the line

```
run gfx2("curxy",10,7)
```

just before

```
print "hello world"
```

and

```
run gfx2("curxy",0,14)
```

after it.

We could keep going for days. The procedure could graduate to foreign languages or blinking letters. Slight variations on this procedure can print any fixed message on the screen.

TO SUM UP

We have created the simplest program we could imagine. It demonstrated that we could get BASIC09 to do something. There are many possibilities for grander versions of the `Hello` procedure, and we tried a few of them.

It's always best to start with something simple even when you know the final product will be complex. We started with a one-line program and expanded it to two lines, then to four lines. At each stage we were able to test the procedure. We would have found any problems early, while the procedure was as simple as possible. In a four-line procedure, debugging isn't a big issue, but when we get to complicated programs involving several procedures and hundreds of lines, an incremental approach will be mighty useful.

CHAPTER 7

drawing with os-9 primitives

Your CoCo will shine after you learn the techniques in this chapter. We'll experiment line by line with a primitive drawing tool to give you a feel for the way OS-9 drawing tools work. Then, we'll create several procedure files that demonstrate the powerful graphics toolbox hiding inside your Color Computer.

Our first procedure file will draw a number of objects on your screen to show you the five basic geometric shapes you can create with OS-9. Then, we'll fill those objects with the eight different patterns immediately available in OS-9 Level II.

Another procedure file will show you how to create an image by drawing from point to point. We'll then change the size of that image by changing the size of the work area in our window. When we do this, we'll be taking advantage of OS-9's automatic scaling.

We'll save that smaller image in a buffer and put it back on the screen as part of a larger picture later. But, we need to experiment awhile first, so you will know just what to expect from OS-9 when you start creating your own world-class computer art.

A NEW PHILOSOPHY

Computers are getting easier to use every day. This new-found ease of use is the result of a new approach to programming. Instead of approaching problems from the machine's point of view, programmers today are writing programs that attempt to solve problems using the same methods humans do.

For example, at the breakfast table we pick up an apple and eat it. When we're finished, we pick up the dishes and wash them. Later, we may pick up the morning paper and read it.

If you look carefully, you'll see a pattern in the events above. In each example we selected an object, or group of objects, and then did something with them. We selected the apple from the bowl and we ate it. We selected the dirty dishes and washed them. We selected the paper from the newsstand and read it.

We can often use the same problem-solving approach while working on our personal computers. We select a program by pointing to it with a mouse or joystick. Then, we run it by clicking a button on the same mouse.

We select a document by pointing to its name in a list or to a graphics icon that represents it on our screen. Then, we open it so we can complete our work.

Operating systems like OS-9 Level II make it all possible. Several Color Computer programs already let you work in this manner. Soon, most of them will. But let's ponder how we can apply the same philosophy to our drawing lesson.

Watch for a pattern as you type in the procedure files. You'll notice that in many places you are sending one set of display codes to select an object — a graphics cursor perhaps. Then, you'll immediately send another set of codes to do something with the object you selected — display that graphics cursor at a specific location on your window, for example. You'll select a pattern and fill a box with it. Or select a special font and print a message using it. Or select a border and change its color.

With almost every step you take, you'll select an object and then act on that object with a verb. When you take this approach to the drawing tools and OS-9 Level II windowing environment, you'll begin to understand what is happening. But more importantly, you'll understand what you need to do to make things happen.

To make your job easier, we have organized the OS-9 drawing and windowing display codes into a table with three columns. The first column lists action verbs that describe a task you may want to perform. The second lists the display code you must type to make it happen. The third column lists additional information that you must give OS-9 when you type the display codes.

TABLE 7-A: OS-9 Drawing and Windowing Tools

To:	Send This Code:	And Supply this Parameter:
Change Background Color	1B 33	Color Number
Change Border Color	1B 34	Color Number
Change Default Color	1B 30	None
Change Foreground Color	1B 32	Color Number
Change Palette Color	1B 31	Palette Number, Color Table Number
Change Working Area	1B 25	*** Location, Size
Create Overlay Window	1B 22	*** Save Switch, Location, Size
Create Window Device	1B 20	*** Type, Location, Size, Colors
Display Bold Text	1B 3D	Plain = 0, Bold Text = 1
Display Proportional Text	1B 3F	Plain = 0, Proportional Text = 1
Display Transparent Text	1B 3C	Plain = 0, Transparent Text = 1
Draw Arc	1B 52	Radius, Area
Draw Bar	1B 4A	Location of Opposite Corner
Draw Bar Relative	1B 4B	Offset to Opposite Corner
Draw Box	1B 48	Location of Opposite Corner
Draw Box Relative	1B 49	Offset to Opposite Corner
Draw Circle	1B 50	Radius
Draw Ellipse	1B 51	Horizontal and Vertical Radius
Draw Line	1B 44	Location of Opposite End
Draw Line and Move	1B 46	Location of Opposite End
Draw Line Relative	1B 45	Offset to Opposite End
Draw Line Relative and Move	1B 47	Offset to Opposite End
Draw Point	1B 42	Location
Draw Point Relative	1B 43	Offset to Location
Fill Screen Area With Pattern	1B 4F	None
Get Screen Pixel Image in Buffer	1B 2C	Group #, Buffer #, Location, Size
Kill Buffer	1B 2A	Group #, Buffer #
Kill Overlay Window	1B 23	None
Kill Window Device	1B 24	None
Position Draw Pointer	1B 40	Location

Continued

Position Draw Pointer Relative	1B 41	Offset to New Location
Position Graphics Cursor	1B 4E	Location
Preload Screen Image in Buffer	1B 2B	Group #, Buffer #, Type, Size, and Number of Bytes
Protect Window Device	1B 36	Do Not Protect = 0, Protect = 1
Put Pixel Image on Screen	1B 2D	Group #, Buffer #, Location
Reserve Memory for Buffer	1B 29	Group #, Buffer #, Buffer Length
Select Drawing Logic	1B 2F	None = 0, AND = 1, OR = 2, XOR = 3
Select Font	1B 3A	Group #, Buffer #
Select Graphics Cursor	1B 39	Group #, Buffer #
Select Pattern	1B 2E	Group #, Buffer #
Select Window	1B 21	None
Turn Scaling On/Off	1B 35	Scaling Off = 0, Scaling On = 1

*** Use character location (80 by 24) or (40 by 24). Other locations are based on pixels (640 by 192).

*** All pixel locations are entered by typing the high and low Hex byte of the horizontal position followed by the high and low byte of the vertical position.

DRAWING A BOX

The point and line are the most basic graphics elements and OS-9 lets you draw both. We'll use line drawing commands later to create a custom-shaped object. We begin our experiments now with the special codes that let you print a box in a Color Computer window.

While we're experimenting you can use Table 7-B to help find your way around the Color Computer's windows while you're learning to speak Hex. We plotted our positions on a piece of student graph paper first and then used the table to translate those positions into Hex values we could feed to our windows with the `Display` tool.

The graph paper we purchased was numbered from 0 to 24 along the longest axis and from 0 to 18 along the shortest. We multiplied every position on the long axis by 30 and numbered the positions of pixel numbers 0 through 660. Remember the screen is 640 pixels wide. We multiplied each numbered position on the shorter axis by 10. That side of our graph paper was numbered 0 to 180. The paper was roughly the same shape as the 640- by 160-pixel screen we are using to draw our first pictures.

TABLE 7-B: Pixel Locations

Decimal	You Type
0	00
10	0 a
20	0 14
30	0 1e
40	0 28
50	0 32
60	0 3c
70	0 46
80	0 50
90	0 5a
100	0 64
110	0 6e
120	0 78
130	0 82
140	0 8c
150	0 96
160	0 a0
170	0 aa
180	0 64
190	0 be
200	0 c8
210	0 d2
240	0 f0
270	1 0e
300	1 2c
330	1 4a
360	1 68
390	1 86
420	1 a4
450	1 c2
480	1 e0
510	1 fe
540	2 1c
570	2 3a
600	2 58
630	2 76
660	2 94

We'll start our drawing experiments by placing the draw pointer at a location 16 pixels down from the top of the window and 16 pixels to the right of the left edge. The draw pointer is invisible, so you'll need to remember where you left it each time you execute a command. Yet, if you think about it, you'll realize that you want it to be invisible. If it was visible you would be left with a bunch of highlighted pixels cluttering up your windows. To position OS-9's draw pointer, type:

```
display 1b 40 0 10 0 10 >/w1
```

Notice that we didn't type 16, 16 to tell OS-9 where we wanted it to print our cursor. Rather, we typed 0 10 0 10. Sixteen decimal pixels translates into 10 hexadecimal pixels.

Notice also that, when we send location codes to OS-9 with the Display tool, we must type both the high and low byte of a 16-bit long Hex value. We must do this because one byte can only count up to 256 decimal pixels, or $FF Hex pixels.

Our window is 640 decimal pixels, or 280 Hex pixels, wide. We must do something with that extra '2' so we send it out separately. Therefore, if we wanted to place the draw pointer on the same line at the far-right edge of the screen, we would need to type:

```
display 1b 40 2 80 0 10  >/w1
```

Now that we have placed the invisible draw pointer where we want it, let's draw an 80-pixel wide box with its upper-left corner on the draw pointer and its lower-right corner on the very bottom of our 160-pixel deep window. If you moved your draw pointer by testing the last command line, make sure you move it back to a position 16 pixels from the top and 16 pixels from the left edge of your window. Do you remember how to move it? Now let's try for a box, type:

```
display 1b 48 0 60 0 a0  >/w1
```

It looks nice, but why isn't the bottom of the box running along the edge of our window? The box we just drew looks like it is about 80 pixels, or 10 character spaces, wide. It should be 60 Hex minus 10 Hex is 50 Hex — or 80 pixels. But a0 Hex is 160 decimal, the bottom line of pixels in our window. What happened?

Do you think our box is shorter because the OS-9 scaling feature is turned on? Let's turn it off just to make sure. Then, we'll draw that box again.

```
display c  >/w1 ; *  erase it first
display 1b 35 0  >/w1
display 1b 48 0 60 0 a0  >/w1
```

Error #189! Wonder what that means. Let's find out. Type:

```
error 189
```

"189 — Illegal Coordinates." Maybe we're trying to draw the box one line too low on the screen. A0 is most likely the first line of pixels in our green command window. Let's try something else.

```
display 1b 48 0 60 0 9f  >/w1
```

Perfect! The bottom of the box runs along even with the bottom of our drawing window. Just what we wanted. Now, leave this box on the screen while we turn the scaling back on and draw it again. When you draw a box, the draw pointer returns to its starting position so we should be ready to roll. Type:

```
display 1b 35 1  >/w1
display 1b 48 0 60 0 9f  >/w1
```

That's interesting, the size relationship between our new scaled box and the full-size box is approximately the same as the relationship between the size of our 160-pixel deep drawing window and the entire 192-pixel deep screen. Amazing! Now we know what OS-9's automatic scaling function can do for us.

It's easier to draw large images accurately than it is to draw small images — especially if you are using a mouse. If we draw our images large — on a full 640- by 192-pixel window perhaps — and then reduce them down to a small screen size, they will look much better.

Now, clear your display window and we'll redraw the box and try to fill it with a pattern. Type:

```
display c  >/w1
display 1b 48 0 60 0 9f  >/w1
```

Remember, we must always redirect the output of our Display codes to our drawing window, /w1. Just for fun, go through some of the steps above and leave off the >/w1. You'll see a very short and stubby box appear on the green command window for an instant. Then OS-9 will issue another prompt and the top half of your new drawing will scroll into that large bit bucket in the sky.

There are several lessons here. First, you usually must display your drawings in one window and type your display codes in another. The scrolling caused by your characters from the keyboard will tear up your drawings before you get to enjoy them. And second, OS-9 gives you a way to redirect your standard output path. This is what makes it possible for you to type in one window and display your output in another. You have been doing that very thing in this chapter by typing the >/w1 at the end of your command lines.

Redirection saved the day here. And it's very useful for a number of other jobs. For example, you may need to print a hard copy listing of your name and address file to take with you on a business trip. To do that, if your printer device is named /p, you need to change the /w in the command lines above to a /p. For example:

```
list names  >/p
```

Let's move on now and see if we can put a pattern in our new box. Try this:

```
display 1b 2e cc 5 >/w1
display 1b 4f >/w1
```

Nothing happened! The fill display codes didn't work. Did you wonder what the manual meant when it said, "Fills the area where the background is the same color as the draw pointer. Filling starts at the current draw pointer position"?

Let's see! Our draw pointer is sitting in the upper-left corner of the box we just drew. The box is made up of blue pixels. The draw pointer is invisible so it must be blue, too. If the `fill` command followed the scenario above, it must have retraced the outline of the box and set all the pixels blue again. Maybe if we move the draw pointer inside the box, we will see the pattern we selected. Type:

```
display 1b 41 0 4 0 4 >/w1
display 1b 2e cc 5 >/w1
display 1b 4f >/w1
```

There are the slanted lines promised in the book. I wonder if we can change their color. Try typing:

```
display 1b 32 3 >/w1
display 1b 4f >/w1
```

Error 186! Looks like we are stuck with the pattern we first drew in the box. Oh well! Let's erase the box and start over.

```
display c >/w1
display 1b 40 0 10 0 10 >/w1
display 1b 48 0 60 0 9f >/w1
```

That's a funny looking box. Let's try to fill it anyway!

```
display 1b 41 0 40 4 >/w1
display 1b 2e cc 5 >/w1
display 1b 4f >/w1
```

Whoops! Better make sure you have a solid line around any area you try to fill in the future. Remember, also, that you must be very careful with the color number you select if you start changing colors during a drawing session.

With a four-color screen set up the way we are running it now, we only have white, blue, black and green available. White is already the background color so we can't use it. If we do, our drawing commands will work, but we'll never see the results. For example, on our present screen if we set the foreground color to white, OS-9 will draw a white box on a white background. We'll never know it.

It's easy to forget about this. Moments ago, we forgot we were working with a four-color screen and decided to change the foreground color to red — or number four. After we issued the command, we couldn't see anything we drew on the screen. After OS-9 went through white, blue, black and green — or colors zero, one, two and three — it rotated back to white again with number four. We lost everything. The moral of the story? Be very careful when you select your foreground and background color combinations. In a later chapter we'll be showing you how to work with OS-9 Level II's color palettes to change colors on the fly. For now, we'll stick to the four colors we're using on this screen.

We'll look now at a procedure file that will draw each OS-9 graphics primitive and fill it with a different pattern. When you finish it, you'll be able to see them all on your screen at one time.

THE LISTING: Shapes

```
*
* Start with a clear screen
* and a black foreground color
*
display c
display 1b 32 2
*
* Position the cursor for the first box
* and draw it.
*
display 1b 40 0 46 0 a
display 1b 48 0 8c 0 3c
*
* Now position the circle and draw it.
*
display 1b 40 1 4a 0 20
display 1b 50 0 32
*
* Now another box
*
display 1b 40 1 e0 0 14
display 1b 48 2 60 0 28
*
*An Ellipse is next
*
display 1b 40 0 68 0 5a
display 1b 51 0 58 0 12
*
* Now another rectangular box
*
display 1b 40 0 e8 0 46
display 1b 48 1 a8 0 60
*
* Another ellipse would be nice
*
display 1b 40 2 1a 0 5a
display 1b 51 0 40 0 12
*
* Another Rectangle
```

```
*
display 1b 4Ø Ø 1Ø Ø 8Ø
display 1b 48 Ø c8 Ø 96
*
* Time for a circle again
*
display 1b 4Ø 1 4a Ø 8Ø
display 1b 5Ø Ø 3Ø
*
* And finally a bar filled
* with a different foreground color
*
* First, we must change the color
*
display 1b 32 3
*
* That should make it green
*
display 1b 4Ø 1 eØ Ø 8Ø
display 1b 4a 2 6Ø Ø 96
*
* Now we should return the foreground color
* to the way we found it.
*
display 1b 32 2
*
* Now for the patterns
*
* We'll move back to the circle first
*
display 1b 4Ø 1 4a Ø 8c
*
* Select a dot pattern
*
display 1b 2e CC Ø1
*
* and use the OS-9 Flood fill display
* commands to put the pattern in the circle
*
display 1b 4f
*
* Back to the Rectangle in the lower left
* hand corner of the screen.
*
display 1b 4Ø Ø 2Ø Ø 9Ø
*
* Notice we can put the draw pointer
* anywhere inside the rectangle.
*
* Let's put a green pattern in this rectangle
*
display 1b 32 3
*
```

```
* And we'll use vertical lines for the pattern.
*
display 1b 2e CC Ø2
display 1b 4f
*
* Now we'll set the color to blue before we
* move on to fill the two ellipses.
*
display 1b 32 1
*
* The one on the right first
*
display 1b 4Ø 2 3a Ø 5a
*
* Let's go for a horizontal line pattern this time
*
display 1b 2e CC Ø3
*
* Do it!
*
display 1b 4f
*
* Now to the other ellipse
*
display 1b 4Ø Ø 78 Ø 5a
*
* Where we'll put a Cross Hatch Pattern
*
display 1b 2e CC Ø4
*
* Let's keep it blue and go for it
*
display 1b 4f
*
* Back to the rectangle in the center of the screen
*
display 1b 4Ø 1 4a Ø 5Ø
*
* where we'll fill with black left slanted line
*
display 1b 32 2
display 1b 2e cc Ø5
display 1b 4f
*
* Now, to the rectangle in the upper right hand corner
* We'll use green right slanted lines here
*
display 1b 4Ø 1 fØ Ø 2Ø
display 1b 2e CC Ø6
display 1b 32 3
display 1b 4f
*
* Now, some small blue dots in the circle in the top row.
```

```
*
display 1b 2e CC 7
display 1b 32 1
display 1b 40 1 4a 0 28
display 1b 4f
*
* And finally, we could use some Large green dots in
* our first square box in the upper left hand corner
*
display 1b 40 0 50 0 28
display 1b 32 3
display 1b 2e CC 8
display 1b 4f
*
display 1b 2e 0 0
*
* Let's dress up our window with a simple blue border
*
display 1b 32 1
display 1b 40 0 5 0 5
display 1b 48 2 7b 0 9b
*
* Always say goodbye!"
*
* Position the cursor first.
*
display  2 29 33
*
* Then send the messages!'
*
display 20 54 68 61 74 27 73 20 41 4c 4c 20 46 6f 6c 6b 73 21 20
*
* If we had used the echo command we would have
* sent a carriage return to the window and ruined our
* nice artwork.  So we just displayed words as
* hex characters.  Tricky!
*
* We'll clean up and return to Black cursor
*
display 1b 32 2
*
* That's All Folks !
*
```

After you type in Procedure Shapes, move your cursor to the OS-9 prompt in your four-line green command window, which is just below the four color, 20-line drawing window you made with the procedure file ReadyDraw. Now type:

```
display 1b 35 0  >/w1
display 1b 2e 00 00  >/w1
display c  >/w1
shapes  >/w1
```

With those four OS-9 command lines, you turned off the automatic scaling in the window named /w1 and cleared that window. You also "de-selected" the current pattern. Then you ran your new procedure file and redirected its output to window /w1.

Since you turned off the automatic scaling feature in your display window, OS-9 printed the objects you defined exactly where you told it to with the display codes in your procedure file. If you want to adjust the position or size of an object, you can do so by editing the proper line in the procedure file. You can automate the display process from your command window, /w2, by using a line like this:

```
display c >/w1 ; shapes >/w1
```

If you leave OS-9's automatic scaling off, the procedure file named Shapes will print its final message as part of the blue border. If, however, you have the scaling turned on when you run Shapes, the message will appear by itself on the bottom line of your display window. Try it both ways!

Each time you come back to this window to try a new version of the procedure file, you need only hold down the CTRL key and press A. OS-9 will reprint the command line above and leave your cursor sitting at the end of the line. As soon as you press ENTER, it will rerun the procedure file.

Better yet, you could put the clear screen code, display c, into your procedure file. Then you won't need to type it each time you test your procedure. That's the way we handled it. If you do it this way, your command line will look like this:

```
shapes >/w1
```

Of course, you can still use the CTRL-A shortcut to keep from typing this command line over and over while you're testing your procedure. It may be a short line, but we bet you didn't buy your Color Computer to practice typing!

Since you ran the procedure file StartApps and have your editor program running continuously in another window, when you want to make a quick change in the script of your procedure file, you only need to press CLEAR until your cursor returns to the window running your editor. Once there, you can make the change, save the procedure file to disk, and then press CLEAR again until your cursor returns to the four-line command window. Once there, simply press CTRL-A followed by ENTER and you'll see the output of your new version of Shapes immediately.

After you get the output from Shapes looking the way you want it to, type:

```
shapes >s
```

This command line runs your procedure file, but it sends the output to a file named s instead of a window. Now type:

```
merge s >/w1
```

The OS-9 Merge tool gives you an excellent way to display drawing commands rapidly. When you send display codes to a window this way, OS-9 receives them as fast as it can display them.

For example, you could handcraft a procedure file that creates a window and displays the StartUp screen you want to see each time you start a particular application on your Color Computer. After you perfect your drawing, you can merge the output of that procedure file into a file named StartUpScreen. Then if you put this line in your StartApps procedure file, you will see your special screen each time you start that application.

```
merge StartUpScreen >/wx
```

You will need to make sure that you redirect the output of the merge command above to the same window that you created in your procedure file.

Now, let's move on to a procedure file that draws a full-size figure on your display screen. Then, we'll scale it down, save it in a buffer and display it at several different positions on the screen.

USING THE LINE DRAWING COMMANDS

We've shown you how you can use most of the OS-9 primitive graphics tools to draw common geometric objects almost everywhere on the screen. Now, we'll show you how to draw an object that isn't one of the standard drawing shapes. We'll use the "draw a line and move" primitive to get the job done. Another procedure file shows you how to draw your own letter X and fill it with a pattern made up of blue slashes.

THE LISTING: DrawX

```
*
* First, clear the screen
*
display c
*
* and use a black foreground for the outline
*
display 1b 32 2
*
* Position the draw pointer at the start
*
display 1b 40 0 20 0 30
*
* Now draw the rest of the letter
```

```
*
display 1b 46 Ø 3Ø Ø 2Ø
display 1b 46 Ø 5Ø Ø 4Ø
display 1b 46 Ø 8Ø Ø 2Ø
display 1b 46 Ø 9Ø Ø 3Ø
display 1b 46 Ø 6Ø Ø 5Ø
display 1b 46 Ø 9Ø Ø 8Ø
display 1b 46 Ø 8Ø Ø 9Ø
display 1b 46 Ø 5Ø Ø 6Ø
display 1b 46 Ø 3Ø Ø 9Ø
display 1b 46 Ø 2Ø Ø 8Ø
display 1b 46 Ø 4Ø Ø 5Ø
display 1b 46 Ø 2Ø Ø 3Ø
display 1b 4Ø Ø 24 Ø 3Ø
*
* Let's select a pattern of blue slanted lines
* for the center or our letter
*
* First, the pattern
*
display 1b 2e cc 5
*
* Now, the Color
*
display 1b 32 1
*
* Apply them with the flood fill command code
*
display 1b 4f
*
* We must always turn the patterns off
* after we're finished.
*
display 1b 2e Ø Ø
*
* And, put the color back the way we found it
*
display 1b 32 2
*
* That's all it takes to draw and X
*
```

Store the procedure `DrawX` in your current data directory. Then test it by typing:

```
drawx >/w1
```

If you like what you see and don't want to make any modifications of your own, type:

```
drawx >dx
merge dx >/w1
```

Now that we have defined the basic shape of our letter, we need to save a copy of it in a GET-PUT buffer so we can draw it anywhere on the screen. Use the procedure file GetX to do the job for you.

THE LISTING: GetX

```
*
* This procedure file changes the working
* area on the screen to a much smaller area.
*
* It then turns on OS-9's scaling and uses the
* Merge dx command to print a smaller version
* of the "X" we made with the DrawX procedure file.
*
* We then Get the Screen image of the small "X"
* into buffer number 5Ø hex, group number 1
*
* After we have loaded the small "X" into a buffer
* we change the working area of window /Wl back
* to the full window.
*
* We are then free to draw our small "X's" anywhere
* we want on the screen.
*
* We'll do that last task in a separate procedure
* file named PutX.
*
display lb 25 Ø Ø 28 6     ;* Change Working Area code
display display c          ;* clear screen
display lb 35 1            ;* make sure scaling is turned on
merge dx                   ;* display "X" in small window
*
* Now get pixel image in grp 8Ø, buffer 1
*
display lb 2c 5Ø 1 Ø 9 Ø 9 Ø 88 Ø 88
display lb 25 Ø Ø 5Ø 14  ;* back to full sized window now
display c                ;* clear that screen
*
* That's all for GetX folks!
```

After you run GetX, you will have that small X you drew earlier stored in a GET-PUT buffer in your Color Computer's memory. The group number of that buffer is 80 or 50 Hex. The buffer number is 1. Now that the procedure file GetX has loaded it into memory, you can display it any time. One of the easiest ways to use GetX is in another procedure file. Maybe we should have named this one "Tic Tac Toe."

THE LISTING: PutX

```
* This procedure file will display the small "X"
* loaded into GET/PUT Group Number 8Ø, Buffer 1
* at several locations on your Color Computer's screen
```

```
*
* In hex that's Group number 5Ø, Buffer 1
*
* In fact it will display three copies of the
* small "X" on the screen in a manner similar
* to a successful tic tac toe game.
*
* We'll even add the grid.  You can draw, scale, get
* and put the "O's" for practice.
*
display c
display 1b 4Ø Ø fØ Ø 18
display 1b 44 Ø fØ Ø 9Ø
*
* One line down, so we'll move the draw pointer
* and do another!
*
display 1b 4Ø 1 86 Ø 18
display 1b 44 1 86 Ø 9Ø
*
* Time to add the horizontal lines
*
display 1b 4Ø Ø 1e Ø 3c
display 1b 44 2 54 Ø 3c
*
* One more!
*
display 1b 4Ø Ø 1e Ø 6e
display 1b 44 2 54 Ø 6e
*
* Now we need three "X's" to win!
*
display 1b 2d 5Ø 1 Ø 64 Ø B
*
* Here's comes the second!
*
display 1b 2d 5Ø 1 1 14 Ø 3F
*
* and the winning move!
*
display 1b 2d 5Ø 1 1 a4 Ø 6F
*
* Now let's frame our good work!
*
display 1b 4Ø Ø 8 Ø 8
display 1b 48 2 7Ø Ø 98
*
```

If you've worked through the examples in this chapter, you should have a pretty good handle on the OS-9 Level II high resolution graphics primitives. Use our procedure files as models. Make a few copies of the tables and charts in the last three chapters and keep them handy while you work. We hope you'll find them a big help.

Pay special attention to the details of scaling. If you are preparing an original drawing, you need to know if it is being scaled or not, so you can make sure the final drawing looks right.

DOING THE SAME THING WITH RUNB

Now that you understand the basics of the primitives that supply the graphics power to OS-9 Level II, we'll show you the easy way to use them.

BASIC09, which we introduced in the last chapter, is a high-level, PASCAL-like language that comes with OS-9 Level II. BASIC09 includes a special graphics module named `gfx2`. This module gives you access to a number of English language-like commands that you can use to draw with your Color Computer. To help you compare the `gfx2` commands to the OS-9 graphics primitives, we rewrote most of the procedure files from the early part of this chapter into BASIC09 code that uses `gfx2`. `Shapes_BASIC09` is first.

In this book, BASIC09 listings will have a four-digit Hex number at the beginning of each line. Do *not* type these numbers when entering a line. They are internally supplied by your computer and only show up when you list a file.

THE LISTING: `Shapes.Bas`

```
PROCEDURE MyShapes
 0000     (* Basic09 emulation of an OS-9 procedure file
 0036
 0037     DIM myW:BYTE
 003E     OPEN #myW,"/W1":WRITE
 004C
 004D     RUN gfx2(myW,"clear")
 005F     RUN gfx2(myW,"pattern",0,0)
 0079
 007A     RUN gfx2(myW,"box",70,10,140,60)
 0096     RUN gfx2(myW,"color",3,0)
 00AE     RUN gfx2(myW,"pattern",204,8)
 00C8     RUN gfx2(myW,"fill",72,12)
 00DF
 00E0     RUN gfx2(myW,"color",2,0)
 00F8     RUN gfx2(myW,"pattern",0,0)
 0112     RUN gfx2(myW,"circle",330,32,50)
 012F     RUN gfx2(myW,"pattern",204,7)
 0149     RUN gfx2(myW,"color",1,0)
 0161     RUN gfx2(myW,"fill")
 0172     RUN gfx2(myW,"pattern",0,0)
 018C     RUN gfx2(myW,"color",2,0)
 01A4     RUN gfx2(myW,"box",480,20,608,40)
 01C2     RUN gfx2(myW,"pattern",204,6)
```

```
01DC        RUN gfx2(myW,"color",3,0)
01F4        RUN gfx2(myW,"fill",600,30)
020C        RUN gfx2(myW,"pattern",0,0)
0226        RUN gfx2(myW,"color",2,0)
023E        RUN gfx2(myW,"ellipse",104,90,88,18)
025E        RUN gfx2(myW,"pattern",204,4)
0278        RUN gfx2(myW,"color",1,0)
0290        RUN gfx2(myW,"fill")
02A1        RUN gfx2(myW,"pattern",0,0)
02BB        RUN gfx2(myW,"color",2,0)
02D3        RUN gfx2(myW,"box",232,70,424,96)
02F0        RUN gfx2(myW,"pattern",204,5)
030A        RUN gfx2(myW,"fill",240,74)
0321        RUN gfx2(myW,"pattern",0,0)
033B
033C        RUN gfx2(myW,"ellipse",538,90,64,18)
035D        RUN gfx2(myW,"pattern",204,3)
0377        RUN gfx2(myW,"color",1,0)
038F        RUN gfx2(myW,"fill")
03A0        RUN gfx2(myW,"pattern",0,0)
03BA        RUN gfx2(myW,"color",2,0)
03D2
03D3        RUN gfx2(myW,"box",16,128,200,150)
03EF        RUN gfx2(myW,"pattern",204,2)
0409        RUN gfx2(myW,"color",3,0)
0421        RUN gfx2(myW,"fill",18,130)
0438        RUN gfx2(myW,"color",2,0)
0450        RUN gfx2(myW,"pattern",0,0)
046A
046B        RUN gfx2(myW,"circle",330,128,48)
0488        RUN gfx2(myW,"pattern",204,1)
04A2        RUN gfx2(myW,"fill")
04B3        RUN gfx2(myW,"pattern",0,0)
04CD
04CE        RUN gfx2(myW,"color",3,0)
04E6        RUN gfx2(myW,"bar",480,128,608,150)
0504
0505        RUN gfx2(myW,"color",1,0)
051D        RUN gfx2(myW,"box",4,4,632,157)
053A        RUN gfx2(myW,"curxy",4,19)
0552        PRINT #myW," That's All Folks ";
```

The BASIC09 version of Shapes requires a lot of typing. However, it is much easier to understand than the OS-9 display code procedure file. Run them both and compare the way they put graphics objects on the screen.

Notice: Before you run these BASIC09 procedures, you should run the OS-9 procedure file ReadyDraw. These BASIC09 programs assume that the prep work done in ReadyDraw has been completed before they are run. If you are really ambitious, you may want to add the functions performed by ReadyDraw to these programs. If you do, they will stand alone. Don't forget to create the DX file before running GetX.Bas.

THE LISTING: DrawX.Bas

```
PROCEDURE MyX
(* We have already created window /W1 so we won't do
(* it again here.  However, we must open a path to it.

DIM myW:BYTE
OPEN #myW,"/W1":WRITE
RUN gfx2(myW,"clear")
RUN gfx2(myW,"color",2,0,4)
RUN gfx2(myW,"setdptr",32,48)
RUN gfx2(myW,"line",48,32)
RUN gfx2(myW,"line",80,64)
RUN gfx2(myW,"line",128,32)
RUN gfx2(myW,"line",144,48)
RUN gfx2(myW,"line",96,80)
RUN gfx2(myW,"line",144,128)
RUN gfx2(myW,"line",128,144)
RUN gfx2(myW,"line",80,96)
RUN gfx2(myW,"line",48,144)
RUN gfx2(myW,"line",32,128)
RUN gfx2(myW,"line",64,80)
RUN gfx2(myW,"line",32,48)

(* Now select a pattern

RUN gfx2(myW,"pattern",204,5)

(* Change the color of the fill

RUN gfx2(myW,"color",1,0)

(* And finally, do the fill

RUN gfx2(myW,"fill",40,50)

(* Put things back the way they were

RUN gfx2(myW,"pattern",0,0)
RUN gfx2(myW,"color",2,0)
CLOSE #myW

(* That's all folks
```

THE LISTING: GetX.Bas

```
PROCEDURE myGet
(* Draw a small "X" on the screen
(* then save it a GET/PUT buffer
(* so you can use it later

DIM myW:BYTE
OPEN #myW,"/W1":WRITE
```

```
RUN gfx2(myW,"cwarea",0,0,40,6)
RUN gfx2(myW,"clear")
RUN gfx2(myW,"scalesw","ON")
SHELL "merge dx >/w1"
RUN gfx2(myW,"GET",80,1,9,9,136,136)
RUN gfx2(myW,"CWArea",0,0,80,20)
RUN gfx2(myW,"clear")

PRINT #myW,"We have now put the 'X' in a buffer."
PRINT #myW,"Now, we'll display it three times."

RUN gfx2(myW,"put",80,1,150,18)
RUN gfx2(myW,"put",80,1,276,63)
RUN gfx2(myW,"put",80,1,420,109)
RUN gfx2(myW,"killbuff",80,1)
```

After you have typed in these BASIC09 procedures and debugged them, you can run them from the four-line green command window /w2, which ReadyDraw created on the same screen as your display window, /w1. Working from the OS9: shell prompt in your command window, change the current data directory to the directory where you have stored your BASIC09 source code files. If you have loaded BASIC09 into memory with a prep file such as StartApps, you will see your handiwork in a few seconds when you type:

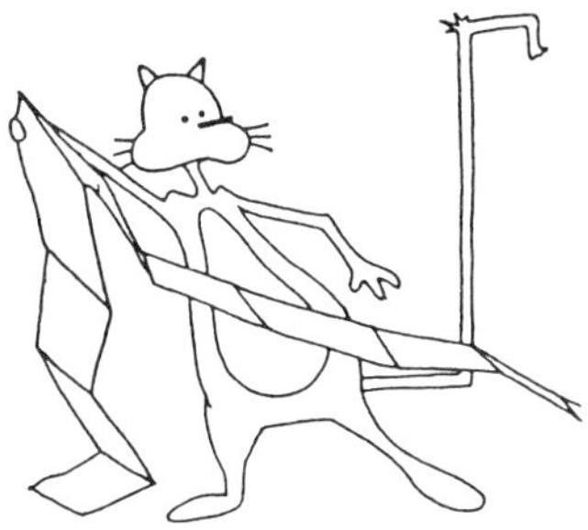

```
chd /dd/BASIC09_DIRECTORY
basic09 Shapes.Bas
```

Also remember: BASIC09, RunB, Gfx2, SysCall and InKey must be stored in your current execution directory (usually /d0/CMDS) or in memory before you can type a command line like the one above. When you take your two Radio Shack disks out of the package, you'll find that the program files above are stored in a CMDS directory on your Config disk. You'll want to copy them on to your working system disk. It'll make life easier.

We learned the hard way that you cannot redefine a GET/PUT buffer. In the above program, we originally had 10's instead of 9's in the GET statement. Since we had just run the procedure file for Getx, our system had defined our buffer that way. When we ran the above BASIC09 program, it crashed. Since we had called the buffer "group 80, buffer 1" in both cases, it tried to redefine the buffer and couldn't. Another way to circumvent this would have been to use a different group and/or buffer number.

If you want to run these programs before you get around to creating a working system disk with them in your CMDS directory, you can load them into memory from your Config disk and then run them. If you have two disk drives, you could put the Config disk in Drive /d1 and type:

```
load /d1/cmds/basic09
load /d1/cmds/runb
load /d1/cmds/Gfx2
load /d1/cmds/SysCall
load /d1/cmds/InKey
basic09 Shapes.Bas
```

If you operate this way, a procedure file with these command lines in it would be a very handy tool.

One of the things you'll notice when you type in long listings is how nice it would be if you had some commands you could type and run automatically without holding down the SHIFT key to type quote marks and a dozen parameters.

Since the Gfx2 file has plenty of room before it fills its 8K memory block and there is additional room available in the RunB block, we'll create some BASIC09 tools you can pack and keep resident in memory. They'll be ready to answer your call in a split second, both from within BASIC09 and from the OS-9 command line. That's a job for the next chapter.

CHAPTER 8

building friendly tools

In this chapter we'll show you how to use BASIC09 and a few OS-9 tools from the CMDS directory on your working system disk to make life simpler while you're using your Color Computer 3.

By the time you finish this chapter, you will have created scores of English language graphics and windowing commands and loaded them into memory. You'll be able to use them from the OS-9 command line as well as from within BASIC09 at a moment's notice.

You'll also learn how to set up the optional high resolution graphics mouse and how to read it. Then, we'll watch over your shoulder as you create a simple drawing program that uses the high resolution mouse and a short program that lets you use OS-9's "alarm clock" function.

ENGLISH LANGUAGE COMMANDS MAKE SENSE

While you were working your way through our exercises in Chapter 7, you most likely decided that it is much easier to tap OS-9's graphics and windowing ability from within BASIC09 than it is from the OS-9 command line. You're right!

In this chapter we'll take you one step further as we help you build a set of tools that will bring some of BASIC09's power to the OS-9 command line. We hope it will make your Color Computer easier to use.

Let's start by looking at several different methods we could use to do the same job — clear a window on our Color Computer's screen. We can do it from the OS-9 command line by typing:

```
display c
```

We can do the same thing from within a BASIC09 program by typing:

```
run gfx2("clear")
```

`Display c` doesn't mean much to most people. And while the verb `clear` is easy to understand in English, the phrase `run gfx2` doesn't mean a whole heck of a lot to anyone. To complicate matters, typing `("clear")` is especially clumsy. Wouldn't it be nice if we could just type `clear` or possibly something shorter like `cls` to clear a window? You could accomplish this by typing in the following program:

```
PROCEDURE cls
(* This procedure clears a Color Computer Window *)

run gfx2("clear")
end
```

After you type in the procedure above — and as long as you stay within BASIC09 — you can run it by typing:

```
run cls
```

BASIC09 is a nice language, but who wants to run it all the time? Can we set you up so you can clear a window from the OS-9 command line by simply typing `cls`?

The first thing you must do to accomplish this goal is save the source code of your procedure. Do this immediately after typing it in with:

```
save
```

If you typed in several additional procedures before you decided to save `cls`, you will need to type:

```
save cls
```

Remember: You must always save a BASIC09 procedure before you pack it. When you run the BASIC09 `Pack` command, your source code is gone forever — unless you have previously saved it to a disk file. And don't forget, you will need the source code if you must change your procedure later.

After you have saved your source code with the command line above, you can turn it into a packed I-code module (which you can run from the OS-9 command line) by typing:

```
pack cls
```

When you type this command, BASIC09 stores an executable i-code module named cls in your current execution directory. Usually this is the directory /d0/CMDS. After you have run this command line, you will be able to clear your screen at any time by typing:

```
cls
```

Since the command is now designed to work from the OS9 prompt, in order to run it from within BASIC09, you will need to type:

```
$cls
```

When you type cls, OS-9 looks in its module directory for a module with the name cls. If it finds a module by that name, it links to it and runs it. If it does not find a module named cls, OS-9 looks in your current execution directory. It should find it there since you just used BASIC09's Pack command to store it there. When it finds the file, OS-9 loads it and links to the module it contained — cls.

When it links to cls, OS-9 learns that the module is a BASIC09 i-code module. This tells it that it *must* also load RunB, or link to it if it is already in memory. Finally, after RunB is in place, OS-9 executes RunB with cls as a parameter, and your desire for a clean window will be fulfilled.

If OS-9 can't find RunB, you will be greeted with an Error 216 message. To be safe, you might want to load it into memory. If you followed our StartUp file, it will already be in memory.

OS-9 keeps all of the preceding actions transparent. You do not need to know about them. You must only remember to type cls. After following the above scenario sentence by sentence, you probably concluded that you could clear your windows faster if the module cls were available in memory all the time. You are correct. However, if you loaded the module cls alone, you would be wasting a lot of memory.

GAINING EFFICIENCY BY COMBINING MODULES

The module cls is only 56 bytes long. However, because of the way the memory management hardware inside the Color Computer 3 works, you will be using an entire 8K memory block when you load cls. The answer is to merge a number of modules into one file. At first glance you would think you could put up to 8K or 8,192 bytes into your file.

However, because a 512-byte long block is mapped into each 64K workspace used by a task, you will want to keep your files no longer than 7,680 bytes. If you do this, OS-9 will be able to load your modules at the very top of memory in each 64K workspace.

If you run the OS-9 `Ident` tool to determine the size of the module `gfx2`, you'll notice something interesting. Try it! Type:

```
ident -x gfx2
```

That is interesting! The module `gfx2` is only 2,250 bytes long. There must be a lot of space left in the 8K memory block it is using! Let's see — 7,680 minus 2,250 equals 5,430. That's 5,430 bytes we can use for our English language commands.

The original `gfx2` module plus the packed versions of the BASIC09 procedures listed here add up to only 6,586 bytes. You could even add the medium resolution graphics package `gfx`, and your file would still fit in an 8K memory block. It is only 501 bytes long.

THE LISTING: `English.Language.Tools`

```
PROCEDURE beep
 0000      (* This command will cause your Color Computer to Beep
 0036
 0037      RUN gfx2("bell")
 0043      END
 0045
PROCEDURE Blink
 0000      (* This command will cause characters typed after you
 0036      (* run it to blink.  Works with text type windows only.
 006D
 006E      RUN gfx2("blnkon")
 007C      END
 007E
PROCEDURE NoBlink
 0000      (* Use this command to turn off blink function.
 002F      (* However, characters sent after you typed
 005B      (* Blink will continue to blink.  Characters
 0087      (* typed later won't.  Only works with text type windows.
 00C0
 00C1      RUN gfx2("blnkOff")
 00D0      END
 00D2
PROCEDURE bold
 0000      (* Makes characters typed appear in BOLD type
 002D      (* Works only in a graphics window.
 0050
 0051
 0052      RUN gfx2("boldsw","on")
 0065      END
 0067
```

```
PROCEDURE NoBold
 0000       (* Turns off the bold switch so characters typed appear
 0038       (* normal
 0041       (* Only works in a graphics window
 0063
 0064       RUN gfx2("boldsw","off")
 0078       END
 007A
PROCEDURE BorderBlue
 0000       (* This command will turn border of your screen to blue
 0037
 0038       RUN gfx2("border",1)
 0049       END
 004B
PROCEDURE BorderWhite
 0000       (* This command will turn border of your screen to white
 0038
 0039       RUN gfx2("border",0)
 004A       END
 004C
PROCEDURE BorderBlack
 0000       (* This command will turn border of your screen to black
 0038
 0039       RUN gfx2("border",2)
 004A       END
 004C
PROCEDURE BorderRed
 0000       (* This command will turn border of your screen to red
 0036
 0037       RUN gfx2("border",4)
 0048       END
 004A
PROCEDURE BorderGreen
 0000       (* This command will turn border of your screen to green
 0038
 0039       RUN gfx2("border",3)
 004A       END
 004C
PROCEDURE BorderYellow
 0000       (* This command will turn border of your screen to yellow
 0039
 003A       RUN gfx2("border",5)
 004B       END
 004D
PROCEDURE BorderCyan
 0000       (* This command will turn border of your screen to cyan
 0037
 0038       RUN gfx2("border",7)
 0049       END
 004B
```

```
PROCEDURE cls
 0000      (* This command will clear your screen
 0026
 0027       RUN gfx2("clear")
 0034       END
 0036
PROCEDURE LettersBlue
 0000      (* This command will give you Blue letters
 002A
 002B       RUN gfx2("color",1)
 003B       END
 003D
PROCEDURE LettersBlack
 0000      (* This command will give you Black letters
 002B
 002C       RUN gfx2("color",2)
 003C       END
 003E
PROCEDURE LettersGreen
 0000      (* This command will give you Green letters
 002B
 002C       RUN gfx2("color",3)
 003C       END
 003E
PROCEDURE LettersRed
 0000      (* This command will give you Red letters
 0029
 002A       RUN gfx2("color",4)
 003A       END
 003C
PROCEDURE LettersYellow
 0000      (* This command will give you Yellow letters
 002C
 002D       RUN gfx2("color",5)
 003D       END
 003F
PROCEDURE WindowRed
 0000      (* This command will give you a Red window
 002A
 002B       RUN gfx2("color",0,4)
 003E       END
 0040
PROCEDURE WindowBlack
 0000      (* This command will give you a Black window
 002C
 002D       RUN gfx2("color",0,2)
 0040       END
 0042
PROCEDURE WindowCyan
 0000      (* This command will give you a Cyan window
 002B
```

```
 002C      RUN gfx2("color",0,7)
 003F      END
 0041
PROCEDURE WindowBlue
 0000      (* This command will give you a Blue window
 002B
 002C      RUN gfx2("color",0,1)
 003F      END
 0041
PROCEDURE LettersWhite
 0000      (* This command will give you White letters
 002B
 002C      RUN gfx2("color",0)
 003C      END
 003E
PROCEDURE WindowWhite
 0000      (* This command will give you a White window
 002C
 002D      RUN gfx2("color",1,0)
 0040      END
 0042
PROCEDURE Cursor
 0000      (* This command turns on your cursor
 0024
 0025      RUN gfx2("curon")
 0032      END
 0034
PROCEDURE NoCursor
 0000      (* This command turns your cursor OFF
 0025
 0026      RUN gfx2("curoff")
 0034      END
 0036
PROCEDURE WorkInTop
 0000      (* This command sets your working area to the top half of
 003A      (* the screen
 0047
 0048      RUN gfx2("cwarea",0,0,80,12)
 0062      END
 0064
PROCEDURE WorkInFullScreen
 0000      (* This command gives you back the full screen after
 0035      (* working
 003F      (* in the top or bottom half only
 0060
 0061      RUN gfx2("cwarea",0,0,80,24)
 007B      END
 007D
PROCEDURE WorkInBottom
 0000      (* This command sets your working area to the bottom half
 003A      (* of the screen
```

```
 004A
 004B       RUN gfx2("cwarea",0,12,80,12)
 0065       END
 0067
PROCEDURE KillWindow
 0000       (* This command will remove a window.
 0025       (* You must redirect its output to the
 004B       (* window you want to kill.
 0066
 0067       RUN gfx2("DWEnd")
 0074       END
 0076
PROCEDURE MakeTextWindow
 0000       (* This command will make an 80 column window
 002D       (* out of an unused window device.
 004F
 0050       (* It will have blue letters on a white background.
 0083       (* The border will also be white.
 00A4
 00A5       RUN gfx2("DWSet",2,0,0,80,24,1,0,0)
 00CA       END
 00CC
PROCEDURE Make4ColorWindow
 0000       (* This command will make an 80 column graphics window
 0036       (* out of an unused window device.
 0058
 0059       (* Four colors will be available in this window.
 0089       (* It sports a pixel resolution of 640 horizontal by 192
 00C2       (* vertical.
 00CE
 00CF       (* It will have blue letters on a white background.
 0102       (* The border will be blue.
 011D
 011E       RUN gfx2("DWSet",7,0,0,80,24,1,0,1)
 0143       END
 0145
PROCEDURE Make16ColorWindow
 0000       (* This command will make an 40 column window
 002D       (* out of an unused window device.
 004F
 0050       (* Sixteen colors will be available in this window.
 0083       (* It sports a pixel resolution of 320 horizontal by 192
 00BC       (* vertical.
 00C8
 00C9       (* It will have blue letters on a cyan background.
 00FB       (* The border will be red.
 0115
 0116       RUN gfx2("DWSet",8,0,0,40,24,1,7,4)
 013B       END
 013D
PROCEDURE LettersBig
 0000       (* This command will switch you to the larger (8 x 8)
```

```
 ØØ36      (* character font
 ØØ47
 ØØ48      RUN gfx2("font",2ØØ,1)
 ØØ5A      END
 ØØ5C
PROCEDURE circle
 ØØØØ      (* This command draws a large circle in the middle of a
 ØØ38      (* window
 ØØ41
 ØØ42      RUN gfx2("circle",32Ø,96,4Ø)
 ØØ5A      END
 ØØ5C
PROCEDURE NoPattern
 ØØØØ      (* This command turns off all patterns
 ØØ26
 ØØ27      RUN gfx2("pattern",Ø,Ø)
 ØØ3C      END
 ØØ3E
PROCEDURE LettersSmall
 ØØØØ      (* This command will switch to the smaller (6 x 8 )
 ØØ34      (* character font
 ØØ45
 ØØ46      RUN gfx2("font",2ØØ,2)
 ØØ58      END
 ØØ5A
PROCEDURE GraphicsFont
 ØØØØ      (* This command selects the graphics character font
 ØØ33
 ØØ34      RUN gfx2("font",2ØØ,3)
 ØØ46      END
 ØØ48
PROCEDURE HourGlass
 ØØØØ      (* This command selects the Hour Glass Graphics Cursor
 ØØ36
 ØØ37      RUN gfx2("gcset",2Ø2,4)
 ØØ4A      END
 ØØ4C
PROCEDURE MakeOverlay4Ø
 ØØØØ      (* This command will create an overlay window covering the
 ØØ3B      (* top
 ØØ41      (* top half of your screen.  It will save the screen
 ØØ76      (* underneath
 ØØ83      (* it.
 ØØ89
 ØØ8A      RUN gfx2("owset",1,2,2,36,12,1,Ø)
 ØØAC      END
 ØØAE
PROCEDURE MakeOverlay8Ø
 ØØØØ      (* This command will create an overlay window covering the
 ØØ3B      (* top
 ØØ41      (* top half of your screen.  It will save the screen
```

```
 ØØ76      (* underneath
 ØØ83      (* it.
 ØØ89
 ØØ8A      RUN gfx2("owset",1,2,2,76,12,1,Ø)
 ØØAC      END
 ØØAE
PROCEDURE ReverseOn
 ØØØØ      (* This command turns on reverse video
 ØØ27      (*
 ØØ2A
 ØØ2B      RUN gfx2("revon")
 ØØ38      END
 ØØ3A
PROCEDURE reverseoff
 ØØØØ      (* This command turns off reverse video
 ØØ28      (*
 ØØ2B
 ØØ2C      RUN gfx2("revoff")
 ØØ3A      END
 ØØ3C
PROCEDURE ScaleOn
 ØØØØ      (* This command turns on OS-9's scaling feature
 ØØ3Ø
 ØØ31      RUN gfx2("scalesw","on")
 ØØ45      END
 ØØ47
PROCEDURE ScaleOff
 ØØØØ      (* This command turns off OS-9's scaling feature
 ØØ31
 ØØ32      RUN gfx2("scalesw","off")
 ØØ47      END
 ØØ49
PROCEDURE Select
 ØØØØ      (* This command selects the window you redirect this
 ØØ35      (* command to
 ØØ43
 ØØ44      RUN gfx2("select")
 ØØ52      END
 ØØ54
PROCEDURE FillWithHorizLines
 ØØØØ      (* This command selects a horizontal line pattern
 ØØ31      (* It works only in a 16, type 8, window
 ØØ59
 ØØ5A      RUN gfx2("pattern",2Ø5,3)
 ØØ6F      RUN gfx2("fill",1,1)
 ØØ81
 ØØ82      (* Now turn off the pattern
 ØØ9D      RUN gfx2("pattern",Ø,Ø)
 ØØB2      END
 ØØB4
```

```
PROCEDURE FillWithSlantedLines
 0000      (* This command selects a line pattern slanted right
 0034      (* It works only in a 16, type 8, window
 005C
 005D      RUN gfx2("pattern",205,6)
 0072      RUN gfx2("fill",1,1)
 0084
 0085      (* Now turn off the pattern
 00A0      RUN gfx2("pattern",0,0)
 00B5      END
 00B7
PROCEDURE FillWithVertLines
 0000      (* This command selects a vertical line pattern
 002F      (* It works only in a 16, type 8, window
 0057
 0058      RUN gfx2("pattern",205,2)
 006D      RUN gfx2("fill",1,1)
 007F
 0080      (* Now turn off the pattern
 009B      RUN gfx2("pattern",0,0)
 00B0      END
 00B2
PROCEDURE FillWithDots
 0000      (* This command selects a large dot pattern
 002B      (* It works only in a 16, type 8, window
 0053
 0054      RUN gfx2("pattern",205,8)
 0069      RUN gfx2("fill",1,1)
 007B
 007C      (* Now turn off the pattern
 0097      RUN gfx2("pattern",0,0)
 00AC      END
 00AE
PROCEDURE FillWithCrossHatch
 0000      (* This command selects a crosshatch pattern
 002C      (* It works only in a 16, type 8, window
 0054
 0055      RUN gfx2("pattern",205,4)
 006A      RUN gfx2("fill",1,1)
 007C
 007D      (* Now turn off the pattern
 0098      RUN gfx2("pattern",0,0)
 00AD      END
 00AF
PROCEDURE KillOverlayWindow
 0000      (* This command will remove an overlay window.
 002E      (* You must redirect its output to the
 0054      (* window you want to kill.
 006F
 0070      RUN gfx2("OWEnd")
```

```
 ØØ7D      END
 ØØ7F
PROCEDURE Underline
 ØØØØ      (* This command will cause characters typed after you
 ØØ36      (* run it to be underlined.
 ØØ51
 ØØ52      RUN gfx2("undlnon")
 ØØ61      END
 ØØ63
PROCEDURE NoUnderline
 ØØØØ      (* Use this command to turn off the underline function.
 ØØ37      (* However, characters sent after you typed "Underline"
 ØØ6F      (* will continue to be underlined.  Characters
 ØØ9D      (* typed later won't.
 ØØB2
 ØØB3      RUN gfx2("undlnoff")
 ØØC3      END
 ØØC5
PROCEDURE Transparent
 ØØØØ      (* Makes characters typed appear transparent --
 ØØ3Ø      (* You will not see their background.  Works only
 ØØ61      (* in a graphics window.
 ØØ79
 ØØ7A
 ØØ7B      RUN gfx2("TCharSw","on")
 ØØ8F      END
 ØØ91
PROCEDURE NoTransparent
 ØØØØ      (* Turns off the transparent switch so characters
 ØØ31      (* typed appear normal.  Only works in a graphics window.
 ØØ6A
 ØØ6B      RUN gfx2("TCharSw","off")
 ØØ8Ø      END
 ØØ82
PROCEDURE NoGraphicsCursor
 ØØØØ      (* This command turns off the Graphics Cursor
 ØØ2D
 ØØ2E      RUN gfx2("gcset",Ø,Ø)
 ØØ41      END
 ØØ43
PROCEDURE Pointer
 ØØØØ      (* This command selects the Pointer as a Graphics Cursor
 ØØ38
 ØØ39      RUN gfx2("gcset",2Ø2,1)
 ØØ4C      END
 ØØ4E
PROCEDURE Pencil
 ØØØØ      (* This command selects the Pencil as a Graphics Cursor
 ØØ37
 ØØ38      RUN gfx2("gcset",2Ø2,2)
 ØØ4B      END
```

```
ØØ4D
PROCEDURE CrossHair
 ØØØØ       (* This command selects the small CrossHair as a Graphics
 ØØ3A       (* Cursor
 ØØ43
 ØØ44       RUN gfx2("gcset",2Ø2,7)
 ØØ57       END
```

Using these commands is almost self-explanatory. For example, to generate a beep tone in the speaker of your CM-8 monitor, you only need to type:

```
beep
```

To change the color of the window you are working in, you could answer an OS-9 command line prompt like this:

```
windowcyan ; lettersblue ; borderred
```

We'll let you experiment with the rest!

These BASIC09 procedures define a set of English language commands you may find easy to remember. If you would rather have commands with shorter names, rename the procedures when you type them using BASIC09's editor. Just remember, six months from now it may be hard to remember that wc means WindowCyan and not Word Count.

GETTING YOUR TOOLS IN GFX2

After you type these procedures, you'll want to pack them and put them all in your gfx2 file. When we started that process, our current data directory was named /DD/BOOK/B09_SRC. We started the production process by creating a special directory where we could store all of our packed i-code modules. We didn't want to clutter up our /d0/CMDS directory with another 50 filenames. We did this by typing:

```
makdir BIN
chx /dd/book/b09_src/bin
```

Immediately after we typed each procedure, we saved it by typing:

```
save
```

When we did this, BASIC09 saved the source code of our procedure in a file with the same name as our procedure. It stored them in our current data directory, /DD/BOOK/B09_SRC. Immediately after we ran the BASIC09 Save command, we typed:

```
pack
```

When we typed this command line, BASIC09 created an i-code module with the same name as the procedure we had just typed. It stored that module in a file it created in our current execution directory, /DD/BOOK/B09_SRC/BIN.

We repeated the steps above for every procedure we created. Then we merged all of the files in our current execution directory into several temporary files. Like this:

```
merge beep blink noblink bold nobold borderblue  >temp1
merge borderwhite borderblack borderred bordergreen  >temp2
merge borderyellow bordercyan cls lettersblue lettersblack  >temp3
merge lettersgreen lettersred lettersyellow letterswhite  >temp4
merge windowred windowblack windowcyan windowblue  >temp5
merge windowwhite cursor nocursor workintop workinfullscreen  >temp6
merge workinbottom killwindow maketextwindow make4colorwindow  >temp7
merge make16colorwindow lettersbig letterssmall circle nopattern  >temp8
merge graphicsfont hourglass pointer pencil crosshair nographicscursor  >temp9
merge makeoverlay40 makeoverlay80 reverseon reverseoff  >temp10
merge scaleon scaleoff select fillwithhorizlines fillwithvertlines  >temp11
merge fillwithdots fillwithcrosshatch killoverlaywindow underline  >temp12
merge nounderline transparent notransparent  >temp13
```

You can type longer command lines and place more i-code modules in each temporary file if you like. In fact, you may type up to 198 characters on each line — or just over two and a half lines before pressing ENTER.

Now, you can merge your temporary files into one large new gfx2 file and store it in your normal execution directory /d0/CMDS. Here's one way to do it:

```
chx /d0/cmds
rename /d0/cmds/gfx2 gfx2_original
chd /dd/book/b09_src/bin

merge /dd/cmds/gfx2_original temp1 temp2 temp3 temp4
temp5 temp6 temp7 temp8 temp9 temp10 temp11 temp12
temp13 >/dd/cmds/gfx2

attr /dd/cmds/gfx2 e pe -w -pw
load gfx2
```

If you also want SysCall, Inkey and Gfx in the new gfx2 file, you could merge them into temp14 and include it in the above.

Notice: When you use the OS-9 `Merge` tool, the "execute" attributes of your new file are not set. You must manually run the OS-9 `Attr` command to set the execute attributes as we did above. If you do not do this, you will not be able to load or run the modules stored in a file created with the `Merge` tool.

Once you have merged your new English language commands into the `gfx2` file, you will find they execute quickly. In fact, you will probably want to load this new `gfx2` file from your OS-9 start-up procedure file. If you do this, your new commands will be available at the first `OS9` prompt.

MAKING A MINI-DRAWING PROGRAM

Now that your OS-9 toolbox has grown, we'll move on to create a short drawing program you can use to have fun with your Color Computer 3. We'll show you how to set up OS-9 to use the optional high resolution mouse adapter and how to read that mouse. Then, we'll create three BASIC09 procedures that will let you use the mouse to draw boxes, circles and lines.

You would be surprised how many things you can draw when you combine these three basic shapes. After you have played with our `LetsDraw` program, you'll probably want to use it as the starting point for your own `CoCoDraw`. These short procedures are only the beginning!

THE LISTING: `LetsDraw`

```
PROCEDURE DrawObjects
 0000      DIM button:BYTE
 0007      DIM horiz,vert:INTEGER
 0012      DIM choice:STRING[1]
 001E
 001F      (* First, clear the window
 0039      RUN gfx2("clear")
 0046
 0047      (* And greet them with a boldfaced message
 0071      RUN gfx2("boldsw","on")
 0084      PRINT "Welcome to CoCo Draw!"
 009D
 009E      (* Don't forget to turn bold printing off
 00C7      RUN gfx2("boldsw","off")
 00DB
 00DC      (* and prepare OS-9 for the High Resolution Mouse *)
 0110      RUN SetUpMouse
 0114
 0115      REPEAT
 0117        (* We'll put the window in an
 0134        (* overlay window
 0145        RUN gfx2("owset",1,5,5,30,10,2,4)
```

```
Ø167
Ø168     (* We should turn on the text cursor
Ø18C     RUN gfx2("curon")
Ø199
Ø19A     (* and turn off the graphics cursor for now
Ø1C5     RUN gfx2("gcset",Ø,Ø)
Ø1D8
Ø1D9     (* Here's our menu
Ø1EB     PRINT "You may draw one object."
Ø2Ø7     PRINT
Ø2Ø9     PRINT "     1. A box"
Ø21A     PRINT "     2. A circle"
Ø22E     PRINT "     3. A line"
Ø24Ø     PRINT
Ø242     PRINT "     Ø. To Quit"
Ø255
Ø256     PRINT
Ø258
Ø259     (* Draw attention to our prompt
Ø278     RUN gfx2("revon")
Ø285     PRINT "Which one: ";
Ø295
Ø296     (* But after we get their attention
Ø2B9     (* we want to return to normal print
Ø2DD     RUN gfx2("revoff")
Ø2EB
Ø2EC     (* Now, wait for their response
Ø3ØB     REPEAT
Ø3ØD       RUN inkey(choice)
Ø317     UNTIL choice<>""
Ø322
Ø323     (* When they answer, we'll
Ø33D     (* turn off the cursor and
Ø357     (* close our window to give
Ø372     (* them a full screen to draw in
Ø392     RUN gfx2("curoff")
Ø3AØ     RUN gfx2("owend")
Ø3AD
Ø3AE     (* We must run the drawing program
Ø3DØ     (* they have selected.
Ø3E6     IF choice="1" THEN
Ø3F3       RUN gfx2("curoff")
Ø4Ø1       RUN drawbox
Ø4Ø5     ELSE
Ø4Ø9       IF choice="2" THEN
Ø416         RUN gfx2("curoff")
Ø424         RUN drawcircle
Ø428       ELSE
Ø42C         IF choice="3" THEN
Ø439           RUN gfx2("curoff")
Ø447           RUN drawline
```

```
Ø44B            ENDIF
Ø44D          ENDIF
Ø44F        ENDIF
Ø451      UNTIL choice="Ø"
Ø45D
Ø45E
Ø45F
PROCEDURE SetUpMouse
 ØØØØ      (* This procedure uses the program 'SysCall' to
 ØØ2F      (* do a set status call which sets up OS-9 to treat
 ØØ62      (* the Color Computer Mouse as a high resolution device
 ØØ99      (* using the right joystick port.  Because, this change is
 ØØD3      (* system wide, another program using the mouse later will
 Ø1ØD      (* also need to know how to use the optional high
 Ø13F      (* resolution mouse adapter.
 Ø15B
 Ø15C      (* Since this set status call can also be used to change the
 Ø198      (* key repeat start constant and delay speed, it tells
 Ø1CE      (* OS-9 to leave those parameters unchanged.
 Ø1FA
 Ø1FB      (* Notice that all system calls use a similar format
 Ø22F
 Ø23Ø      TYPE registers=cc,a,b,dp:BYTE; x,y,u:INTEGER
 Ø255
 Ø256      DIM regs:registers
 Ø25F      DIM path,callcode:BYTE
 Ø26A      DIM packet(32):BYTE
 Ø276
 Ø277      (* Now set up the mouse parameters
 Ø299
 Ø29A      regs.a:=Ø
 Ø2A5      regs.b:=$94
 Ø2B1      regs.x:=$Ø1Ø1
 Ø2BD      regs.y:=$FFFF
 Ø2C9      callcode:=$8E
 Ø2D1
 Ø2D2      RUN syscall(callcode,regs)
 Ø2E1
 Ø2E2      END
 Ø2E4
 Ø2E5
 Ø2E6
PROCEDURE drawbox
 ØØØØ      (* Program to draw a box at location pointed
 ØØ2C      (* to by high resolution mouse.
 ØØ4B
 ØØ4C      (* Uses procedure GetMouse
 ØØ66      (* Called by procedure DrawObjects
 ØØ88
 ØØ89      DIM horiz,vert,Horiz1,vert1:INTEGER
 ØØ9C      DIM button:BYTE
```

```
00A3
00A4        (* We'll use a pencil for our graphics cursor
00D1        RUN gfx2("gcset",202,2)
00E4
00E5        (* We must back up and erase our original banner
0115        (* before printing a new one.
0132        RUN gfx2("curup")
013F        RUN gfx2("erline")
014D        PRINT "Point to first corner of box and click mouse."
017E
017F        (* Notice how we pass empty parameters to the
01AC        (* procedure getmouse.  GetMouse will place a
01D9        (* value in each of the parameters listed before
020A        (* it exits.
0216        RUN getmouse(horiz,vert,button)
022A        Horiz1:=horiz
0232        vert1:=vert
023A
023B        (* We'll place one corner of the box where
0265        (* they first click the mouse.
0283        RUN gfx2("setdptr",Horiz1,vert1)
029C        RUN gfx2("POINT",Horiz1,vert1)
02B3
02B4        (* Then, we need to tell them what to do next.
02E2        RUN gfx2("curup")
02EF        RUN gfx2("erline")
02FD        PRINT "Point to location of opposite corner and click again."
0336
0337        (* We then run GetMouse again to let them
0360        (* point to the opposite corner of the box.
038B
038C        RUN getmouse(horiz,vert,button)
03A0
03A1        (* Use the second point to draw the box
03C8        RUN gfx2("box",horiz,vert)
03DD
03DE        (* Then, ring the bell and return.
0400        RUN gfx2("bell")
040C        END
040E
040F
0410
PROCEDURE drawcircle
0000        (* Program to draw circle at location pointed
002D        (* to by high resolution mouse.
004C
004D        (* Uses procedure GetMouse
0067        (* Called by procedure DrawObjects
0089
008A        (* Notice how drawcircle works in a manner
00B4        (* identical to drawbox.  the same is true of
```

```
ØØE1      (* our last procedure, drawline.
Ø1Ø1
Ø1Ø2      DIM horiz,vert,HorizCen:INTEGER
Ø111      DIM button:BYTE
Ø118
Ø119      RUN gfx2("gcset",2Ø2,1)
Ø12C
Ø12D      RUN gfx2("curup")
Ø13A      RUN gfx2("erline")
Ø148
Ø149      PRINT "Point to where you want a circle and click the mouse button."
Ø18E
Ø18F      RUN getmouse(horiz,vert,button)
Ø1A3      HorizCen:=horiz
Ø1AB      RUN gfx2("setdptr",horiz,vert)
Ø1C4      RUN gfx2("POINT",horiz,vert)
Ø1DB      RUN gfx2("curup")
Ø1E8      RUN gfx2("erline")
Ø1F6      PRINT "Move horizontally the length of the radius and click again."
Ø235      RUN getmouse(horiz,vert,button)
Ø249      RUN gfx2("circle",ABS(HorizCen-horiz))
Ø26Ø      RUN gfx2("bell")
Ø26C      RUN gfx2("gcset",Ø,Ø)
Ø27F      END
Ø281
Ø282
Ø283
PROCEDURE drawline
ØØØØ      (* Program to draw line at location pointed
ØØ2B      (* to by high resolution mouse.
ØØ4A
ØØ4B      (* Uses procedure GetMouse
ØØ65      (* Called by procedure DrawObjects
ØØ87
ØØ88      DIM horiz,vert,horiz1,vert1:INTEGER
ØØ9B      DIM button:BYTE
ØØA2
ØØA3      RUN gfx2("gcset",2Ø2,1)
ØØB6
ØØB7      RUN gfx2("curup")
ØØC4      RUN gfx2("erline")
ØØD2      PRINT "Point to first end of line and click mouse."
Ø1Ø1
Ø1Ø2      RUN getmouse(horiz,vert,button)
Ø116      horiz1:=horiz
Ø11E      vert1:=vert
Ø126      RUN gfx2("setdptr",horiz1,vert1)
Ø13F      RUN gfx2("POINT",horiz1,vert1)
Ø156      RUN gfx2("curup")
Ø163      RUN gfx2("erline")
Ø171      PRINT "Now point to other end of line and click."
```

```
  RUN getmouse(horiz,vert,button)
  RUN gfx2("line",horiz,vert)
  RUN gfx2("gcset",0,0)
  END
PROCEDURE GetMouse
  (* Reads the present location of the mouse and
  (* returns the status of the button.
  TYPE registers=cc,a,b,dp:BYTE; x,y,u:INTEGER
  DIM regs:registers
  DIM path,callcode:BYTE
  DIM packet(32):BYTE
  PARAM horiz,vert:INTEGER
  PARAM button:BYTE
  REPEAT
    regs.a:=0
    regs.b:=$89
    regs.x:=ADDR(packet)
    regs.y:=1
    callcode:=$8D
    RUN syscall(callcode,regs)
    (* We get our location and the the status of
    (* the mouse button from the packet
    (* returned by the get status call.
    horiz:=packet(25)*256+packet(26)
    vert:=packet(27)*256+packet(28)
    button:=packet(9)
    (* We use then print the graphics cursor
    (* at the location returned.  The graphics
    (* cursor tells them where they are pointing
    (* on the screen.
    RUN gfx2("putgc",horiz,vert)
    (* When they click the button, we return
  UNTIL button<>0
  END
```

These BASIC09 procedures are designed to run in a four-color, 640-by-192 pixel window. Before you run them, you must merge the information in the files `/dd/sys/stdptrs` and `/dd/sys/`

stdpats_4 into a window. You can do this by running the procedure file ReadyDraw, which we created in Chapter 7.

You must also merge the information contained in the /dd/sys/stdfonts file into a window before you run these procedures. We did that in our sample start-up file in the last chapter. Finally, InKey and Syscall, which are supplied with OS-9 Level II of the CMDS directory of the BASIC09 disk, need to be in your current execution directory or in memory.

As you experiment with our LetsDraw program, think about how you would like your Color Computer 3 to respond to the mouse while you're drawing. Then, modify it to make it run your way. For example, by changing the control loops in the procedure GetMouse and the procedures DrawBox, DrawCircle and DrawLine, you can write a version of LetsDraw that will let you drag the mouse from one corner of the box to the opposite — or from one end of a line to the opposite. Enjoy!

SETTING A COCO ALARM!

An alarm clock on your Color Computer could be quite handy. Who wants to forget and leave their dinner in the microwave? This alarm clock, written by Brian Lantz, will beep at you several times when it goes off. Notice the way he uses the program SysCall to exercise the OS-9 F$Alarm system call. The format is identical to the one we showed you in the GetMouse procedure. Only the data in the 6809 registers has been changed to protect the innocent — or make it work!

THE LISTING: Alarm

```
PROCEDURE Alarm
 0000      DIM choice:STRING[1]
 000C      DIM pass:INTEGER
 0013      TYPE registers=CC,A,B,DP:BYTE; X,Y,U:INTEGER
 0038      DIM regs:registers
 0041      DIM callcode:BYTE
 0048      DIM packet(6):BYTE
 0054      DIM junk:STRING
 005B
 005C      RUN GFX2("OWSET",1,5,4,30,10,2,4)
 007E
 007F      callcode:=$1E
 0087      regs.X:=ADDR(packet)
 0095
 0096      FOR pass=0 TO 1 STEP 0
 00AB        PRINT CHR$(12);
 00B1        PRINT "     Alarm Update Program"
 00CE        PRINT "   (c) 1987 Brian A. Lantz"
 00EC        PRINT
 00EE        PRINT " Time:"; RIGHT$(DATE$,8); "  Date:"; LEFT$(DATE$,8
              )
 010C        PRINT
```

```
010E         PRINT "  0 - End Alarm Program"
0129         PRINT "  1 - Set the Alarm"
0140         PRINT "  2 - Turn off the Alarm"
015C         PRINT "  3 - Display the Alarm"
0177         PRINT "      ";
0182
0183         RUN GFX2("BELL")
018F         RUN GFX2("REVON")
019C         PRINT "Your Choice ";
01AD         RUN GFX2("REVOFF")
01BB
01BC         INPUT " ",choice
01C5
01C6         IF choice="0" THEN RUN GFX2("OWEND")
01DF           RUN GFX2("CURUP")
01EC           RUN GFX2("ERLINE")
01FA           RUN GFX2("CURUP")
0207           RUN GFX2("ERLINE")
0215           END
0217         ENDIF
0219
021A         IF choice="1" THEN PRINT CHR$(12);
022C           packet(2):=VAL(MID$(DATE$,4,2))
023C           packet(1):=VAL(LEFT$(DATE$,2))
024A           packet(3):=VAL(MID$(DATE$,7,2))
025A
025B           INPUT "Set Alarm for other day ? ",choice
027D           IF choice="y" THEN GOTO 4
028D           ENDIF
028F
0290           IF choice="Y" THEN GOTO 4
02A0           ENDIF
02A2
02A3           GOTO 5
02A7
02A8 4         INPUT "Enter Alarm Month--> ",packet(2)
02CB           INPUT "Enter Alarm Day--> ",packet(3)
02E9           INPUT "Enter Alarm Year--> ",packet(1)
0308
0309 5         INPUT "Enter Alarm Hour--> ",packet(4)
032B           INPUT "Enter Alarm Minute--> ",packet(5)
034C
034D           regs.A:=0
0358           regs.B:=1
0363
0364           RUN SysCall(callcode,regs)
0373           PRINT
0375           PRINT "Alarm is Set!!"
0387           GOSUB 1000
038B           GOTO 100
```

```
038F        ENDIF
0391
0392        IF choice="2" THEN regs.A:=0
03A9          regs.B:=0
03B4
03B5          RUN SysCall(callcode,regs)
03C4          PRINT CHR$(12); "Alarm is now off!"
03DD          GOSUB 1000
03E1          GOTO 100
03E5        ENDIF
03E7
03E8        IF choice="3" THEN regs.A:=0
03FF          regs.B:=2
040A
040B          RUN SysCall(callcode,regs)
041A          PRINT CHR$(12); "The Alarm is now set at:"
043A          PRINT
043C
043D          IF packet(2)=1 THEN PRINT "January";
0456          ENDIF
0458          IF packet(2)=2 THEN PRINT "February";
0472          ENDIF
0474          IF packet(2)=3 THEN PRINT "March";
048B          ENDIF
048D          IF packet(2)=4 THEN PRINT "April";
04A4          ENDIF
04A6          IF packet(2)=5 THEN PRINT "May";
04BB          ENDIF
04BD          IF packet(2)=6 THEN PRINT "June";
04D3          ENDIF
04D5          IF packet(2)=7 THEN PRINT "July";
04EB          ENDIF
04ED          IF packet(2)=8 THEN PRINT "August";
0505          ENDIF
0507          IF packet(2)=9 THEN PRINT "September";
0522          ENDIF
0524          IF packet(2)=10 THEN PRINT "October";
053D          ENDIF
053F          IF packet(2)=11 THEN PRINT "November";
0559          ENDIF
055B          IF packet(2)=12 THEN PRINT "December";
0575          ENDIF
0577
0578          PRINT " "; packet(3); ", 19"; packet(1)
0590          PRINT "at "; packet(4); ":";
05A2
05A3          IF packet(5)<10 THEN PRINT "0";
05B6          ENDIF
05B8
05B9          PRINT packet(5); ":00"
```

```
05C6          PRINT
05C8          PRINT "Alarm is now o";
05DB
05DC          IF regs.B=1 THEN PRINT "n"
05EF          ELSE
05F3            PRINT "ff"
05F9          ENDIF
05FB
05FC          GOSUB 1000
0600          GOTO 100
0604        ENDIF
0606
0607        PRINT CHR$(12)
060C        PRINT "Invalid Selection!!"
0623        GOSUB 1000
0627 100  NEXT pass
0635
0636 1000 PRINT
063B      RUN GFX2("REVON")
0648      PRINT "Press <ENTER> to Continue";
0666      RUN GFX2("REVOFF")
0674      INPUT " ",junk
067D      RETURN
```

Notice the similarity between the code Lantz used to display his menu and the code we used in the procedure DrawObjects earlier. There are often many ways to do the same job on a computer. Also, compare the standard BASIC structure Lantz used in the decision tree following his menu to the standard BASIC09 structure we used in DrawObjects. He chose to use the standard BASIC GOTO command to handle program flow. We opted for several control structures unique to BASIC09: REPEAT-UNTIL and WHILE-DO.

The more you use BASIC09 to solve your computing problems, the more you'll like it. We'll have a lot more BASIC09 programs you can use as examples in later chapters. For now, we must return to the OS-9 command line where we can show you a few more tricks and review basic OS-9 operation.

CHAPTER 9

# of file trees and other things os-9

If you've been faithful and stuck with us through the first eight chapters, you have received a practical introduction to most of the OS-9 tools available with Color Computer OS-9 Level II. If you've typed in and run the many procedure files and BASIC09 procedures, you are nearing the top of the learning curve. Now, the age-old saying takes charge — practice will make perfect. In this chapter, we'll pick up a few stragglers, pass out more shortcuts and tips, and present a philosophical overview of OS-9.

GETTING ORGANIZED

One of these days you may purchase a hard disk for your Color Computer. When you do, your approach to computing will change radically. Your enjoyment level will soar, too.

You will, however, eventually need to get organized (hard drive or not). If you don't, you'll find yourself lost in a sea of directories and subdirectories.

Many people have asked us the questions, "How should I set up my disk directories? Is it best to use a tall, skinny directory structure or should I spread my directories out in a horizontal fashion?"

Organizing a disk is a very personal matter, but perhaps we can help with an overview of the possibilities available to OS-9 users. As we begin, remember that it was a tall, skinny directory structure you were forced to use if your first operating system was RS-DOS, CP/M or even one of the earlier versions of MS-DOS. Remember the long lists you had to search when you needed to find a stray file? Bet you thought those searches would take forever! Let's move forward now and show you how you can use OS-9's hierarchical file system to get organized.

The most basic element in the OS-9 filing system is the individual file. Files usually contain data you need. OS-9 files can also contain directories that tell the system how to find other information and the programs you need to manipulate your information. As you begin to learn about the OS-9 filing system, think of each mounted disk as a large filing cabinet. Inside that filing cabinet you'll find a number of individual directories. These directories perform the same duty as file drawers in a real filing cabinet.

Other OS-9 directories stored within the first-level directories are called subdirectories. They are similar to the file folders you place in file drawers. The individual OS-9 files that contain your data can be compared to the individual pieces of paper you store in the file folders in the real drawers of that filing cabinet in your den.

The top level of the OS-9 filing system on any particular disk is the root directory of that disk. The directories stored in the root directory usually give you access to applications programs and other system data.

For example, the standard OS-9 Level II system disk that you purchase from Tandy contains five files and two individual directories. Two of the files, `OS9Boot` and `Startup`, are used when you boot your Color Computer. Three other files contain OS-9 procedure files that you can run to create several different windows. The two directories hold programs and other information about your computer.

The `CMDS` directory contains the OS-9 tools you have been using throughout this book. The `SYS` directory contains information that OS-9 uses occasionally. For example, in one of the files you'll find a list of English language error messages. You can ask to see one of them when you receive a numerical error message you don't understand. Another file holds help messages that show you the syntax for each OS-9 tool. Additional files in the `SYS` directory contain data that defines the standard fonts, graphics cursors and background patterns available with OS-9 Level II.

On multiuser OS-9 based computers, the system manager often sets up a directory for each user. These "user" directories are almost always placed in the root directory of the disk. It is up to the individual user to organize the data in his or her own directory. Since you are the "user," the system manager's move places the ball squarely in your court. Let's look at one way to play the game.

We'll start by assuming that you don't have a hard disk. You will still want to set up directories on your floppy disks to match the many jobs you need to do. For example, if you supervise a large staff, do the billing, keep track of an inventory and oversee the sales team, you will want to set up at least four directories in the root directory of your personal disk. The first few levels of your filing system might look like this:

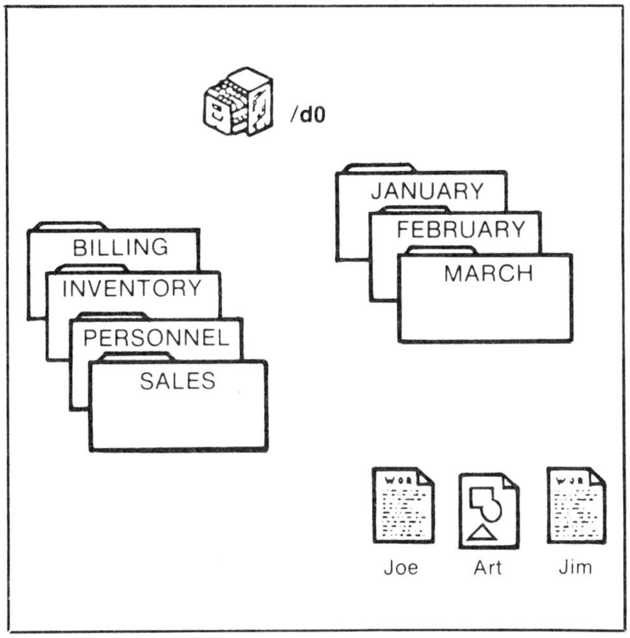

In the directory named `BILLING`, you could create two subdirectories, or folders, `Sent` and `Paid`.

In `INVENTORY` you might need to set up folders for `Completed_Widgets` and `Spare_Parts`.

In the `PERSONNEL` directory you will need at least two folders, one for `Evaluations` and another for `Payroll`.

And finally, in the `SALES` folder you will need to create 12 folders or subdirectories, one for each month. Each folder will hold individual files that contain reports from each salesperson for the month plus any charts or graphics you need to make a clear and concise report to your boss.

If you are the only user and are setting up your filing system on your own floppy disk, the structure of your disk will be similar to that in the illustration above.

If you are working in an office with two other managers and using a hard disk for storage, the system manager will probably create three directories — one for each of you — in the root directory of the hard disk. If this is the case, you will need to copy the top directory on your floppy disk and its contents into your user directory on the hard disk. For example, if your name is Fred and one of the three user directories set up by the system manager is named FRED, then the pathlist to your BILLING folder will be:

```
/h0/FRED/BILLING
```

The complete pathlist to Jim's sales report for January will be:

```
/h0/FRED/SALES/January/Jim
```

You will find that it is easy to find a particular file after you have set up a logical filing system similar to the one above. For example, if you need to check out Sam's last personnel evaluation, you need to look in a file with a pathlist like this:

```
/d0/FRED/PERSONNEL/Evaluations/February/Sam
```

Isn't it easy to find a file when it is stored in a logical place? Typing a long pathlist like this could get old very fast, but since you probably do all of your personnel reports at one time, you can take advantage of another handy OS-9 feature and set your current data directory to the current month's evaluations. You can do that with a command line like this:

```
chd /d0/FRED/PERSONNEL/Evaluations/February
```

Then, all you will need to type is:

```
edit Sam
```

The first command line above sets the current data directory to /D0/FRED/PERSONNEL/Evaluations/February. You'll find that OS-9's hierarchical directory structure lets you organize your data directories the same way you have organized your business. That's good because you know your business better than anyone else.

After you organize your data directories in a structure parallel to your business, you will be able to find your files quickly. Once you have organized your disk, OS-9's chd command will make it easy for you to change your current data directory to the particular directory that contains the files needed to accomplish the day's work.

OS-9 HELPS ORGANIZE PROGRAMS, TOO

OS-9 files can also contain programs, and its designers moved one up on UNIX when they added a second working directory to the file system. This second working directory is called the current execution directory. It holds files that contain 6809 object code or "intermediate" code that runs with the many OS-9 programming languages you can use on your Color Computer.

WHY CURRENT WORKING DIRECTORIES ARE IMPORTANT

When you boot Color Computer OS-9 Level II on a floppy disk-based system, a program named `cc3go` executes automatically. It sets up your current directories for you. After `cc3go` runs, your current execution directory will be `/d0/CMDS` and your current data directory will be `/d0`.

If you own a Tandy hard disk and have installed its device descriptor, `/h0`, and device driver, `cc3hdisk`, in your `OS9Boot` file, `cc3go` automatically sets your current execution directory to `/h0/CMDS` and your current data directory to `/h0` each time you start up your Color Computer.

These "current" directories apply only to the disk physically mounted in drive `/d0` when you boot OS-9. If you remove that disk and insert another, OS-9's records will no longer be "current." You will need to use the OS-9 `chd` tool to change your current data directory to the root directory of the new disk. Likewise, you will need to use the `chx` tool to change the current execution directory to the `CMDS` directory on the new disk.

If you do not use `chd` and `chx` to update OS-9's records, it will get lost because it will continue to look for your directories on the new disk at the same physical location it found them on the old disk. Most of the time it will not find them in the same location, and it will load something totally inappropriate into memory. Strange things will happen and you'll wind up reading an obscure error message.

HOW OS-9 FINDS YOUR PROGRAMS

When you decide to run a program, `Dir` for example, OS-9 looks for `Dir` and runs it. However, before OS-9 looks on your disk drives, it checks to find out if the program you want to run is already in memory. To do this it looks for the name you typed on the command line in its module directory. If OS-9 finds `Dir` in its module directory, it links to it and runs it immediately. No disk access will be needed.

But what if Dir is not in memory? In this case, OS-9 looks in the current execution directory and tries to find a file named Dir. If it finds a file with this name in this directory, it assumes it is executable code, loads it into memory and runs it.

And finally, if OS-9 doesn't find Dir in the current execution directory, it makes one more try — this time it looks in the current data directory. But, if OS-9 finds a file named Dir in the current data directory, it doesn't treat it like a program. It treats it like a data file. More specifically, it assumes this data file contains an OS-9 procedure file and uses it accordingly.

An OS-9 procedure file is similar to a UNIX script file — it contains a list of OS-9 commands that are read and executed by the shell. Each time OS-9 reads a command line from a procedure file, it executes it, just as if you had typed it. In fact, OS-9 reads and executes command lines from the procedure file until it receives an end-of-file signal.

BASIC09 I-CODE IS EXECUTED AUTOMATICALLY

When it runs into "intermediate" code (i-code) from an OS-9 language like BASIC09, the OS-9 shell runs the language's run-time package automatically. For example, packed BASIC09 programs are executed by a run-time interpreter named RunB.

When you type the name of a file stored in your current execution directory that contains packed BASIC09 code, OS-9 loads this i-code into memory just as if it were 6809 object code. However, before OS-9 runs the code in any module, it checks the information in the module header to find out what type of code is in the module.

When the shell finds out that you have loaded a packed BASIC09 i-code module, it knows that it needs RunB to run your program. So, the shell automatically loads RunB and executes it with the name of your module as a parameter. All of this work is transparent to you, and all you will see on your screen is the output of your BASIC09 program.

SUBDIRECTORIES HELP YOU ORGANIZE YOUR TOOLS

When you first purchase OS-9 Level II for the Color Computer 3, you'll find there are enough tools stored in the /d0/CMDS directory on the OS-9 System Master Disk to fill several screen pages with filenames. After you add a few dozen of your own favorite applications programs and third-party tools, it will become almost impossible to find a file when you look through a directory listing on the screen. The problem is further complicated by the fact that the Dir utility command in the 6809 version of OS-9 does not alphabetize the directory listing for you.

If you move up to a hard disk and buy or write hundreds of new programs, you will need to organize a set of CMDS directories on your hard disk using a method similar to the one you used to organize your data directories. For example, if you own more than one set of advanced utility programs, you'll find that many of the vendors give their programs the same name. The standard UNIX utilities, ls and mv, are perfect examples. Almost every third-party utility package contains them.

The names aren't the only problem. Even though these utilities have the same name, most require a different syntax on the command line. Also, OS-9 won't let you store more than one program with the same filename in the same directory. Besides, it was six months ago when you moved that utility to your CMDS directory — which version did you load?

These problems inspired us to get our utility programs organized. We did this by creating subdirectories in our current execution directory, /h0/CMDS. For typing ease we used two- or three-letter names for the directories we created to store the various programs and utilities from the various third-party vendors. Here is a look at the subdirectories in our CMDS directory.

```
                    /h0/CMDS
      cw     dpj     fhl     mw     rs     sg
```

Computerware's utilities are stored in the directory cw; D.P. Johnson's hackers kits live in dpj; *OPak, Xlist* and other products from Frank Hogg Laboratory are stored in fhl; Microware's toolkit is saved in mw; Tandy products live in rs and, finally, Steve Goldberg's *Utilipak Too* tools are run from a subdirectory named sg.

Using the standard OS-9 Level II shell, we type the pathlist to a tool in one of these directories when we need to run it. That's why we used short directory names. For example, if we want to run Steve Goldberg's version of ls, we merely type:

```
sg/ls
```

ORGANIZE YOUR TOOLS BY SUBJECT

Ask 100 people how they organize their hard disk and you'll most likely wind up with 99 different answers. But there are some basics you should consider. To get in the mood, study these approaches.

```
/h0/LANGUAGES/BASIC09/SOURCE/INVENTORY/PROGRAMS
/h0/INVENTORY/PROGRAMS/SOURCE/BASIC09
```

Here's the issue. What is more important — the job or the program that wrote the program that does the job? The first example above emphasizes the computer, instead of the job. The latter takes the opposite approach.

For most of us, the fact that a file is related to inventory is more important than the fact that it was created by BASIC09. Another way of saying it is that some nouns are more important than their adjectives.

And what happens when someone else sits down at your Color Computer keyboard? Will they be able to find things quickly if everything is stored by language rather than by subject? Wouldn't they find it a real drag to look through a half-dozen different language subdirectories to find one inventory program?

USING MODPATCH TO SET DISK DRIVE STEP RATE

It's time for you to meet Modpatch, another OS-9 Level II tool. Modpatch will come in handy when you need to patch a module in memory. For example, if you own disk drives that step at a rate faster than 30 milliseconds, you will want to patch the device descriptors.

You can create a new OS9Boot file that contains the double-sided device descriptor you need to use your double-sided drives with the OS-9 Config tool. Then, you can use Modpatch to change the stepping rate in the new device descriptors.

ModPatch reads a file containing the patches you want to make to a module in memory. Here's the patch file you need to change your disk drive's stepping rate to six milliseconds. Type it into a file named Patch using the OS-9 Build tool.

```
L d0
C 14 00 03
V
L d1
C 14 00 03
V
```

This script file lets you patch the device descriptors that work with both /d0 and /d1 in one Modpatch run. Here's how it works.

In the first line, the script tells Modpatch to link to the device descriptor module named d0. In the second line, it changes the byte at an offset of 14 Hex bytes from the beginning of the file from 00 to 03. This changes the step rate from 30 milliseconds to six milliseconds. The official OS-9 speak name of that byte in a device descriptor is IT.STP.

The third line in the script tells Modpatch to verify the module d0. It updates the CRC of that module so that it may be loaded into memory and run again. Remember: If you attempt to load a module with a bad CRC, OS-9 will refuse to accept it. In the fourth line the process starts over and makes the same changes to the device descriptor module named d1.

To make the patch, you must have created the file named Patch in your current data directory. After you have done this, type:

```
ModPatch patch
```

While we're speaking of patches, if you have any device descriptors you want to upgrade to OS-9 Level II, you need to change the byte at an offset of 14 decimal from FF to 07. To do this, use the OS-9 Build tool to create a ModPatch patch file like this.

```
L H0
C 0E FF 07
V
```

After you have created this patch file, you must run it with Modpatch like you did with the step rate change above.

USING MODPATCH TO SET REPEAT KEY SPEED

If your keyboard seems inclined to echo an extra lowercase letter every time you hold down the SHIFT key to start a new sentence or capitalize a proper noun, you might want to try this patch file.

```
l cc3io
c 7e 1e 3e
c 86 03 06
v
```

After you create this patch file, run it with Modpatch. It almost doubles the delay time OS-9 uses before it starts repeating a key you hold down. It also increases the delay between repeated characters if you continue to hold the key down.

Once you have used the OS-9 Modpatch tool to install these changes, you will want to evaluate them. If you like the new step rate — or the increased key repeat delay — you can make them permanent by running the OS-9 Cobbler tool. Type:

```
cobbler /d0
```

When you run Cobbler, it creates a new OS-9 boot file on the disk mounted in drive /d0. That new OS9Boot file contains the same set of modules it did when you last started your Color Computer. However, the new OS9Boot file contains the patched versions of d0, d1 and cc3IO — or any other module you may have changed using the Modpatch tool. The next time you start your Color Computer, those changes will be in effect.

Caution: If you plan on installing these changes in your OS9Boot file, make sure that you do not forget the V, for verify, step in your Modpatch script file.

THE MAGIC OF /DD

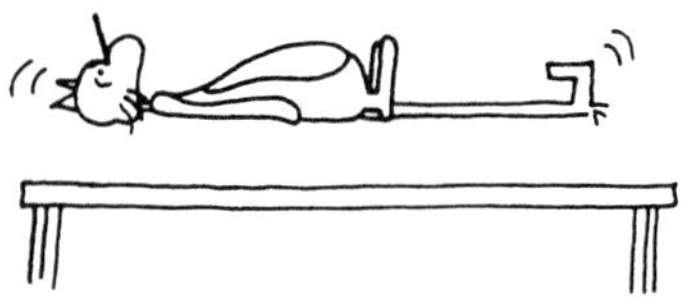

One great new feature of OS-9 Level II is the device descriptor /dd. The "dd" stands for default drive. Microware and Tandy hope that all software developers will use this device descriptor when they must "hard code" a pathlist in an OS-9 program.

When you first boot OS-9 Level II, the device descriptor /dd is merely a copy of the standard /d0 device descriptor installed in your OS9Boot file.

Why should you care? Follow this scenario. Immediately after booting our new OS-9 Level II system, we created a new boot file that contained /d0 and /d1 device descriptors set at 40 tracks, double-sided with a step rate of 6 ms. We left /dd in the boot file. In fact, we didn't even notice that it was present.

Later, we encountered a new error number while creating some new windows. We immediately typed error 192 and waited for OS-9 to tell us what we had done wrong. No such luck!

"Couldn't open path to /dd/sys/errmsg," the message said. Why?

The disk that now contained our system and Errmsg was a double-sided disk. The default drive, /dd, was still set to look like the original /d0, a single-sided, 35-track drive. When the error utility command tried to read the Errmsg file from the SYS directory on our double-sided disk, it couldn't access it. Foiled! But protected at the same time.

Later, after we installed our hard disk drivers, we made a copy of the /h0 device descriptor and patched it to so that the module it contained was named /dd. We verified it to update the CRC and then used OS9Gen to generate a new OS9Boot file with our new dd module replacing the original.

We had already copied the Errmsg file into the SYS directory on our hard disk, so the next time we received an error message we called upon the OS-9 Error tool again. This time the hard disk started clicking immediately, and, a second later, OS-9 reported the English language version of the sin we had committed.

If you use a RAM disk instead of a hard disk, you can create a default device descriptor, /dd, that points to your RAM disk. Then, if you copy your SYS directory to your RAM disk, the Error utility command will respond almost instantly. So will the Help utility command for that matter, if you copy the file Helpmsg to the SYS directory on your RAM disk.

In summary, the default device descriptor /dd is just a copy of the device descriptor of the drive where you store files that must always be found quickly.

Using our current Color Computer 3 installation as an example, /dd is simply a copy of /h0. Both /dd and /h0 are still in the boot file — and both can be used to access the hard disk drive. Both device descriptors have the same drive number and the same address, only the name of the device is different. We can use either name when we send a file to the drive manually.

If we all get behind this Microware standard, it will one day be much easier to write programs that can be used easily, no matter where our current data directory is located. It won't make any difference if we are using a 40-track, double-sided floppy disk, a RAM disk, an 80-track, quad-density floppy, or a hard disk drive, if our programs look in /dd/sys/errmsg for English language messages they will find them, if we have copied the sys/errmsg file to that media.

ONLY PATCH WHEN YOU MUST

Earlier in this chapter, we showed you a few tricks you can pull with the OS-9 Modpatch tool. For the most part, however, the secret of success with OS-9 is not to patch.

OS-9 Level II gives you tools to handle most jobs right on the command line. TMode is a good example. You use this tool to tell OS-9 what your hardware looks like. For example:

```
tmode upc -pause
```

This command line tells OS-9 that you want the terminal on the standard output path to print only uppercase letters, and you do not want it to stop and wait for you to give it a go-ahead at the end of a screen page. The following command does just the opposite.

```
tmode -upc pause
```

After you give this command, OS-9 will pause and let you catch up on your reading when it fills your screen. It prints lowercase letters on your screen.

The moral of our story: Don't use a sledge hammer to kill a flea. Take the time to study the outstanding manual that comes with OS-9 Level II. A small investment here can save you much time later.

TMODE VS XMODE

Here's another point we often forget. When you first boot Color Computer OS-9, it gets information about your hardware from device descriptors. However, it immediately stores this information in path descriptors.

Processes started later get their information about your hardware devices from these original path descriptors, not from the device descriptors.

When you run `Tmode`, it modifies the most recent path descriptor, not the device descriptor. If you kill the process that created the path descriptor modified by `Tmode`, you also kill the changes made by `Tmode`. This means that if you want to make a "permanent" change, you must run `Xmode` almost immediately after you boot OS-9.

Remember, to make temporary changes, use `Tmode`. To make permanent changes, use `Xmode`. After you change system parameters using the OS-9 `Xmode` tool, you can run `Cobbler` to make those changes permanent in your `OS9Boot` file. After you do this, your system will be set up the way you want it when you first start up OS-9.

MAKING NEW SYSTEM DISKS

We'll show you several different ways to build new OS-9 system disks. You may find them handy, especially if you are fortunate enough to be using a Color Computer equipped with a hard disk. We'll start by taking a look at `Config`, an excellent tool for the OS-9 beginner.

`Config` gives you a menu and lets you select the device descriptors you want to have available on your new system disk. The program is stored in a directory named `CMDS`. The files that hold the modules containing all the required OS-9 device descriptors, device drivers, file managers, etc., are stored in a directory named `MODULES`.

You start by booting your system using a backup copy of your OS-9 System Disk. After you see the `OS9` prompt, you must take out the System Disk and insert the disk containing `Config`. Do not skip the following steps:

```
chx /d0/cmds
chd /d0
```

Now, type `Config` and follow the directions on the menu. You move from row to row on the menu using the up and down arrow keys. You select a device by pressing S. If you want more information about a device, you can get it by pressing H.

When you have finished selecting device descriptors for all the devices you will be using, `Config` creates a new `OS9Boot` file and asks if you would like a disk with no commands, a basic command set, a full command set, or a set of individually selected commands.

A note of caution is in order. Make sure you tell `Config` to include all of the window device descriptors, including `/w`. OS-9 uses this descriptor when you ask for the next available window. Don't worry about using a lot of memory. Each window descriptor only uses 66 bytes.

After you have spent what seems like weeks waiting for your computer to copy all of your files onto a new system disk, you will come to the realization that you really don't need to have all your files on each and every system disk you own. It is much easier to boot with one disk that contains only the files you need to start the system, i.e., `OS9Boot`.

As soon as the system is running, you can remove that disk and insert the disk that contains the files you use all the time. In fact, you may want to load one disk with the tools you use while writing and another with the tools you need while programming with BASIC09.

Remember: If you use these stripped-down system disks to start OS-9, you must always let OS-9 know you have swapped disks immediately. Do this by typing:

```
chx /d0/cmds
chd /d0
```

Once you move up to a hard disk, you won't even need to swap disks. OS-9 will automatically select `/h0/CMDS` as your current execution directory and `/h0` as your current data directory when you start OS-9. You'll only need the file named `OS9Boot` on the floppy you use to boot OS-9.

CONFIG A SYSTEM DISK USING A PIPE

Once you know your way around OS-9, you'll discover there are a lot of ways to skin a cat. For example, using an unformatted directory list utility like `d` or `ls` from a third-party vendor and a pipeline to `OS9Gen`, you can configure new system disks quickly.

First, format a new disk to hold your module library. Then, create a directory with a name that describes the configuration you want on your new system disk.

For example, we use directory names like STOCKRS, STOCKHD and HDONLY. The first directory contains the modules needed to create a standard Tandy OS-9 system disk. The second contains the same modules plus a device descriptor and device driver for our hard disk. The third contains the hard disk drivers, but leaves out the floppy disk driver and descriptor to save space on an OS-9 Level I system.

You can use the MakDir utility command to make your new directories. How do you get the modules into those directories? We started by merging the standard modules we need in each and every boot file — regardless of the hardware configuration — in a file called StdBoot. We used a command line like this.

```
chd /dd/modules
merge IOMan RBF.mn SCF.mn Pipeman.mn Piper.dr Pipe.dd
CC3go >StdBoot
```

If you forget which modules are in a file a few months after you have created your directory, you can use the OS-9 Ident tool to find out.

```
ident -s StdBoot
```

There are several ways to get the right modules in your directories. For example, several third-party vendors and the national OS-9 Users Group sell Modbuster or Splitmod tools you can use to split a file containing a number of OS-9 modules into individual files that contain one module each. Here's how you do it. Start by making a new directory where you can store your new files:

```
makdir /d0/ConfigItMyWay
```

Now, make the new directory your working data directory:

```
chd /d0/ConfigItMyWay
```

It's time to run modbuster:

```
modbuster /d1/OS9Boot
```

When Modbuster finishes, you'll find a directory containing a file for each module in the OS9Boot file on the disk you had mounted in drive /d1. You can now use the OS-9 Del tool to delete the files you do not want in your new System Disk. After you have finished deleting the unwanted files, use the OS-9 Copy command to copy any additional module files you may need in your OS9Boot file into the directory ConfigItMyWay.

You are now ready to perform pipeline magic with OS-9. Insert a freshly formatted disk in drive /d1 and type:

```
chd /d0/ConfigItMyWay
ls ! os9gen /d1
```

If you don't believe in magic and want to confirm that the proper modules are in your OS9Boot file after the ls/os9gen team complete their handiwork, type:

```
ident -s /d1/os9boot
```

Once you have created a directory containing the modules needed in the OS9Boot file on your first customized system disk, you are almost home free. From here on out, you can create new directories and copy module files back and forth. Each directory will hold the module files you use with a specific type of hardware configuration. When you're done, make sure to save the disk with these directories so you can use it in the future.

BACKING UP A SINGLE-SIDED ORIGINAL DISK ON A DOUBLE-SIDED DUPLICATE

In the first chapter we showed you how to make a backup of your System Master Disk using the OS-9 Backup tool. Unfortunately, however, the Backup tool will not let you back up a disk to a disk of another size or type. You cannot use Backup to move files from a 35-track disk to a 40-track disk. Nor can you back up a single-sided, 40-track disk to a double-sided, 40-track disk.

To back up all the files on a disk of one format onto a disk formatted differently, you must use the OS-9 DSave utility command. Here's one way to do the job with DSave.

```
dsave /d1 /d0 ! Shell
```

Notice that this command assumes you have two disk drives in operation. After you have used OS-9 a few hours, you'll discover that two disk drives are indeed a necessity, not a luxury. The exclamation point in the command line above causes Dsave to send its output to the OS-9 command line interpreter named shell.

DSave's output takes the form of a number of individual OS-9 copy commands. When the shell receives those command lines through the pipeline above, it executes them. In a few minutes you will have all of the files from the disk mounted in drive /d1 saved on the disk mounted in drive /d0. One word of warning: The DSave command assumes that the Copy command is in your current execution directory and will try to load it from there. Make sure DSave will find Copy in your current execution directory.

ABOUT CUSTOMIZING YOUR DISKS

One of the most important advantages of OS-9 is the fact that it lets you customize your system to your heart's desire. Unfortunately, this ability also makes a tremendous contribution to the myth that OS-9 is difficult to use and hard to understand.

Take the pledge right now to stick with the basics until you are ready to start modifying your system. Practice running the utility commands stored in the /d0/CMDS directory of your working system disk.

Hopefully, we have given you enough information to get you started and pointed out a few of the pitfalls you will want to avoid. Hang in there and practice. Stick with the simple utilities until you thoroughly understand what is happening when you run them. After you conquer a command, move on to another. Before long, you'll be able to control your Color Computer like you never could before.

Follow the directions in the OS-9 users manual or *The Complete Rainbow Guide To OS-9* carefully. Once you understand what happens when you run each command, you will gain confidence and will be able to modify your operating system safely.

TESTING A PROCEDURE FILE WHILE YOU TYPE IT

Here's another neat trick for your portfolio. Would you rather test a procedure file while you're typing? Try this:

```
ex shell t -p >>NewProcedureFile
```

This command line creates a shell that echoes your command lines and doesn't print any prompts. Since you have redirected the standard error output path to a file, you will wind up with a file that runs as a procedure file.

If each command line you typed ran perfectly when you typed it live, it will run properly from the script NewProcedureFile. If, however, you ran into an error with your typing, you will need to edit NewProcedureFile. Since you actually ran the code you typed, you'll know which typos need to be fixed. Nifty!

SPLITTING THE SHELL MODULE FROM THE SHELL FILE

If you would like to customize your Shell file and load it with the OS-9 tools you think you would like to have in memory all the time, follow these steps.

First, type in and run this BASIC09 procedure file to create a file that contains only the Shell module.

```
PROCEDURE StripShell
 ØØØØ       DIM Char,Inpath,Outpath:BYTE
 ØØØF       DIM Count:INTEGER
 ØØ16
 ØØ17       OPEN #Inpath,"/dd/cmds/shell":READ
 ØØ3Ø       CREATE #Outpath,"/dd/cmds/Shell_Only"
```

```
004C
004D        FOR Count=1 TO 1532
005E          GET #Inpath,Char
0068          PUT #Outpath,Char
0072        NEXT Count
007D
007E        CLOSE #Inpath
0084        CLOSE #Outpath
008A        END
```

After you have run this short BASIC09 procedure, you will have a new file named Shell_Only stored in your CMDS directory. You can now merge it with the other files you want in memory at all times. For example, you could type:

```
chd /dd/cmds
rename Shell Shell_Original
merge Shell_Only pxd pwd rename tmode >Shell
attr Shell e pe
```

The OS-9 tools we merged into the new Shell file above are only an example. You must decide what you want in memory and then build your own Shell file containing those modules.

Remember, however, to make sure that the total length of the modules in the Shell file is less than 7,680 bytes long. If you keep it shorter than this, OS-9 will be able to load it at the very top of a 64K workspace.

The top 512 bytes of each 64K workspace is used by the hardware devices that let your Color Computer communicate with the outside world. This means you actually have 8,192 bytes minus 512 bytes, or 7,680 bytes you can use if you want the Shell and other modules in your file to load at the top of a 64K workspace.

NAMING A PROGRAM AUTOEX OR STARTUP

If you want OS-9 to run a particular program, BASIC09 for example, when you start your computer, use the OS-9 Rename tool to name the program you want to run AutoEx.

```
rename /dd/cmds/Basic09 AutoEx
```

OS-9 will find AutoEx (which is really BASIC09) and start it for you automatically.

Caution: If you use this AutoEx technique, make sure you create at least one window and start an OS-9 shell running in it. Do this in your StartUp file. It will give you a place to go home to if you accidentally terminate the program you started as AutoEx. If it happens, you can get to the safety window by pressing the CLEAR key until it rests next to the OS9: prompt.

WHEN YOU GET LOST

If you get lost while navigating an OS-9 disk full of subdirectories, don't forget you can call upon the OS-9 `pwd` and `pxd` commands to find the name of your current data directory and current execution directory, respectively.

HOW TO TELL A DEVICE FROM A FILE

And finally, if you've wondered how you can tell an OS-9 hardware device from a file, read on. If a pathlist starts with a slash (/), the first name in that pathlist is a device. For example, the pathlist `/d0/CMDS/dir` tells us that `/d0` is a device. `CMDS` is a subdirectory stored in the root directory of the device `/d0`. `Dir` is a file stored in the subdirectory named `CMDS`.

Sometimes, a device doesn't know about directories. Such is the case with your printer or an RS-232 communications cartridge. However, you'll know they are devices because of the slash in their names — `/P` and `/T2`.

That's it for our overview of OS-9, the operating system. From here on we'll concentrate on a few fantastic tools you can build with BASIC09. Enjoy!

CHAPTER 10

a real basic09 program:

The BASIC09 program, `Hello`, that we wrote in Chapter 6 is enough of a program to get you used to BASIC09 and to prove that you can write a program. There is something special about discovering that you can control your computer. Granted, printing a phrase on the screen is not the same as writing the great American program, but it's the first step on that path. Feel proud!

Now we're going to write a program with a little more meat on its bones. We'll attack it the same way we did `Hello`: a first try followed by refinements. This time, however, the first try will be a flop. If you haven't read it yet, skim the BASIC09 manual before you move on to this step.

A LITTLE BACKGROUND

Your computer stores characters and small numbers in chunks of memory called bytes. A byte can have 256 possible values. The first 128 of them are defined by the ASCII (American Standard Code for Information Interchange) code. Without ASCII or a similar code, bytes would just be little numbers. The code lets your computer translate bytes into characters — some printable, others special control codes. Most programmers can't remember which numbers go with which characters, so some of them keep tables of all the character values near their computers, and others write programs that print the tables on the screen any time they need them.

A PROGRAM TO PRINT THE ASCII TABLE

The CHR$ function in BASIC09 makes it easy to print a crude ASCII table.

THE LISTING: First_Try

```
PROCEDURE One_1
 ØØØØ      DIM i:INTEGER
 ØØØ7      FOR i:=Ø TO 4Ø
 ØØ17        PRINT i,CHR$(i)
 ØØ21      NEXT i
```

Please note, when typing in these BASIC09 programs, we don't type in the four numbers at the left of each line. These numbers are for system use; your Color Computer will put them in the procedure all by itself.

The program declares one integer variable named i. The FOR loop runs i through all the values from 0 to 40 while the PRINT statement prints the numeric value of i and the character that goes with it.

A generous person might say that the procedure works (barely), but there are plenty of problems with it. Mainly, it doesn't fit enough data on one screen, and it acts very strangely with non-printable characters (the values between 0 and 32).

There are two ways to deal with the problem of fitting 256 lines of data on one screen. We can select some small part of the range to print or we can use several columns. Both solutions are useful, so we'll try each of them.

DEALING WITH THE UNPRINTABLE CHARACTERS

The first 32 characters (numbers 0 through 31) are control characters. Some of them — like tab, backspace and bell — have an effect on the screen when you print them, but most of them are completely unprintable. Fortunately, the control characters have names. We'll make the table complete by printing a character's name when we can't print the character.

If a procedure is going to print names, we need to somehow include them in the procedure. The BASIC09 DATA statement is a clean way to put constant data in a procedure, but it's only easy for a program to read names from DATA statements in order. That doesn't sound good. We don't want to restrict ourselves to using the names in a preset order. We could get them in any order by fooling around with line numbers and the BASIC09 RESTORE statement, but it's easier to read the names from the DATA statements into an array. Whenever we want to print the name of an unprintable character, we'll pick it out of the array.

THE LISTING: Second_Try

```
PROCEDURE Second_Try
 0000      (* Print a range of characters and
 0022      (* the corresponding numbers
 003E      DIM i:INTEGER
 0045      DIM LowChars(33):STRING[8]
 0056      DIM str:STRING[8]
 0062      DIM high,low:INTEGER
 006D      BASE 0
 006F
 0070      DATA "nul","soh","stx","etx"
 008C      DATA "eot","enq","ack","bel"
 00A8      DATA "bs","tab","lf","vt"
 00C1      DATA "ff","cr","so","si"
 00D9      DATA "dle","dc1","dc2","dc3"
 00F5      DATA "dc4","nak","syn","etb"
 0111      DATA "can","em","sub","esc"
 012C      DATA "fs","gs","rs","us"
 0144      DATA "sp"
 014D
 014E      (* Get limits on the range of
 016B      (* characters to print
 0181      INPUT "Bottom of range: ",low
 019A      INPUT "Top of range: ",high
 01B0
 01B1      (* Copy strings from DATA into
 01CF      (* LowChars array
 01E0      FOR i=0 TO 32
 01F0        READ LowChars(i)
 01F9      NEXT i
 0204
 0205      (*
 0208      (* Print the decimal, hexadecimal, and character values
 023F      (* for a range of numbers.
 0259      (*
 025C      PRINT " Dec  Hex  Char"
 026F      FOR i=low TO high
 0281        IF i<=32 THEN
 028D          str=LowChars(i)
 0298        ELSE
 029C          str=CHR$(i)
 02A5        ENDIF
 02A7        PRINT USING "I4>,T7,H2^,T12,S8",i,i,str
 02C9      NEXT i
 02D4      END
```

The procedure is divided into five parts. The first part declares four variables.

- The variable `i` is going to be the loop index for two different loops later in the procedure. A tradition dating back to the early

FORTRAN days of programming suggests that loop indexes should be named i, j, k, l, n, o or p. When imagination fails to invent a better name, programmers fall back on the old standard. We only need one, so it is named `i`.

- The variable `str` will be a general-purpose string variable in this procedure.
- Names for the unprintable characters will be loaded into `LowChars`.
- The variables named `high` and `low` will be used as limits on a loop.

The second part of the procedure is a big block of `DATA` statements that hold the names of the unprintable characters. It doesn't matter to BASIC09 where in a procedure `DATA` statements are (though their order is important). There are three common rules for placing `DATA` statements:

- Put them at the beginning.
- Put them at the end.
- Put them near the statements that use them.

For very long procedures, the last option is the best. You should be able to find the `DATA` statements that go with a `READ` without a major search. The second option is appropriate if you feel that the `DATA` statements distract attention from the main point of the procedure. Since they are the main point of this procedure, they stand proudly near its beginning.

Since a list of all 256 possible character values would cover many screens, we're going to ask for a range of values to print. The person running this program (we'll call him the "user") will probably select a small range of numbers to print, often only one number. Of course there is nothing preventing him from selecting the entire range. The two `INPUT` statements get the limits for the range we will print, `low` and `high`. These variables will pop up again in the last part of the procedure.

All the character names in the `DATA` statements need to be copied into the `LowChars` array. The `FOR` loop in the fourth section of the procedure reads the names from the `DATA` statements into the array.

Notice the `BASE` statement before the `FOR` loop. Normally, BASIC09 arrays have indexes that start at one. This is sensible. We usually think of the first entry in an array as being in position one. In this case an array that starts at one is inconvenient. The first unprintable character is number zero. It would be possible to leave the first character out of `LowChars` or shift all the values by one (so the value for zero would be stored in `LowChars(1)`), but everything lines up nicely if the `LowChars` array starts at zero. The `BASE 0` statement tells BASIC09 that we want arrays to start at zero in this procedure. Warning: the BASE statement applies to *all* arrays in a procedure.

The last section of Second_Try prints the data the user requested. First it prints a title line. This is where you discover that we're going to print decimal (ordinary base 10), hexadecimal (base 16) and character values. The FOR loop in this section drives i from low to high. Inside the loop, i will run through the range of values the user selected.

Some values will correspond to unprintable characters; the program should find names for these in LowChars. The BASIC09 CHR$ function will return the characters corresponding to the printable values.

After the IF statement, everything is ready for printing. The name of the character is in str, and PRINT USING knows how to print the decimal and hexadecimal values. Find PRINT USING in your BASIC09 manual and see if you can figure out how this statement works.

ANOTHER APPROACH

We could fit several columns of the output from Second_Try on a screen. It's a good idea because it would let the user see a wider range of values on one screen. If we could drop the decimal and hexadecimal values and just print the names of the characters, the columns would get narrower and even more values could be squeezed on a screen.

The 256 possible character values fit neatly in a 16-by-16 table. Those dimensions fit with the hexadecimal representation of the values (like a 10-by-10 table would with decimal). Once you have found a character in the table, you can find the hexadecimal number by remembering that the column number is the left digit and the row number is the right digit. If this is unclear, bear with us. It will be easier to see when you have a table on your screen.

We're not going to do the entire 16-by-16 table here. It would be too big to fit comfortably on a 32-column screen. The first eight columns of the table contain all the standard ASCII characters, so we'll make an 8-by-16 table.

It is still hard to get the table on a screen. A 16-row by 8-column table will fit on a 32-by-16 screen without a line to spare. Unfortunately, the table is a little hard to read without a title row across the top. If you use a low resolution screen, experiment; you may like the table better without its title.

The procedure Third_Try makes the ASCII table.

THE LISTING: Third_Try

```
PROCEDURE Third_Try
 ØØØØ      (* Print a table of ASCII
 ØØ19      (* values
 ØØ22      DIM i,j:INTEGER
 ØØ2D      DIM LowChars(33):STRING[8]
 ØØ3E      DIM str:STRING[8]
 ØØ4A      BASE Ø
 ØØ4C
 ØØ4D      DATA "nul","soh","stx","etx"
 ØØ69      DATA "eot","enq","ack","bel"
 ØØ85      DATA "bs","tab","lf","vt"
 ØØ9E      DATA "ff","cr","so","si"
 ØØB6      DATA "dle","dc1","dc2","dc3"
 ØØD2      DATA "dc4","nak","syn","etb"
 ØØEE      DATA "can","em","sub","esc"
 Ø1Ø9      DATA "fs","gs","rs","us"
 Ø121      DATA "sp"
 Ø12A
 Ø12B      FOR i=Ø TO 32
 Ø13B        READ LowChars(i)
 Ø144      NEXT i
 Ø14F
 Ø15Ø      (*
 Ø153      (* Print the entire ASCII table as compactly as possible
 Ø18B      (*
 Ø18E      PRINT "    Ø    1   2 3 4 5 6 7"
 Ø1A7      FOR i=Ø TO 15
 Ø1B7        PRINT USING "h1",i;
 Ø1C3        PRINT USING "' ',S3,' ',S3",LowChars(i),LowChars(i+16);
 Ø1E7        FOR j=2 TO 7
 Ø1F7          IF i=15 AND j=7 THEN
 Ø2ØA            PRINT " del";
 Ø213          ELSE
 Ø217            PRINT USING "' ',S1",CHR$(j*16+i);
 Ø22F          ENDIF
 Ø231        NEXT j
 Ø23C        PRINT
 Ø23E      NEXT i
 Ø249      END
```

The beginning of Third_Try should look familiar by now. It fills LowChars with the names of the unprintable characters. The section of code starting at the comment "Print the entire ASCII table as compactly as possible" does just what the comment says. The general outline of the code is:

```
PRINT title
FOR each line
  PRINT sidebar and control characters
  (the first two columns of the table)
```

FOR columns 2 through 7
  PRINT the character that belongs here (The bottom-right side of the table has another control character that needs special treatment)

Each row of the table has three parts. First is a title that runs down the side labeling each row. The labels are 0, 1, 2, 3, 4, 5, 6, 7, 8, 9, A, B, C, D, E and F, the digits in hexadecimal. Since the label is the same as the row number, printing i in hexadecimal gives the label. After the label come two names that have to come out of LowChars table. In the first row, the first column will be LowChars(0), and the second column will be LowChars(16). The rule that will work for all the rows is: In Row i, Column 1 should contain LowChars(i) and Column 2 should contain LowChars(i+16). The other six columns of each row (columns 3 through 8) contain printable characters. We can print them all with a FOR loop.

There is a problem character at the lower-right side of the ASCII table. It is another unprintable character named del. We have to put an IF statement in the FOR loop to handle that one special case.

PUTTING IT TOGETHER

We have developed two ways to put the same information on the screen. They are both useful procedures. What is the best way to combine their functions? Three choices come to mind:

- Don't combine anything. Leave it just the way it is.
- Combine everything. Make one procedure that combines the two.
- Make a separate procedure out of the DATA statements and the code that reads them into LowChars.

The first choice is wasteful because the exact same code appears in two places and error prone because it would be easy to change a DATA statement in one procedure without making the same change in the other procedure. The second choice is much better, but, as a general rule, it is best if a procedure does one thing. If you don't see the two different ways of printing ASCII values as one function, the third option is the best one.

One option puts too much into one procedure and another divides a single function between two procedures. Since the choice may not be obvious, let's try both and see what they look like.

First we'll combine Second_Try and Third_Try into one procedure.

THE LISTING: DisplayCharacters

```
PROCEDURE DisplayCharacters
      (* Display characters and their numeric
      (* values.  If terse is true, display all the
      (* ASCII characters in a table.  If terse is
      (* false, display a subrange of the ASCII characters
      (* in a list.
      PARAM low,high:INTEGER
      PARAM Terse:BOOLEAN

      DIM i,j:INTEGER
      DIM LowChars(33):STRING[8]
      DIM str:STRING[8]

      DATA "nul","soh","stx","etx"
      DATA "eot","enq","ack","bel"
      DATA "bs","tab","lf","vt"
      DATA "ff","cr","so","si"
      DATA "dle","dc1","dc2","dc3"
      DATA "dc4","nak","syn","etb"
      DATA "can","em","sub","esc"
      DATA "fs","gs","rs","us"
      DATA "sp"

      BASE 0

      FOR i=0 TO 32
        READ LowChars(i)
      NEXT i

      IF Terse THEN
        (*
        (* Print the entire ASCII table as compactly as possible
        (*
        PRINT "    0   1  2 3 4 5 6 7"
        FOR i=0 TO 15
          PRINT USING "h1",i;
          PRINT USING "' ',S3,' ',S3",LowChars(i),LowChars(i+16);
          FOR j=2 TO 7
            IF i=15 AND j=7 THEN
              PRINT " del";
            ELSE
              PRINT USING "' ',S1",CHR$(j*16+i);
            ENDIF
          NEXT j
          PRINT
        NEXT i
      ELSE


```

```
Ø3ØB
Ø3ØC        (*
Ø3ØF        (* Print the decimal, hexadecimal, and character values
Ø346        (* for a range of numbers.
Ø36Ø        (*
Ø363        PRINT " Dec  Hex  Char"
Ø376        FOR i=low TO high
Ø388          IF i<=32 THEN
Ø394            str=LowChars(i)
Ø39F          ELSE
Ø3A3            str=CHR$(i)
Ø3AC          ENDIF
Ø3AE          PRINT USING "I4>,T7,H2^,T12,S8",i,i,str
Ø3DØ        NEXT i
Ø3DB      ENDIF
Ø3DD      END
```

Almost everything in the DisplayCharacters procedure should look familiar. The main change is a new IF statement that makes the procedure act like Third_Try if the variable terse is true and Second_Try if terse is false. You can see that the code between the IF terse THEN and the corresponding ELSE is straight out of Third_Try, and the code after the ELSE is from Second_Try.

DisplayCharacters doesn't take any input. It gets everything it needs as a parameter. You can run it from BASIC09 command mode:

```
run DisplayCharacters(20,30,false)
run DisplayCharacters(1,1,true)
```

or from another BASIC09 procedure.

A procedure to run DisplayCharacters might look like:

THE LISTING: Prompter

```
PROCEDURE prompter
 ØØØØ       DIM terse:BOOLEAN
 ØØØ7       DIM high,low:INTEGER
 ØØ12       INPUT "Terse (t,f)? ",terse
 ØØ27       IF NOT(terse) THEN
 ØØ31         INPUT "Lowbound: ",low
 ØØ43         INPUT "Highbound: ",high
 ØØ56       ENDIF
 ØØ58       RUN DisplayCharacters(low,high,terse)
 ØØ6C       END
```

Prompter contains the input statements we removed from Second_Try and Third_Try when we combined them into DisplayCharacters. It collects the values DisplayCharacters will need, then runs DisplayCharacters with those values as parameters.

BASIC09 doesn't permit procedures to have a variable number of parameters. This is a little bit inconvenient because, when `terse` is true, the other two parameters are not used. We can live with that if we must, but let's see what we get when we keep the functions of `Second_Try` and `Third_Try` separate.

THE LISTING: `ASCII_Table`

```
PROCEDURE ASCII_Table
 0000      DIM i,j:INTEGER
 000B      DIM LowChars(33):STRING[8]
 001C      DIM str:STRING[8]
 0028      BASE 0
 002A
 002B      (* Get the strings that name
 0047      (* the non-printable characters
 0066      RUN Control_Names(LowChars)
 0070
 0071      (*
 0074      (* Print the entire ASCII table as compactly as possible
 00AC      (*
 00AF      PRINT "    0   1  2 3 4 5 6 7"
 00C8      FOR i=0 TO 15
 00D8        PRINT USING "h1",i;
 00E4        PRINT USING "' ',S3,' ',S3",LowChars(i),LowChars(i+16);
 0108        FOR j=2 TO 7
 0118          IF i=15 AND j=7 THEN
 012B            PRINT " del";
 0134          ELSE
 0138            PRINT USING "' ',S1",CHR$(j*16+i);
 0150          ENDIF
 0152        NEXT j
 015D        PRINT
 015F      NEXT i
 016A      END
```

THE LISTING: `ASCII_List`

```
PROCEDURE ASCII_List
 0000      (* Print a range of ASCII characters and the
 002C      (* corresponding numbers
 0044      PARAM low,high:INTEGER
 004F      DIM i:INTEGER
 0056      DIM LowChars(33):STRING[8]
 0067      DIM str:STRING[8]
 0073      BASE 0
 0075
 0076      (* Get the strings that name the unprintable
 00A2      (* characters
 00AF      RUN Control_Names(LowChars)
 00B9
```

```
(*
(* Print the decimal, hexadecimal, and character values
(* for a range of numbers.
(*
PRINT " Dec  Hex  Char"
FOR i=low TO high
  IF i<=32 THEN  \REM A non-printable value
    str=LowChars(i)
  ELSE  \REM a printable value
    str=CHR$(i)
  ENDIF
  PRINT USING "I4>,T7,H2^,T12,S8",i,i,str
NEXT i
```

THE LISTING: Control_Names

```
PROCEDURE Control_Names
(* Return a list of the names of
(* the non-printable (control) characters

PARAM LowChars(33):STRING[8]

DIM i:INTEGER
DIM str:STRING[8]
BASE 0

DATA "nul","soh","stx","etx"
DATA "eot","enq","ack","bel"
DATA "bs","tab","lf","vt"
DATA "ff","cr","so","si"
DATA "dle","dc1","dc2","dc3"
DATA "dc4","nak","syn","etb"
DATA "can","em","sub","esc"
DATA "fs","gs","rs","us"
DATA "sp"


FOR i=0 TO 32
  READ LowChars(i)
NEXT i
END
```

THE LISTING: Prompter2

```
PROCEDURE prompter2
DIM terse:BOOLEAN
DIM high,low:INTEGER

INPUT "Terse (t,f)? ",terse

IF NOT(terse) THEN
```

```
ØØ33        INPUT "Lowbound: ",low
ØØ45        INPUT "Highbound: ",high
ØØ58        RUN ASCII_List(low,high)
ØØ67      ELSE
ØØ6B        RUN ASCII_Table
ØØ6F      ENDIF
ØØ71      END
```

This time we've got four procedures instead of two:

- `ASCII_Table` prints the ASCII table.
- `ASCII_List` prints a range of characters with values.
- `Control_Names` fills a table of character names.
- `Prompter2` requests values from the user.

Each procedure does one thing, they are all short, and there are never useless parameters. This is definitely better.

The last procedure in this chapter is a little mysterious. It wraps `Prompter2` up in a loop and adds a menu. The menu only gives the user a choice of getting ASCII values or quitting, and the loop only keeps swapping between the menu display and an ASCII display until it quits. Let's leave it mysterious for a moment and look at the code.

THE LISTING: `Menu`

```
PROCEDURE Menu1
 ØØØØ      DIM InputChr,WaitChr:STRING[1]
 ØØ1Ø      DIM low,high:INTEGER
 ØØ1B      DIM Terse:BOOLEAN
 ØØ22
 ØØ23      REPEAT
 ØØ25        RUN gfx2("clear")
 ØØ32        PRINT "            Menu  "
 ØØ47        PRINT " a:   Display ASCII Table"
 ØØ64        PRINT " q:   Quit"
 ØØ72        PRINT "            Selection:";
 ØØ8B        GET #Ø,InputChr
 ØØ94        IF InputChr="a" OR InputChr="A" THEN
 ØØA9          RUN gfx2("clear")
 ØØB6          INPUT "Terse?",Terse
 ØØC4          IF NOT(Terse) THEN
 ØØCE            INPUT "Lowbound:",low
 ØØDF            INPUT "Highbound:",high
 ØØF1            RUN ASCII_List(low,high)
 Ø1ØØ          ELSE
 Ø1Ø4            RUN ASCII_Table
 Ø1Ø8          ENDIF
 Ø1ØA          GET #Ø,WaitChr
 Ø113        ENDIF
 Ø115      UNTIL InputChr="q" OR InputChr="Q"
 Ø129      RUN gfx2("clear")
```

There are a couple of interesting tricks in Menu. The first GET #0 is for the menu selection. The program waits at that GET until the user makes a selection, then it passes the character to the subsequent comparisons. The other GET #0 in the loop appears to be useless. You won't find another reference to WaitChr in the procedure. So why do we make the user enter it?

If you remove the second GET #0 from the menu procedure, you will find that the menu continues to work well as a selector, but you never get a chance to look at the output from the procedures it calls. You make a selection, the information flashes by on the screen, then the screen clears and the menu comes up again. We needed to slow the procedure down between the time it runs a report and the time it displays a new menu. Using GET #0 to wait for the user to press a key — any key — is a good way to make the procedure wait.

BASIC09 offers a programmer many ways to build loops. There's the FOR statement, the WHILE statement, the REPEAT/UNTIL, and the LOOP. There's also GOTO of course — the ultimate, powerful and dangerous statement. In this case we chose REPEAT/UNTIL. You'll want to use REPEAT/UNTIL when you build a loop that will always execute at least once. For this procedure we know that we'll display the menu at least once so REPEAT/UNTIL is our choice.

We created the Menu procedure because these procedures are the first parts of a system. Compare this menu to the final product in Chapter 17.

WHAT HAVE WE LEARNED?

In this chapter we built several programs that display the names for values defined in the ASCII character set. We started with a very simple program. The program was fine if you only cared about printable characters and didn't mind several screens of output. We tried two other ways to print ASCII values and decided that we wanted to keep them both.

It didn't make sense to have identical code for finding the names of unprintable characters in two different procedures. We tried two ways of eliminating the duplicate code. First we combined the two procedures into one, then we separated the duplicated code into its own procedure and let the other procedures run it. The second solution seemed simpler.

It's a good idea to think of procedures as input procedures, output procedures, or compute procedures. Those classes help keep procedures short and simple.

A procedure that is about one screen of code is probably not too long. That doesn't mean longer procedures are always too long, only that you should look for clean ways to divide them into several smaller procedures.

The REPEAT/UNTIL loop construct should be used for loops that will always execute at least once.

It is useful to write a simple program before you dive into something complicated. The simple program might be just what you need, and you will save yourself lots of work. If it's not just what you need, it might be close enough that you can make simple modifications to get to what you want. Even if it is nothing like what you want, it might uncover some issues you hadn't considered.

POSSIBLE ENHANCEMENTS

If you use 80-column windows, consider adding the values between 128 and 255 to the ASCII table. They aren't ASCII values, but many of them are defined on the Color Computer.

Try using two menu selections to determine whether to use ASCII_List or ASCII_Table. It will probably work better than what we did.

If you use OS-9 windows, you can try beautifying the displays with fonts and graphics. Try putting boxes around things. Use bold print for ASCII values and proportional spacing for titles. Consider the use of color.

The functions of the procedures can be defined in another way that may be better than the division we chose. Control_Names would be more useful if it were Character_Name. It could have two parameters. We could pass it a number in one parameter and it would return the name of the corresponding ASCII character in the other. ASCII_List and ASCII_Table would become considerably shorter, and Character_Name would be at most a little longer than Control_Names. Warning: This is a fairly difficult change to make.

CHAPTER 11

selecting colors: the palette

It's a bit of a puzzle. Your Color Computer is able to display 64 different colors. It says so right in the manual. Another place in the manual says that you can display two colors, four colors, or 16 colors. What happened to the 64 colors?

If you are serious about painting, the word palette might be all you need to hear. Ask a painter how many colors they can use and you might hear, "Here's my box of paints. It has about 50 tubes of paint in it, mostly different colors." Another painter might understand the question differently and tell you, "I can use any color I can imagine. See, I take a little paint from each of these tubes and mix them on my palette. I can mix colors until I have exactly the color I want."

The palette is the key. You almost never see a painter using paint straight from the tube. It goes on the palette for mixing before it is used. A Color Computer is not as versatile as a painter. It can only keep two, four, or 16 different mixed colors on its palette. It only has three colors, and it is seriously limited in how it can mix the colors.

The 64 colors that the Color Computer can display are the different mixtures that you can put on the computer's palette. You have red, green, and blue at your disposal, and you can use 0, 1, 2, or 3 dabs of each color. So how do four possible amounts of each of three colors add up to 64 colors?

Imagine that the color mixture either had each color or not. How many mixtures does that give you?

	R	G	B
1	—	—	—
2	—	—	X
3	—	X	—
4	—	X	X
5	X	—	—
6	X	—	X
7	X	X	—
8	X	X	X

Three colors and two amounts (yes or no) for each color gives eight mixtures. If there were three possible amounts for each color in the mixture — none, a tad, or a big glob — we'd have 27 possible mixtures. With four possible amounts of each color, we get 64 mixtures. If you like math, it works like this. With n different colors in x different amounts, we get x^n mixtures.

COLOR IDENTIFIERS

The type of window on the screen affects the way OS-9 uses the palette. There are always 16 colors in the palette, and you can always choose them from the 64 color mixtures. If the window on the screen is a two-color window, OS-9 will ignore all but the first two colors on the palette. If the window is in four-color mode, OS-9 will ignore all but the first four colors on the palette. Only the 16-color mode uses the entire palette.

A two-color window ignores most of the palette, but it conserves memory. A pixel (that's a single dot) in a two-color window can be stored as one bit. It only needs two possible values: black or white, green or yellow, or whatever pair of colors you choose as the first two colors in your palette.

A four-color window needs two bits for each pixel. That means a four-color window uses twice as much memory as a two-color window. A 16-color window uses four bits for each pixel; that's twice as much memory as a four-color window, or half a byte for each pixel! The following table gives the binary codes that OS-9 uses for colors.

TABLE 11-A: Binary Codes for Colors

Color	Two Color	Four Color	Sixteen Color
0	0	00	0000
1	1	01	0001
2	NA	10	0010
3	NA	11	0011
4	NA	NA	0100
5	NA	NA	0101
6	NA	NA	0110
7	NA	NA	0111
8	NA	NA	1000
9	NA	NA	1001
10	NA	NA	1010
11	NA	NA	1011
12	NA	NA	1100
13	NA	NA	1101
14	NA	NA	1110
15	NA	NA	1111

TEXT WINDOWS ARE DIFFERENT

Graphics windows (window types 5, 6 and 7) choose foreground and background colors out of the same range of selections from the palette. Text windows (window types 1 and 2) use the first eight colors in the palette for background colors and the second eight colors for foreground. This is an interesting twist.

If the palette contains two copies of the same colors, you won't be able to tell that foreground Color 1 is not the same as background Color 1. This is the default color scheme:

TABLE 11-B: Default Color Scheme

Palette		Color
0	8	white
1	9	blue
2	10	black
3	11	green
4	12	red
5	13	yellow
6	14	magenta
7	15	cyan

If you ask for Color 2 as a foreground color, you will get Color 10. Both Color 2 and Color 10 are black, so you don't care, but what if you alter the colors in the palette? The command:

```
display 1b 31 0A 26
```

will turn the foreground a greenish red. If you didn't know about magic going on under the hood, you'd wonder why changing the 10th color in the palette affected the second color. You might be even more surprised if you set the border to Color 2 and found the foreground version of Color 2 was greenish red and the border version of the same color was black. It's done with mirrors, but so long as you remember that foreground Color *x* shows up at position *x*+8 in the palette, it all makes sense.

Note that letters on a text screen show up in the foreground color. Background, border and the cursor show up in background colors.

MIXING COLORS FOR THE PALETTE

Let's mix some colors. This involves some serious fussing with bits, so brace yourself. Each color mixture in the palette is stored as a byte, but only six bits in the byte are used. The six bits allow two bits for each of the three colors. The bits each mean something. If we call the least significant bit (the one farthest to the right) Bit 0, then:

Bit	Means
0	faint blue
1	faint green
2	faint red
3	blue
4	green
5	red

They might be easier to understand this way:

00RGBrgb

We should be able to get three different shades of pure blue — four shades if you count black as a shade of blue. The palette codes for those blues are: 00001001, 00001000, 00000001 and 00000000. The first code is an intense blue; after that, each code gives a dimmer blue until the last one is black.

We could add a little red to the blue like this: 00001101. That adds a faint helping of red to the brightest blue.

The tables above let you find the codes for any of the 64 colors, but the code will be in binary. You will have to convert it to hexadecimal before you can use it with `Display` or BASIC09. The following table will help you with the conversion.

TABLE 11-C: Binary to Hexadecimal Conversion Chart

		B	G	GB	R	R B	RG	RGB
	000	001	010	011	100	101	110	111
000	$00	$08	$10	$18	$20	$28	$30	$38
b 001	$01	$09	$11	$19	$21	$29	$31	$39
g 010	$02	$0A	$12	$1A	$22	$2A	$32	$3A
gb 011	$03	$0B	$13	$1B	$23	$2B	$33	$3B
r 100	$04	$0C	$14	$1C	$24	$2C	$34	$3C
rb 101	$05	$0D	$15	$1D	$25	$2D	$35	$3D
rg 110	$06	$0E	$16	$1E	$26	$2E	$36	$3E
rgb 111	$07	$0F	$17	$1F	$27	$2F	$37	$3F

If you want the code for the color RG_b, look for the column with the R and G bits on. That's the seventh column. Look for the row with only the b bit on. That's the second row. The second row and the seventh column cross at $31, so that's the code for the color RG_b.

The color codes in the palette are stored in what the Color Computer calls palette registers. There are 16 palette registers numbered 0 through 15.

EXPERIMENTING WITH THE PALETTE

We're going to want the full 16 colors in the palette, so if you don't have a Type 08 window around, set one up. Reminder: Set the window up with the following commands (except that you may want to change /w6 to some other device):

```
iniz /w6
merge /d0/sys/stdfonts >/w6
display 1b 20 08 00 00 28 18 1 0 2 >/w6
shell i=/w6
```

Use CLEAR to get to window six. Now, let's paint some colors on the screen:

```
display Øc
display 1b 4Ø Ø1 EØ ØØ Ø1
display 1b 32 Ø3
display 1b 4b ØØ Øa ØØ be
display 1b 41 ØØ Øc ØØ ØØ
display 1b 32 Ø4
display 1b 4b ØØ Øa ØØ be
display 1b 41 ØØ Øc ØØ ØØ
display 1b 32 Ø5
display 1b 4b ØØ Øa ØØ be
display 1b 41 ØØ Øc ØØ ØØ
display 1b 32 Ø6
display 1b 4b ØØ Øa ØØ be
display 1b 41 ØØ Øc ØØ ØØ
display 1b 32 Ø7
```

```
display 1b 4b ØØ Øa ØØ be
display 1b 41 ØØ Øc ØØ ØØ
display 1b 32 Ø8
display 1b 4b ØØ Øa ØØ be
display 1b 41 ØØ Øc ØØ ØØ
display 1b 32 Ø9
display 1b 4b ØØ Øa ØØ be
display 1b 41 ØØ Øc ØØ ØØ
display 1b 32 ØA
display 1b 4b ØØ Øa ØØ be
display 1b 41 ØØ Øc ØØ ØØ
display 1b 32 ØB
display 1b 4b ØØ Øa ØØ be
display 1b 41 ØØ Øc ØØ ØØ
display 1b 32 ØC
display 1b 4b ØØ Øa ØØ be
display 1b 41 ØØ Øc ØØ ØØ
display 1b 32 ØD
display 1b 4b ØØ Øa ØØ be
display 1b 41 ØØ Øc ØØ ØØ
display 1b 32 ØE
display 1b 4b ØØ Øa ØØ be
display 1b 41 ØØ Øc ØØ ØØ
display 1b 32 ØF
display 1b 4b ØØ Øa ØØ be
display 1b 41 ØØ Øc ØØ ØØ
display 1b 32 Ø1
```

If you build a shell script with all those display commands in it and run it from a Type 08 graphics window, you will see all 16 colors in the palette. Color 0 is your background color; Color 1 is the color the OS-9 prompt and your typing appear in, and Color 3 is the border color. All the other colors in the palette are in bars on the right side of the screen.

Now that we can see all the colors, let's change one. Try:

```
display 1b 31 0e 24
```

The column second from the right will turn red. Try:

```
display 1b 31 0e 3c
```

The column will change to tan. Use CONTROL-A and try all the different colors you like. If you want to change the color of another column, change the 0E to some other code between 00 and 0F. For example:

```
display 1b 31 05 08
```

will turn the third column from the left to light blue.

Generating the color bars from a shell script took a lot of typing. It is easier from BASIC09. This time we'll put up bars for all 16 colors instead of just the 13 colors that aren't already on the screen.

THE LISTING: Bars

```
PROCEDURE Bars
 ØØØØ      DIM color:INTEGER
 ØØØ7      RUN gfx2("clear")
 ØØ14      FOR color:=Ø TO 15
 ØØ24        RUN gfx2("color",color)
 ØØ36        RUN gfx2("bar",48Ø+(color-3)*$ØA,1,49Ø+(color-3)*$ØA,19Ø)
 ØØ65      NEXT color
 ØØ7Ø      RUN gfx2("color",1)
```

Now that we've got the entire palette displayed on the screen, let's run one of the colors in the palette through all 64 possible colors. We'll play with palette register number eight.

THE LISTING: Palette

```
PROCEDURE Palette
 ØØØØ      DIM color:INTEGER
 ØØØ7      DIM delay:REAL
 ØØØE      DIM Decode:STRING[6]
 ØØ1A      DIM c:STRING[1]
 ØØ26      DIM work:INTEGER
 ØØ2D      DIM i:INTEGER
 ØØ34      RUN gfx2("color",8)
 ØØ44      RUN gfx2("bar",24Ø,1,3ØØ,19Ø)
 ØØ5C      FOR color:=Ø TO 63
 ØØ6C        RUN gfx2("palette",8,color)
 ØØ83        Decode:=""
 ØØ8A        work:=color
 ØØ92        RESTORE
 ØØ94        FOR i:=1 TO 6
 ØØA4          READ c
 ØØA9          IF LAND(work,1)=1 THEN
 ØØB8            Decode:=c+Decode
 ØØC4          ELSE
 ØØC8            Decode:="_"+Decode
 ØØD4          ENDIF
 ØØD6          work:=work/2
 ØØE1        NEXT i
 ØØEC        RUN gfx2("curxy",Ø,1Ø)
 ØØFF        RUN gfx2("color",1)
```

```
    PRINT Decode;
    FOR delay:=0 TO 1500
    NEXT delay
  NEXT color
  RUN gfx2("color",1)
  END
  DATA "b","g","r","B","G","R"
```

Since colors on the screen stay attached to their palette register, we have been able to experiment with colors on the screen by changing the palette register without redrawing the screen. We can also get some nice special effects by playing with the palette registers.

The next program displays a moving picture of beads rolling down a slope.

THE LISTING: Marbles

```
PROCEDURE marbles
  DIM color(8):INTEGER
  DIM x,fcolor:INTEGER
  DIM time,i:INTEGER
  BASE 0
  FOR i:=0 TO 7
    READ color(i)
    RUN gfx2("palette",4+i,color(i))
  NEXT i
  RUN gfx2("clear")
  RUN gfx2("color",2)
  RUN gfx2("line",43,25,303,155)
  RUN gfx2("color",1)
  FOR x:=25 TO 155 STEP 4
    RUN gfx2("setdptr",2*x,x)
    fcolor:=MOD(x/4,8)+4
    RUN gfx2("circle",4)
    RUN gfx2("color",fcolor)
    RUN gfx2("fill")
  NEXT x
  FOR time:=1 TO 200
    FOR i:=0 TO 7
      RUN gfx2("palette",MOD(time+i,8)+4,color(i))
    NEXT i
  NEXT time
  DATA $3F,$24,$36,$09,$13,$26,$12,$1B
```

A less obvious use of the palette is to make things appear and disappear. If an object is painted in a color that is the same as the background, you can't see it. Normally it would take a while to paint it with a different color, but if it's already painted with a different palette register that happens to hold the same color mixture as the background, you can change the color of the object by changing a palette register, bringing the object out of the background instantly.

THE LISTING: Bounce

```
PROCEDURE Bounce
       DIM i:INTEGER
       DIM time:INTEGER
       DIM x,y:INTEGER
       RUN gfx2("clear")
       RUN gfx2("color",1,0,0)
       FOR i:=1 TO 15
         READ x,y
         RUN gfx2("setdptr",x,y)
         RUN gfx2("circle",10)
         RUN gfx2("color",i)
         RUN gfx2("fill")
       NEXT i
       FOR i:=0 TO 15
         RUN gfx2("palette",i,0)
       NEXT i
       FOR time:=1 TO 600
         RUN gfx2("palette",MOD(time,15)+1,$24)
         RUN gfx2("palette",MOD(time-1,15)+1,0)
         FOR i:=1 TO 100
         NEXT i
       NEXT time
       RUN gfx2("defcol")
       RUN gfx2("color",1,0,2)
       END
       DATA 20,20
       DATA 50,25
       DATA 80,35
       DATA 110,50
       DATA 140,70
       DATA 170,95
       DATA 200,125
       DATA 230,160
       DATA 260,125
       DATA 290,95
       DATA 310,70
       DATA 340,50
       DATA 370,35
       DATA 400,25
       DATA 430,20
```

The animation can be so fast that the motion blurs. We put a delay loop in the program to slow it down to where the motion is visible.

Colors are not placed directly on the screen. First, colors are chosen and placed on the palette. The colors on the palette can be used on the screen. The palette lets OS-9 offer you a wide choice of colors without using an impossible amount of memory to store a screen. Don't look at the palette as a trick that restricts you to 16 colors. Look at it as a trick that lets you have more than 16 colors to choose from. It also invites you to do some interesting animation tricks.

CHAPTER 12

getting serious: a screen-oriented text editor

So far our programs have been simple enough that we could almost have replaced their code with a bunch of `PRINT` statements. Now we are ready to tackle a program that has much less predictable behavior.

A serious, full-featured, text editor is a big project, but it is surprisingly easy to write a simple screen-oriented editor.

A text editor is used to enter and modify text. A screen-oriented text editor gives you a screen of text and lets you modify it on the screen. If you want to change a word, you move the cursor to the word and type its replacement. Creating new text is a special case; you are replacing empty space with new text.

A good editor uses the screen as a window on the file. When you try to move the cursor off an edge of the screen, it moves the window. This feature lets editors handle more text than can fit on one screen. For example, moving the cursor down from the last line on the screen moves the cursor onto a line that used to be right below the screen. It also changes the screen so the new line is displayed.

OUR FIRST SCREEN EDITOR

We want to start with the simplest screen editor we can imagine and see where it takes us. The simplest possible screen editor limits itself to one screen. The data is stored in a 24-by-80 array that is painted directly onto the screen. The coordinates of the cursor on the screen are the same as the coordinates of the current location in the array.

We aren't going to give this editor any way to get at disk files. It simplifies the program, but it makes it almost useless as a text editor. It's as if BASIC09 didn't have a load or save command. This is such an important omission that it isn't fair to call the program a text editor; we'll call it a "scratchpad" program.

So far we've only been listing things our program won't do. What do we hope to achieve with this `Scratchpad`? The answer is, as little as possible. We need to display a screen full of blanks, allow characters to be entered anywhere on the screen, and make the cursor keys work. We also need a way to stop the program.

We are going to assume that you are using a 24-line by 80-column window. If you choose to use a smaller window, you will need to go through the procedures that make up `ScratchPad`, changing numbers like 80, 79, 24 and 23 to the smaller numbers that give the dimensions of the window you are using.

THE SCREEN DATA STRUCTURE

The matrix that holds a screen of data will either look like this:

```
DIM Screen(24,80) : BYTE
```

this:

```
DIM Screen(24,80) : STRING[1]
```

or this:

```
DIM Screen(24) : STRING[80]
```

Making the right choice may be important. The wrong data structure could make the program needlessly complicated or slow. There is only one way to find the right option. We will experiment.

Let's start by filling the screen data structure with blanks and displaying it. First with an array of bytes.

THE LISTING: Paint_1

```
PROCEDURE Paint_1
 0000      DIM Screen(24,80):BYTE
 0010      DIM x,y:INTEGER
 001B      BASE 0
 001D      FOR y:=0 TO 23
 002D        FOR x:=0 TO 79
 003D          Screen(y,x)=ASC(" ")
 004D        NEXT x
 0058      NEXT y
 0063
 0064      FOR y:=0 TO 23
 0074        RUN gfx2("curxy",0,y)
 0089        FOR x:=0 TO 79
 0099          PRINT CHR$(Screen(y,x));
 00A6        NEXT x
 00B1      NEXT y
```

The procedure doesn't look bad, but it's intolerably slow. It takes about 15 seconds to display the screen! Usually we ignore speed at this stage because speed is the last thing a programmer should worry about. It's not that speed isn't important, just that it only makes sense to try to improve a correct program. It makes no sense to worry about the speed of a program that may not even work.

We are dealing with an exception to the rule. This procedure is correct, but so slow that it can be thought of as broken unless we can make it faster.

The procedure had to convert bytes to characters with the CHR$ function in the loop that printed the screen. We can eliminate that conversion; the BASIC09 PUT statement will print a byte as a character without conversion. Let's see if it works any better:

THE LISTING: Paint_15

```
PROCEDURE Paint_15
 0000      DIM Screen(24,80):BYTE
 0010      DIM x,y:INTEGER
 001B      BASE 0
 001D      FOR y:=0 TO 23
 002D        FOR x:=0 TO 79
 003D          Screen(y,x)=ASC(" ")
 004D        NEXT x
 0058      NEXT y
 0063
 0064      FOR y:=0 TO 23
 0074        RUN gfx2("curxy",0,y)
 0089        FOR x:=0 TO 79
 0099          PUT #1,Screen(y,x)
 00A9        NEXT x
 00B4      NEXT y
```

Using PUT instead of PRINT and getting rid of the CHR$ conversion might have added a whisker of speed, but not enough to matter. Maybe it will be faster with no conversions at all. Let's try the 24-by-80 array of strings.

THE LISTING: Paint_2

```
PROCEDURE Paint_2
 ØØØØ       DIM Screen(24,8Ø):STRING[1]
 ØØ15       DIM x,y:INTEGER
 ØØ2Ø       BASE Ø
 ØØ22       FOR y:=Ø TO 23
 ØØ32         FOR x:=Ø TO 79
 ØØ42           Screen(y,x):=" "
 ØØ51         NEXT x
 ØØ5C       NEXT y
 ØØ67       FOR y:=Ø TO 23
 ØØ77         RUN gfx2("curxy",Ø,y)
 ØØ8C         FOR x:=Ø TO 79
 ØØ9C           PRINT Screen(y,x);
 ØØA8         NEXT x
 ØØB3       NEXT y
```

It takes almost exactly as long as our first experiment. Let's see if treating lines as long strings works better:

THE LISTING: Paint_3

```
PROCEDURE Paint_3
 ØØØØ       DIM Screen(24):STRING[8Ø]
 ØØ11       DIM x,y:INTEGER
 ØØ1C       BASE Ø
 ØØ1E       FOR y:=Ø TO 23
 ØØ2E         Screen(y):=""
 ØØ39         FOR x:=Ø TO 79
 ØØ49           Screen(y):=Screen(y)+" "
 ØØ5C         NEXT x
 ØØ67       NEXT y
 ØØ72       FOR y:=Ø TO 23
 ØØ82         RUN gfx2("curxy",Ø,y)
 ØØ97         PRINT Screen(y);
 ØØAØ       NEXT y
```

This test procedure seems a little simpler than the others. It also runs a bit faster. It actually displays the data quite a bit faster, but it takes longer to initialize the array than the other experimental procedures did.

We can live with slow initialization if we must. We'll be displaying the screen more often than we'll be initializing it. However, we are probably on the wrong track. The screen display is the fastest we have managed yet, but it's still too slow. We need to find a different approach.

It would be easier to tolerate the time we spend displaying data if interesting things were appearing on the screen, but all we have seen is a wonderfully slow way to clear the screen. Maybe we should just clear the screen with the gfx2 CLEAR function. We know it is fast and correct.

We have found a way to display an empty screen fast, but we still need to choose the data type for the screen array. Our first set of experiments told us:

- Bytes aren't the natural data type for printable data.
- The ASC and CHR$ conversions reminded us that BASIC09 likes to keep characters in strings.
- An array of STRING[1] behaves like an array of bytes except that no conversions are needed.
- An array of STRING[80] is easier to display than the other data structures.

Keeping the screen in an array of bytes didn't seem to offer any advantages so we can tentatively eliminate bytes from consideration. Now we have only two structures to decide between.

An experiment that requires us to change the data in the screen data structure and display the result might help us decide. Let's try to draw a diagonal line down each screen and display the result.

THE LISTING: Exp_1

```
PROCEDURE Exp_1
 ØØØØ       DIM Screen(24,8Ø):STRING[1]
 ØØ15       DIM x,y,i:INTEGER
 ØØ24       BASE Ø
 ØØ26       FOR y:=Ø TO 23
 ØØ36         FOR x:=Ø TO 79
 ØØ46           Screen(y,x):=" "
 ØØ55         NEXT x
 ØØ6Ø       NEXT y
 ØØ6B       FOR y:=Ø TO 23
 ØØ7B         Screen(y,y):="#"
 ØØ8A       NEXT y
 ØØ95       RUN gfx2("clear")
 ØØA2       FOR y:=Ø TO 23
 ØØB2         FOR i:=Ø TO 79
 ØØC2         EXITIF Screen(y,i)<>" " THEN
 ØØD5           RUN gfx2("curxy",Ø,y)
 ØØEA           FOR x:=Ø TO 79
 ØØFA             PRINT Screen(y,x);
 Ø1Ø6           NEXT x
 Ø111         ENDEXIT
 Ø115         NEXT i
 Ø12Ø       NEXT y
```

It works, but doesn't look elegant. It isn't very fast either. Using one string per line looks like this:

THE LISTING: Exp_2

```
PROCEDURE Exp_2
 0000       DIM Screen(24):STRING[80]
 0011       DIM x,y:INTEGER
 001C       BASE 0
 001E       FOR y:=0 TO 23
 002E         Screen(y):=""
 0039         FOR x:=0 TO 79
 0049           Screen(y):=Screen(y)+" "
 005C         NEXT x
 0067       NEXT y
 0072       FOR y:=0 TO 23
 0082         Screen(y):=LEFT$(Screen(y),y)+"#"+RIGHT$(Screen(y),80-(y+ 1))
 00AA       NEXT y
 00B5       RUN gfx2("clear")
 00C2       FOR y:=0 TO 23
 00D2         FOR x:=1 TO 80
 00E2         EXITIF MID$(Screen(y),x,1)<>" " THEN
 00F8           RUN gfx2("curxy",0,y)
 010D           PRINT Screen(y);
 0116         ENDEXIT
 011A         NEXT x
 0125       NEXT y
```

We can make it look a little better by defining a constant string of 80 blanks.

THE LISTING: Exp_3

```
PROCEDURE Exp_3
 0000       DIM Screen(24):STRING[80]
 0011       DIM Blanks:STRING[80]
 001D       DIM y:INTEGER
 0024       BASE 0
 0026       READ Blanks
 002B       FOR y:=0 TO 23
 003B         Screen(y):=Blanks
 0047       NEXT y
 0052       FOR y:=0 TO 23
 0062         Screen(y):=LEFT$(Screen(y),y)+"#"+RIGHT$(Screen(y),80-(y+1))
 008A       NEXT y
 0095       RUN gfx2("clear")
 00A2       FOR y:=0 TO 23
 00B2         IF Screen(y)<>Blanks THEN
 00C2           RUN gfx2("curxy",0,y)
```

```
ØØD7          PRINT Screen(y);
ØØEØ        ENDIF
ØØE2      NEXT y
ØØED      DATA "
"
```

That's probably about as good as we're going to get. We should worry about the messy equation we had to use to replace blanks with #'s, but, if we find out later that representing lines as strings is the wrong choice, we can change our minds.

CONTROLLING THE SCREEN

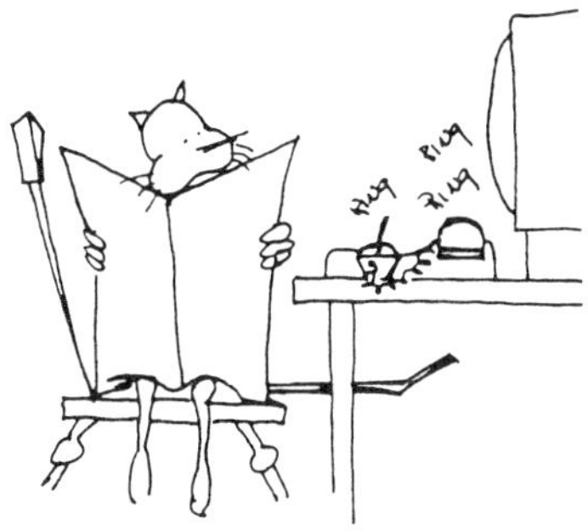

Now that we have a data structure for the screen and we know how to initialize it and display it, we are ready to decide how to change it.

We'll choose the F1 key as the quit button. Now, we need to watch for an F1 (to end the ScratchPad program), but we can ignore all other non-printable characters.

The outline of this superbly stupid ScratchPad program is:

Initialize ScreenData
Clear the screen
Get an input character
While the input isn't an F1
  Print the character on the screen
  Store the character in the right place in ScreenData

We can steal the code for the first two steps from our last experimental procedure. The rest of the outline looks reasonable except the last line. That will probably be very ugly. Let's plan to hide it in a special procedure where we won't have to look at it. While we're at it, we'll shove several other problems into procedures.

Delegating work to other procedures sounds like cheating, but it is a highly respected technique. Difficult problems just melt away when you keep dividing them into a few sub-problems and handing them to other procedures.

The first version of ScratchPad looks like:

THE LISTING: Scratchpad_1

```
PROCEDURE ScratchPad_1
 ØØØØ      DIM ScreenData(24):STRING[8Ø]
 ØØ11      DIM Blanks:STRING[8Ø]
 ØØ1D      DIM InChr:STRING[1]
 ØØ29      DIM x,y:INTEGER
 ØØ34      BASE Ø
```

```
0036
0037       READ Blanks
003C       FOR y:=0 TO 23
004C         ScreenData(y):=Blanks
0058       NEXT y
0063       SHELL "tmode -pause -echo -lf"
007D       RUN gfx2("clear")
008A       x:=0
0091       y:=0
0098
0099       GET #0,InChr
00A2       WHILE InChr<>CHR$($B1) DO
00B0         IF InChr>=" " THEN
00BD           RUN UpdScreenData(ScreenData(y),x,y,InChr)
00D9           PRINT InChr;
00DF           x:=x+1
00EA         ELSE
00EE           RUN ApplyArrow(InChr,x,y)
0102         ENDIF
0104         RUN WrapXY(x,80,y,24)
0119         RUN gfx2("curxy",x,y)
0130         GET #0,InChr
0139       ENDWHILE
013D
013E       SHELL "tmode pause echo lf"
0155       END
0157       DATA "
"
```

We need to write three procedures to handle the work that `ScratchPad` delegates:

THE LISTING: `UpdScreenData`

```
PROCEDURE UpdScreenData
 0000      PARAM Line:STRING[80]
 000C      PARAM x,y:INTEGER
 0017      PARAM InChr:STRING[1]
 0023      Line:=LEFT$(Line,x)+InChr+RIGHT$(Line,80-(x+1))
```

THE LISTING: `ApplyArrow_1`

```
PROCEDURE ApplyArrow
 0000      (* Change x and y coordinates in response to keys that
 0036      (* move the cursor
 0048
 0049      (* So far we ignore all the cursor control characters
 007E      (* so this procedure does nothing
 009F      PARAM InChr:STRING[1]
 00AB      PARAM x,y:INTEGER
 00B6      END
```

THE LISTING: `WrapXY_1`

```
PROCEDURE WrapXY
 0000       PARAM x,xlimit,y,ylimit:INTEGER
 0013       IF x>=xlimit THEN
 0020         x:=0
 0027         y:=y+1
 0032       ELSE IF x<0 THEN
 0041           x:=xlimit-1
 004C           y:=y-1
 0057         ENDIF
 0059       ENDIF
 005B       IF y>=ylimit THEN
 0068         y:=0
 006F       ELSE IF y<0 THEN
 007E           y:=ylimit-1
 0089         ENDIF
 008B       ENDIF
```

Finally we have a working screen editor. It is even fast. Now we can add some brains.

The `ApplyArrow` procedure is empty. Eventually we'll deal with all the cursor movement keys there, but let's start by dealing with the ENTER key.

We need to make the `ApplyArrow` procedure change X and Y when it is passed the ENTER (carriage return) character in `InChr`. ENTER usually moves the cursor to the beginning of the next line. Rephrasing that in terms of X and Y: The effect of the ENTER key is to set X to zero and add one to Y.

The enhanced `ApplyArrow` function is:

THE LISTING: `ApplyArrow_2`

```
PROCEDURE ApplyArrow
 0000       (* Change x and y coordinates in response to keys that
 0036       (* move the cursor
 0048
 0049       (* So far we ignore all the cursor control characters
 007E       (* so this procedure does nothing
 009F       PARAM InChr:STRING[1]
 00AB       PARAM x,y:INTEGER
 00B6       IF InChr=CHR$($0D) THEN
 00C4         x:=0
 00CB         y:=y+1
 00D6       ENDIF
 00D8       END
```

That wasn't hard at all! `ScratchPad` is getting noticeably smarter, but unless your typing is better than ours, you have noticed a serious need for a working backspace key. While we're in there, we'll install code for all four arrow keys.

We need to refer to Appendix C in the OS-9 Commands reference section of your manual for the codes that the arrow keys send. We find that each arrow key can send three different codes by using the SHIFT and CONTROL keys. All the arrow keys together can generate 12 different codes. We could use 12 BASIC09 IF-THEN statements to handle the codes, but that seems clumsy. We will look for a better solution.

THE LISTING: ApplyArrow_3

```
PROCEDURE ApplyArrow
 0000      (* Change x and y coordinates in response to keys that
 0036      (* move the cursor
 0048
 0049      (* So far we ignore all the cursor control characters
 007E      (* so this procedure does nothing
 009F      PARAM InChr:STRING[1]
 00AB      PARAM x,y:INTEGER
 00B6      IF InChr>=CHR$(8) AND InChr<=CHR$($1C) THEN
 00CC        ON ASC(InChr)-7 GOSUB 10,20,30,200,40,50,200,200,60,70,80
               ,90,200,200,200,200,110,120,130,200,140
 012B      ENDIF
 012D      END
 012F 10   REM Backspace
 013E      x:=x-1
 0149      RETURN
 014B 20   REM Forward arrow
 015E      x:=x+1
 0169      RETURN
 016B 30   REM Down
 0175      y:=y+1
 0180      RETURN
 0182 40   REM Up
 018A      y:=y-1
 0195      RETURN
 0197 50   REM Enter
 01A2      x:=0
 01A9      GOSUB 30
 01AD      RETURN
 01AF 60   REM cntl backspace
 01C3 70   REM cntl forward arrow
 01DB 80   REM cntl Down
 01EA 90   REM cntl Up
 01F7 110  REM shift backspace
 020C 120  REM shift forward arrow
 0225 130  REM shift Down
 0235 140  REM shift Up
 0243 200  REM Undefined
 0252      RETURN
 0254      END
```

The ON-GOSUB statement is useful in situations like this. When you have many numbered options to choose between, ON-GOSUB gives you a compact way to write it down. The statement got a bit long. It's hard to type it correctly, and painful to fix errors, but it saved us at least 24 lines of boring code.

We now have full support for typing and moving the cursor around on the screen. This is enough power to uncover an unfixable bug. See if you can find it.

Run ScratchPad and move the cursor to the lower-right corner of the screen. Try to type a letter there. It is impossible. Every time you type a letter in that position, the screen scrolls up a line. We did everything we could to prevent this problem, but it's still there. We have to work around it by taking a little bite out of the lower-right corner of the screen. There is no way to get the program to put a character in that corner, but there is a way to prevent a user from trying to type there and making the screen scroll. We have to modify the WrapXY procedure so it will refuse to let the cursor move to the impossible position. The updated procedure looks like:

THE LISTING: WrapXY

```
PROCEDURE WrapXY
 ØØØØ      PARAM x,xlimit,y,ylimit:INTEGER
 ØØ13      (* Make the lower right corner of the screen "out of bounds."
 ØØ5Ø      IF x=xlimit-1 AND y=ylimit-1 THEN
 ØØ6B        x:=x+1
 ØØ76      ENDIF
 ØØ78      IF x>=xlimit THEN
 ØØ85        x:=Ø
 ØØ8C        y:=y+1
 ØØ97      ELSE IF x<Ø THEN
 ØØA6          x:=xlimit-1
 ØØB1          y:=y-1
 ØØBC        ENDIF
 ØØBE      ENDIF
 ØØCØ      IF y>=ylimit THEN
 ØØCD        y:=Ø
 ØØD4      ELSE IF y<Ø THEN
 ØØE3          y:=ylimit-1
 ØØEE        ENDIF
 ØØFØ      ENDIF
```

We didn't need to do much. We just bumped the cursor over the spot at the beginning of WrapXY and let the rest of the procedure move it to the upper-left corner of the screen.

We've created a ScratchPad program that doesn't do much, but does that very nicely. You could run it in an extra window and keep notes in it. They would last as long as you left the ScratchPad program running, and you could refer to them by bringing up the ScratchPad window with the CLEAR key.

We demonstrated two principles in this chapter: experimentation and decomposition. They are both important techniques when you tangle with a big problem.

When you don't immediately see the right way to approach a problem, don't give up. Don't just close your eyes and pick a direction either. Play around. The procedures that you throw out aren't mistakes, they're experiments.

Decomposition is the art of breaking a large problem into a collection of smaller problems. If a problem looks messy, or even impossible, break it into pieces. The pieces may be easier to solve than the big problem. If the pieces still look difficult, break up the pieces.

Each of the procedures we used to build the ScratchPad problem is reasonably simple. The program would have worked as nicely if the entire thing was wedged into one procedure, but it would have been harder to design and much harder to understand.

CHAPTER 13

souping up scratchpad

In the last chapter we built a primitive screen editor. In this chapter we'll try to give it enough power to be useful. This chapter will be a little different from the previous chapters about programming. We're not going to create a new program. Instead, we'll enhance an old one.

Building from a working base program is a reliable way to build elaborate programs, but there is a special art to it. When you add features to a program, you want to do it with the least possible disturbance. Sneak your change into the program. Imagine that someone is guarding the code, and you want to make changes so subtle they won't be noticed. This isn't always possible. Some changes will require major surgery, and sometimes you will find irresistible ways to improve the base program.

While we're modifying `Scratchpad`, we will have several opportunities to design window support into the program. We will take the opportunities. Support for windows is one of the nice things about OS-9 on the Color Computer. If you've got it, flaunt it!

GOALS

We have two goals for the enhanced ScratchPad:

- It should be able to load and save files.
- It should handle more than one screen full of text.

The most important feature missing from last chapter's ScratchPad program was support for files. You couldn't load a file for editing or save the result. We would like to fix that deficiency if we can.

Once we can edit files, we will feel tempted to work with files that are more than 24 lines long. Even a short letter is likely to use more than 24 lines of text. If we want the program to deserve the name ScratchPad, we should give it something like the usefulness of a scratchpad. It should either support something like sheets that can be torn off and saved or a longer page.

GOING BEYOND ONE SCREEN

The biggest window we can fit on a Color Computer's screen is 24 lines by 80 columns. In the last chapter we pictured an array of strings glued to the window. The location of the cursor in the window was exactly the same as current location in the array. This picture only works if all the text can fit in one window. If we want to edit more text than can fit in a window, we will need to invent a different way of looking at the window.

In order to let a user see more than a 24-by-80 block of text, the window must be able to move over the text. We will design our editor so when the cursor moves to a line that isn't visible through the window, the window will move to keep the cursor visible.

The moving window idea can handle unlimited amounts of text. Lines can be any width, and there can be any number of them. The idea can handle unlimited text, but the Color Computer can't. The limitation is memory. Even if we limit the lines to 80 columns, 100 lines of text need 8,000 bytes of memory.

We might be able to find enough memory for 400 lines if we limit them to 80 characters, or about 300 if we let the lines go to 100 characters. The way BASIC09 stores strings makes the maximum length important even when the string is empty. A variable declared as STRING[80] can hold strings with lengths ranging from zero to 80 characters, but it always uses 80 bytes of memory.

We could get tricky and pack many lines into one string, but we won't. We will plan to edit up to 100 lines of text, and we will store the text in a simple array of strings. Naturally, we will suggest that you look for a better way to store the lines as a possible enhancement.

SUPPORTING FILES

The editor operates on an array of lines in memory. We want to be able to read data into that array from a disk file or write the array out to a disk file. The basic idea is easy; (while there is more data in the file and more room in the array) to read a file into the array, we need to:

- Read a line or 80 characters (whichever comes first)
- Pad the line out to 80 characters

Notice the details. Details are the crucially important drudgework of programming.

- We stop reading when there is nothing left to read or when the array is full.
- A line in the array is a line from the file but no more than 80 characters.
- We always make sure that the strings in the array are filled.

The last detail is the trickiest. The rule that all lines must be exactly 80 characters long is descended from last chapter's version of `ScratchPad`. We didn't make a fuss about the rule (though we *were* careful about it), but we did build it into the code. Look at `UpdScreenData`. The statement there wouldn't work if lines could be anything other than 80 characters long.

Files aren't as fussy as `ScratchPad`'s data array. We can store many lines on a disk, and they can be any length. We could write the entire array with one `PUT` statement, but the file would appear to be a single tremendous line. The `ScratchPad` program could use it, but other programs would not be amused.

We don't need to be careful about writing files, but it makes sense not to be wasteful. There may be a number of empty lines at the end of the array. We can save disk space by writing everything up to the last line with data in it, then stopping. We can save more disk space by trimming the blanks off each line before we write it.

A WINDOW WITH TRIMMING

A user may want to load and save files at any time. We will let him do that by pressing a key and naming an operation. This is why we've been saving the F2 key. The user will press the F2 key and a menu will appear in an overlay window. There'll be a pointer in the menu that indicates the operation `ScratchPad` is ready to perform. The user can move the pointer through the menu like a finicky eater choosing a meal. Pressing the F2 key again orders a service from the menu. Pressing F1 leaves the menu without making a selection.

The OS-9 window support makes it easy to build this type of menu into a program. The general idea is to use the owset function to open an overlay window, display the menu in the overlay window, put a graphics cursor in the window, and let the user move the graphics cursor until we read a function key, then perform the requested operation.

The actual procedure that will handle the menu is almost as simple as the outline. The tricky part of designing the procedure is remembering details like turning the text cursor off before turning the graphics cursor on. Two cursors in one window would be confusing.

AND NOW THE PROGRAM

The main procedure for the ScratchPad program has the same outline it had in the last chapter, but there are important additions. We added the concept of a home line (also a variable named HomeLine). The x and y variables are still the location of the cursor on the screen. HomeLine is the line number of the first line on the screen. Initially, x, y and HomeLine are all zero. That means that the cursor is in the upper-left corner of the screen and that the top line on the screen is the first line in the ScreenData array. HomeLine keeps track of the window's position in the ScreenData array as the window moves up and down through the array.

THE LISTING: ScratchPad

```
PROCEDURE ScratchPad
 ØØØØ      (* The top level routine of a simple editor program
 ØØ33      (* The constant, 1ØØ, is the number of lines the editor
 ØØ6A      (* can handle.  It appears throughout this program as
 ØØ9F      (* 1ØØ or 99 (the last entry in BASE Ø)
 ØØC6      DIM ScreenData(1ØØ):STRING[8Ø]
 ØØD7      DIM InChr:STRING[1]
 ØØE3      DIM x,y,HomeLine:INTEGER
 ØØF2      DIM Scroll:BOOLEAN
 ØØF9      BASE Ø
 ØØFB
 ØØFC      RUN ClearBuf(ScreenData)
 Ø1Ø6      (* Modify the terminal mode to suit this program.
 Ø137      (* We want to echo characters from the program, so we
 Ø16C      (* tell OS-9 not to echo. We also don't want OS-9
 Ø19D      (* pausing the display when it thinks a page has been
 Ø1D2      (* displayed.
 Ø1DF      SHELL "tmode -pause -echo "
```

```
        RUN gfx2("clear")
        x:=0 \y:=0 \HomeLine:=0

        (* The Main loop.  It reads data and commands and
        (* sends them to other procedures for handling.
        GET #0,InChr
        WHILE InChr<>CHR$($B1) DO
          IF InChr>=" " AND InChr<CHR$($80) THEN
            RUN UpdScreenData(ScreenData(y+HomeLine),x,y,InChr)
            PRINT InChr;
            x:=x+1
          ELSE
            RUN ApplyArrow(InChr,x,y)
          ENDIF
          RUN ScrollXY(x,79,y,23,HomeLine,99,Scroll)
          IF Scroll THEN
            RUN ScrollScreen(ScreenData,y,23,HomeLine)
          ENDIF
          RUN gfx2("curxy",x,y)
          IF InChr=CHR$($B2) THEN  \REM F2
            RUN FileMenu(ScreenData,x,y,HomeLine)
          ENDIF
          GET #0,InChr
        ENDWHILE
        RUN QuitMenu(ScreenData,x,y,HomeLine)
        SHELL "tmode pause echo "
```

Moving the cursor around can now include scrolling the display to bring new lines into the window. This is similar to what WrapXY used to do, but different enough that we designed a new procedure named ScrollXY to handle it. ScrollXY needs more information than WrapXY: x, maximum x, y, maximum y, HomeLine and number of lines in ScreenData. It sets a boolean variable, Scroll, to tell ScratchPad whether the cursor has gone off the screen.

If Scroll is true, ScratchPad knows that HomeLine and the screen display need to be updated. The problem sounds hard, so it gets shoved off to another procedure, ScrollScreen.

ScratchPad watches for the F2 key. If it reads the F2 code, it calls a procedure that deals with files. ScratchPad also calls a limited version of the file-handling procedure when the user asks the program to quit. This gives the user a last chance to save the file he's been working on before ScratchPad ends and the data disappears.

WATCHING FOR SCROLLING

The ScrollXY procedure is a modified version of WrapXY. It handles values of x just as WrapXY did, but it has to think harder about y. If y tries to run below 0 or above 23, ScrollXY looks for a chance to scroll.

When HomeLine is 0 and y goes negative, the user is trying to move the cursor into the void before the beginning of ScreenData. We can't let that happen, so we use the WrapXY trick; we drop the cursor to the bottom of the screen. When ScrollXY detects that the last line in ScreenData is on the screen (HomeLine is 76), it won't permit the cursor to move beyond the end of the screen. Again it uses the trick from WrapXY.

THE LISTING: ScrollXY

```
PROCEDURE ScrollXY
  PARAM x,xlimit,y,ylimit:INTEGER
  PARAM Home:INTEGER
  PARAM MaxLines:INTEGER
  PARAM Scroll:BOOLEAN
  (* Make the lower right corner of the screen "out of bounds."
  IF x=xlimit AND y=ylimit THEN
    x:=x+1
  ENDIF

  IF x>xlimit THEN
    x:=Ø
    y:=y+1
  ELSE IF x<Ø THEN
      x:=xlimit
      y:=y-1
    ENDIF
  ENDIF


  Scroll:=FALSE
  IF y>ylimit AND Home<MaxLines-ylimit THEN
    Scroll:=TRUE
    Home:=Home+1
    y:=y-1
  ELSE IF y<Ø AND Home>Ø THEN
      Scroll:=TRUE
      Home:=Home-1
      y:=y+1
    ENDIF
  ENDIF
  IF y>ylimit THEN
    y:=Ø
  ELSE IF y<Ø THEN
      y:=ylimit
    ENDIF
  ENDIF
```

When ScrollXY calls for scrolling, ScratchPad runs ScrollScreen.

THE LISTING: ScrollScreen

```
PROCEDURE ScrollScreen
 0000       PARAM Lines(99):STRING[80]
 0011       PARAM y,ScreenSize:INTEGER
 001C       PARAM HomeLine:INTEGER
 0023       BASE 0
 0025       IF y=0 THEN  \REM Scroll Top
 003E         RUN ScrollTop(Lines(HomeLine))
 004B       ELSE
 004F         RUN ScrollBottom(Lines(HomeLine+ScreenSize),Lines(HomeLine

               +(ScreenSize-1)))
 006F       ENDIF
 0071       END
```

ScrollScreen decides which direction to scroll by seeing whether the cursor is at the top of the screen or the bottom. It runs other procedures to do the scrolling. The procedure called ScrollBottom takes two parameters: the line to scroll onto the bottom of the screen and the line that's currently at the bottom of the screen. Why? Let's look at ScrollBottom.

THE LISTING: ScrollBottom

```
PROCEDURE ScrollBottom
 0000       PARAM Line:STRING[80]
 000C       PARAM OneUp:STRING[80]
 0018       RUN gfx2("curxy",79,23)
 002B       PRINT RIGHT$(OneUp,1); LEFT$(Line,79);
 003B       END
```

Another detail: Remember the trick we played with the lower-right corner of the screen? We couldn't print a character there without causing unwanted scrolling, so we didn't try. Now we're about to move the bottom line on the screen up one line. The bottom line is missing its last character, the one that fell in the lower-right corner of the screen. We have to stick the character back on the line when we move it from Line 23 to Line 22. That's why we need two lines in ScrollBottom.

ScrollTop has a small trick too. It has to scroll backward — adding new lines at the top of the screen. It uses the gfx2 INSLIN function to insert a blank line at the top of the screen, then it fills the line in. It is fortunate that OS-9 gives us INSLIN. If we didn't have this function, we would have to redisplay the whole screen every time a line scrolled in from the top. It would have been impressively slow.

THE LISTING: `ScrollTop`

```
PROCEDURE ScrollTop
 0000      PARAM Line:STRING[80]
 000C      RUN gfx2("curxy",0,0)
 001F      RUN gfx2("inslin")
 002D      PRINT Line;
 0033      END
```

When `ScratchPad` reads the `F2` character, `$B2`, it calls `FileMenu`. We discussed the operation of `FileMenu` earlier. It puts up an overlay window and lets the user move a graphics pointer around in it, then it performs the selected operation. Here's how it goes:

THE LISTING: `FileMenu`

```
PROCEDURE FileMenu
 0000      PARAM ScreenData(100):STRING[80]
 0011      PARAM x,y,HomeLine:INTEGER
 0020      DIM c:BYTE
 0027      DIM i,selection:INTEGER
 0032      DIM filename,Blanks:STRING[80]
 0042      DIM s:STRING[10]
 004E      BASE 0
 0050      Blanks:="
   "
 00A7      RUN gfx2("owset",1,0,0,10,6,0,1)
 00C9      RUN gfx2("curoff")
 00D7      FOR i:=1 TO 5
 00E7        READ s
 00EC        PRINT s
 00F1      NEXT i
 00FC      DATA "File Menu","Load","Save","Clear","Exit"
 0129      RUN gfx2("gcset",202,1)
 013C      selection:=0
 0143      REPEAT
 0145        RUN gfx2("putgc",50,10+selection*8)
 015F        GET #0,c
 0168        IF c=$0A THEN  \REM down arrow
 0182          selection:=MOD(selection+1,4)
 0190        ENDIF
 0192      UNTIL c=$B1 OR c=$B2
 01A6      RUN gfx2("owend")
 01B3      IF c=$B2 THEN  \REM f2  Expand
 01CD        ON selection+1 GOSUB 10,20,30,40
 01E7      ENDIF
 01E9      END
 01EB 10   REM Load a file
 01FC      RUN GetFName(filename)
 0206      RUN ReadFile(filename,ScreenData)
```

```
Ø215        HomeLine:=Ø \x:=Ø \y:=Ø
Ø22A        RUN PaintScreen(ScreenData)
Ø234        RETURN
Ø236 2Ø     REM Save a file
Ø247        RUN GetFName(filename)
Ø251        RUN WritFile(filename,ScreenData)
Ø26Ø        RETURN
Ø262 3Ø     REM Clear workspace
Ø277        RUN ClearBuf(ScreenData)
Ø281        HomeLine:=Ø \x:=Ø \y:=Ø
Ø296        RUN PaintScreen(ScreenData)
Ø2AØ        RETURN
Ø2A2 4Ø     REM exit
Ø2AC        RETURN
```

The FOR loop that reads menu items and prints them in the menu is interesting. This loop is an attractive way to display a constant menu, but it either tries to print everything on one line or puts a carriage return after each line. We chose to put a return after each line. A carriage return after the last line will make the text in the overlay window scroll up unless there is an extra line in the window. We put an extra line in the window. It's ugly, but it works.

The GCSET function selects a graphics cursor. The numbers in the call select a diagonal arrow. Since we are using a graphics cursor, you will have to merge the StdPtr file with a window. If you don't, GCSET will fail when it can't find the cursor description.

Errors at this point are nasty. You are in a tiny window and echo is turned off. If by some chance you get an error in FileMenu, you will want to return the screen to normal. At the D: prompt (which may be hard to find in the mess on the screen) type:

```
$display 1b 23
$tmode echo
```

The first command will close the overlay window and drop you back into the big window. The second command will turn echo back on so you can see what you are typing.

The REPEAT loop in FileMenu ignores all input except down arrows, F1 and F2. The down arrow moves the pointer. The function keys leave the loop.

The file menu can select one of four options: Load a file, Save a file, Clear the workspace, or Exit. Exit is a second escape from the menu. A user can select no operation from the file menu by pressing the F1 key or selecting Exit. The other functions are all performed by other procedures.

THE LISTING: GetFName

```
PROCEDURE GetFName
 0000      PARAM filename:STRING[80]
 000C      RUN gfx2("owset",1,0,0,80,2,3,2)
 002E      RUN gfx2("curon")
 003B      SHELL "tmode echo"
 0049      PRINT "Name of file?"
 005A      INPUT filename
 005F      SHELL "tmode -echo"
 006E      RUN gfx2("owend")
 007B      END
```

THE LISTING: ReadFile

```
PROCEDURE ReadFile
 0000      PARAM filename:STRING[80]
 000C      PARAM ScreenData(100):STRING[80]
 001D      DIM LineNo:INTEGER
 0024      DIM Path:BYTE
 002B      DIM Blanks:STRING[80]
 0037      DIM c:STRING[1]
 0043      BASE 0
 0045      Blanks:="
    "
 009C      RUN ClearBuf(ScreenData)
 00A6      OPEN #Path,filename:READ
 00B2      LineNo:=0
 00B9      ScreenData(0):=""
 00C3      WHILE NOT(EOF(#Path)) AND LineNo<100 DO
 00D5        GET #Path,c
 00DF        IF LEN(ScreenData(LineNo))>=80 OR c=CHR$($0D) THEN
 00F8          ScreenData(LineNo):=ScreenData(LineNo)+LEFT$(Blanks,80-
                LEN(ScreenData(LineNo)))
 0116          LineNo:=LineNo+1
 0121          ScreenData(LineNo):=""
 012C        ELSE
 0130          ScreenData(LineNo):=ScreenData(LineNo)+c
 0143        ENDIF
 0145      ENDWHILE
 0149      CLOSE #Path
 014F      END
```

THE LISTING: WritFile

```
PROCEDURE WritFile
 0000      PARAM filename:STRING[80]
 000C      PARAM ScreenData(100):STRING[80]
 001D      DIM Path:BYTE
 0024      DIM LineNo,i:INTEGER
 002F      DIM Blanks:STRING[80]
 003B      BASE 0
```

```
003D      Blanks:="
  "
0094      CREATE #Path,filename:WRITE
00A0      FOR LineNo:=99 TO 0 STEP -1
00B6      EXITIF ScreenData(LineNo)<>Blanks THEN
00C6      ENDEXIT
00CA      NEXT LineNo
00D5      FOR i:=0 TO LineNo
00E6        PRINT #Path,TRIM$(ScreenData(i))
00F4      NEXT i
00FF      CLOSE #Path
0105      END
```

We haven't made ScratchPad into a competitor for the world's best editor, but it's useful. You might find it better than the line editor that came with OS-9.

This chapter was largely code. Don't let the bulk of it discourage you. If you look at it procedure by procedure, it will be more manageable. We recommend that you read the program "top down" or "bottom up." We discussed the program top down starting with the ScratchPad procedure and working our way out to the procedures it called and so forth.

If you don't like following a program top down, try bottom up. You start by finding procedures that don't call any other procedures. Since they don't call other procedures, they are said to be at the bottom. When you understand the procedures at the bottom, you can look at the procedures that call them. Eventually you'll find yourself at ScratchPad.

If you can guess what procedures do from their place in the procedure that calls them and their name, reading top down works best. You start with the broad picture and work your way down to details. If you have trouble taking procedures that you haven't read on faith, you are forced to work bottom up.

PRINCIPLES

- Build complicated programs from simpler ones.
- When you are enhancing a program, make the smallest changes that do the job. Every change carries a possible error, so keep them to a minimum.
- If a procedure gets unwieldy when you add to it, try to split some of the work off into another procedure.
- Pay attention to the details. This is always important when you are programming, but it is most important when the program gets big.

RECAP

We skipped over uninteresting parts of the ScratchPad program. Here's the entire program in order:

THE LISTING: ScratchPad

```
PROCEDURE ScratchPad
 ØØØØ      (* The top level routine of a simple editor program
 ØØ33      (* The constant, 1ØØ, is the number of lines the editor
 ØØ6A      (* can handle.  It appears throughout this program as
 ØØ9F      (* 1ØØ or 99 (the last entry in BASE Ø)
 ØØC6      DIM ScreenData(1ØØ):STRING[8Ø]
 ØØD7      DIM InChr:STRING[1]
 ØØE3      DIM x,y,HomeLine:INTEGER
 ØØF2      DIM Scroll:BOOLEAN
 ØØF9      BASE Ø
 ØØFB
 ØØFC      RUN ClearBuf(ScreenData)
 Ø1Ø6      (* Modify the terminal mode to suit this program.
 Ø137      (* We want to echo characters from the program, so we
 Ø16C      (* tell OS-9 not to echo. We also don't want OS-9
 Ø19D      (* pausing the display when it thinks a page has been
 Ø1D2      (* displayed.
 Ø1DF      SHELL "tmode -pause -echo "
 Ø1F6      RUN gfx2("clear")
 Ø2Ø3      x:=Ø \y:=Ø \HomeLine:=Ø
 Ø218
 Ø219      (* The Main loop.  It reads data and commands and
 Ø24A      (* sends them to other procedures for handling.
 Ø279      GET #Ø,InChr
 Ø282      WHILE InChr<>CHR$($B1) DO
 Ø29Ø        IF InChr>=" " AND InChr<CHR$($8Ø) THEN
 Ø2A6          RUN UpdScreenData(ScreenData(y+HomeLine),x,y,InChr)
 Ø2C6          PRINT InChr;
 Ø2CC          x:=x+1
 Ø2D7        ELSE
 Ø2DB          RUN ApplyArrow(InChr,x,y)
 Ø2EF        ENDIF
 Ø2F1        RUN ScrollXY(x,79,y,23,HomeLine,99,Scroll)
 Ø313        IF Scroll THEN
 Ø31C          RUN ScrollScreen(ScreenData,y,23,HomeLine)
 Ø333        ENDIF
 Ø335        RUN gfx2("curxy",x,y)
 Ø34C        IF InChr=CHR$($B2) THEN  \REM F2
 Ø35F          RUN FileMenu(ScreenData,x,y,HomeLine)
 Ø378        ENDIF
 Ø37A        GET #Ø,InChr
 Ø383      ENDWHILE
 Ø387      RUN QuitMenu(ScreenData,x,y,HomeLine)
 Ø3AØ      SHELL "tmode pause echo "
```

```
PROCEDURE ClearBuf
 0000      PARAM Buf(100):STRING[80]
 0011      DIM i:INTEGER
 0018      DIM Blanks:STRING[80]
 0024      BASE 0
 0026      Blanks:="
   "
 007D      FOR i:=0 TO 99
 008D        Buf(i):=Blanks
 0099      NEXT i
 00A4      END
PROCEDURE UpdScreenData
 0000      PARAM Line:STRING[80]
 000C      PARAM x,y:INTEGER
 0017      PARAM InChr:STRING[1]
 0023      Line:=LEFT$(Line,x)+InChr+RIGHT$(Line,80-(x+1))
PROCEDURE ApplyArrow
 0000      (* Change x and y coordinates in response to keys that
 0036      (* move the cursor
 0048
 0049      (* So far we ignore all the cursor control characters
 007E      (* so this procedure does nothing
 009F      PARAM InChr:STRING[1]
 00AB      PARAM x,y:INTEGER
 00B6      IF InChr>=CHR$(8) AND InChr<=CHR$($1C) THEN
 00CC        ON ASC(InChr)-7 GOSUB 10,20,30,200,40,50,200,200,60,70,80
               ,90,200,200,200,200,110,120,130,200,140
 012B      ENDIF
 012D      END
 012F 10   REM Backspace
 013E      x:=x-1
 0149      RETURN
 014B 20   REM Forward arrow
 015E      x:=x+1
 0169      RETURN
 016B 30   REM Down
 0175      y:=y+1
 0180      RETURN
 0182 40   REM Up
 018A      y:=y-1
 0195      RETURN
 0197 50   REM Enter
 01A2      x:=0
 01A9      GOSUB 30
 01AD      RETURN
 01AF 60   REM cntl backspace
 01C3 70   REM cntl forward arrow
 01DB 80   REM cntl Down
 01EA 90   REM cntl Up
 01F7 110  REM shift backspace
```

```
 Ø2ØC 12Ø  REM shift forward arrow
 Ø225 13Ø  REM shift Down
 Ø235 14Ø  REM shift Up
 Ø243 2ØØ  REM Undefined
 Ø252      RETURN
 Ø254      END
PROCEDURE ScrollXY
 ØØØØ      PARAM x,xlimit,y,ylimit:INTEGER
 ØØ13      PARAM Home:INTEGER
 ØØ1A      PARAM MaxLines:INTEGER
 ØØ21      PARAM Scroll:BOOLEAN
 ØØ28      (* Make the lower right corner of the screen "out of bounds."
 ØØ65      IF x=xlimit AND y=ylimit THEN
 ØØ7A        x:=x+1
 ØØ85      ENDIF
 ØØ87
 ØØ88      IF x>xlimit THEN
 ØØ95        x:=Ø
 ØØ9C        y:=y+1
 ØØA7      ELSE IF x<Ø THEN
 ØØB6          x:=xlimit
 ØØBE          y:=y-1
 ØØC9        ENDIF
 ØØCB      ENDIF
 ØØCD
 ØØCE
 ØØCF      Scroll:=FALSE
 ØØD5      IF y>ylimit AND Home<MaxLines-ylimit THEN
 ØØEE        Scroll:=TRUE
 ØØF4        Home:=Home+1
 ØØFF        y:=y-1
 Ø1ØA      ELSE IF y<Ø AND Home>Ø THEN
 Ø12Ø          Scroll:=TRUE
 Ø126          Home:=Home-1
 Ø131          y:=y+1
 Ø13C        ENDIF
 Ø13E      ENDIF
 Ø14Ø      IF y>ylimit THEN
 Ø14D        y:=Ø
 Ø154      ELSE IF y<Ø THEN
 Ø163          y:=ylimit
 Ø16B        ENDIF
 Ø16D      ENDIF
PROCEDURE ScrollScreen
 ØØØØ      PARAM Lines(99):STRING[8Ø]
 ØØ11      PARAM y,ScreenSize:INTEGER
 ØØ1C      PARAM HomeLine:INTEGER
 ØØ23      BASE Ø
 ØØ25      IF y=Ø THEN  \REM Scroll Top
 ØØ3E        RUN ScrollTop(Lines(HomeLine))
 ØØ4B      ELSE
```

```
004F        RUN ScrollBottom(Lines(HomeLine+ScreenSize),Lines(HomeLine
              +(ScreenSize-1)))
006F      ENDIF
0071      END
PROCEDURE ScrollTop
0000      PARAM Line:STRING[80]
000C      RUN gfx2("curxy",0,0)
001F      RUN gfx2("inslin")
002D      PRINT Line;
0033      END
PROCEDURE ScrollBottom
0000      PARAM Line:STRING[80]
000C      PARAM OneUp:STRING[80]
0018      RUN gfx2("curxy",79,23)
002B      PRINT RIGHT$(OneUp,1); LEFT$(Line,79);
003B      END
PROCEDURE FileMenu
0000      PARAM ScreenData(100):STRING[80]
0011      PARAM x,y,HomeLine:INTEGER
0020      DIM c:BYTE
0027      DIM i,selection:INTEGER
0032      DIM filename,Blanks:STRING[80]
0042      DIM s:STRING[10]
004E      BASE 0
0050      Blanks:="
   "
00A7      RUN gfx2("owset",1,0,0,10,6,0,1)
00C9      RUN gfx2("curoff")
00D7      FOR i:=1 TO 5
00E7        READ s
00EC        PRINT s
00F1      NEXT i
00FC      DATA "File Menu","Load","Save","Clear","Exit"
0129      RUN gfx2("gcset",202,1)
013C      selection:=0
0143      REPEAT
0145        RUN gfx2("putgc",50,10+selection*8)
015F        GET #0,c
0168        IF c=$0A THEN  \REM down arrow
0182          selection:=MOD(selection+1,4)
0190        ENDIF
0192      UNTIL c=$B1 OR c=$B2
01A6      RUN gfx2("owend")
01B3      IF c=$B2 THEN  \REM f2  Expand
01CD        ON selection+1 GOSUB 10,20,30,40
01E7      ENDIF
01E9      END
01EB 10   REM Load a file
01FC      RUN GetFName(filename)
0206      RUN ReadFile(filename,ScreenData)
```

```
 Ø215       HomeLine:=Ø \x:=Ø \y:=Ø
 Ø22A       RUN PaintScreen(ScreenData)
 Ø234       RETURN
 Ø236 2Ø    REM Save a file
 Ø247       RUN GetFName(filename)
 Ø251       RUN WritFile(filename,ScreenData)
 Ø26Ø       RETURN
 Ø262 3Ø    REM Clear workspace
 Ø277       RUN ClearBuf(ScreenData)
 Ø281       HomeLine:=Ø \x:=Ø \y:=Ø
 Ø296       RUN PaintScreen(ScreenData)
 Ø2AØ       RETURN
 Ø2A2 4Ø    REM exit
 Ø2AC       RETURN
PROCEDURE GetFName
 ØØØØ       PARAM filename:STRING[8Ø]
 ØØØC       RUN gfx2("owset",1,Ø,Ø,8Ø,2,3,2)
 ØØ2E       RUN gfx2("curon")
 ØØ3B       SHELL "tmode echo"
 ØØ49       PRINT "Name of file?"
 ØØ5A       INPUT filename
 ØØ5F       SHELL "tmode -echo"
 ØØ6E       RUN gfx2("owend")
 ØØ7B       END
PROCEDURE ReadFile
 ØØØØ       PARAM filename:STRING[8Ø]
 ØØØC       PARAM ScreenData(1ØØ):STRING[8Ø]
 ØØ1D       DIM LineNo:INTEGER
 ØØ24       DIM Path:BYTE
 ØØ2B       DIM Blanks:STRING[8Ø]
 ØØ37       DIM c:STRING[1]
 ØØ43       BASE Ø
 ØØ45       Blanks:="
   "
 ØØ9C       RUN ClearBuf(ScreenData)
 ØØA6       OPEN #Path,filename:READ
 ØØB2       LineNo:=Ø
 ØØB9       ScreenData(Ø):=""
 ØØC3       WHILE NOT(EOF(#Path)) AND LineNo<1ØØ DO
 ØØD5         GET #Path,c
 ØØDF         IF LEN(ScreenData(LineNo))>=8Ø OR c=CHR$($ØD) THEN
 ØØF8           ScreenData(LineNo):=ScreenData(LineNo)+LEFT$(Blanks,8Ø-
                 LEN(ScreenData(LineNo)))
 Ø116           LineNo:=LineNo+1
 Ø121           ScreenData(LineNo):=""
 Ø12C         ELSE
 Ø13Ø           ScreenData(LineNo):=ScreenData(LineNo)+c
 Ø143         ENDIF
 Ø145       ENDWHILE
 Ø149       CLOSE #Path
 Ø14F       END
```

```
PROCEDURE PaintScreen
 0000      PARAM Screen(100):STRING[80]
 0011      DIM Blanks:STRING[80]
 001D      DIM y:INTEGER
 0024
 0025      BASE 0
 0027      Blanks:="
    "
 007E      RUN gfx2("clear")
 008B      FOR y=0 TO 22
 009B        IF Screen(y)<>"" AND Screen(y)<>Blanks THEN
 00B5          RUN gfx2("curxy",0,y)
 00CA          PUT #1,Screen(y)
 00D7        ENDIF
 00D9      NEXT y
 00E4      RUN gfx2("curxy",0,23)
 00F7      PRINT LEFT$(Screen(23),79);
 0102      RUN gfx2("curhome")
 0111      END
PROCEDURE WritFile
 0000      PARAM filename:STRING[80]
 000C      PARAM ScreenData(100):STRING[80]
 001D      DIM Path:BYTE
 0024      DIM LineNo,i:INTEGER
 002F      DIM Blanks:STRING[80]
 003B      BASE 0
 003D      Blanks:="
    "
 0094      CREATE #Path,filename:WRITE
 00A0      FOR LineNo:=99 TO 0 STEP -1
 00B6      EXITIF ScreenData(LineNo)<>Blanks THEN
 00C6      ENDEXIT
 00CA      NEXT LineNo
 00D5      FOR i:=0 TO LineNo
 00E6        PRINT #Path,TRIM$(ScreenData(i))
 00F4      NEXT i
 00FF      CLOSE #Path
 0105      END
PROCEDURE QuitMenu
 0000      PARAM ScreenData(100):STRING[80]
 0011      DIM c:BYTE
 0018      DIM selection:INTEGER
 001F      DIM filename:STRING[80]
 002B      DIM s:STRING[10]
 0037      BASE 0
 0039      RUN gfx2("owset",1,0,0,10,6,0,1)
 005B      RUN gfx2("curoff")
 0069      FOR i:=1 TO 3
 007B        READ s
 0080        PRINT s
 0085      NEXT i
```

```
DATA "Quit Menu"," Save as"," Quit"
RUN gfx2("gcset",202,1)
selection:=0
REPEAT
  RUN gfx2("putgc",70,10+selection*8)
  GET #0,c
  IF c=$0A THEN  \REM down arrow
    selection:=MOD(selection+1,2)
  ENDIF
UNTIL c=$B1 OR c=$B2
RUN gfx2("owend")
IF selection=0 THEN
  RUN GetFName(filename)
  RUN WritFile(filename,ScreenData)
ENDIF
END
```

POSSIBLE ENHANCEMENTS

The possible enhancements for ScratchPad are almost endless. Many important parts of a real editor are in place. With some work you can add your favorite features and have as much editor-power as you want.

If you want to do serious work with ScratchPad, you should work on error protection. Users (even when the user is yourself) shouldn't find themselves in the debugger when they press the wrong key. There are two places in ScratchPad where you should worry about errors.

If the user accidentally presses the BREAK or ESCAPE keys, ScratchPad will end with an error code. It won't give the user a chance to save the file in ScreenData, and it won't fix the terminal mode or screen parameters.

BASIC09 doesn't give you a way to catch the "signal" that the BREAK key sends or ignore the end of file that the ESCAPE key will send. You can avoid the problem by disabling the troublesome keys. Use Tmode to set the quit key, the interrupt key and the end of file key to zero when you turn off Pause and Echo. Be sure to restore the original values when at the end of ScratchPad. You can find the original values by running Tmode.

Whenever BASIC09 is handling files, it is likely to detect errors. If you try to open a file that isn't there or create a file that is already there, you will get errors. File protection can cause other errors. It is a good idea to protect file operations with ON ERROR GOTO statements.

Installing good error protection in ScratchPad is important, but not exciting. Adding features to the program is more exciting.

We haven't assigned functions to the shifted and controlled arrow keys. They should do something. There is also a keyboard full of ALT keys. You'll probably run out of ideas for functions before you run out of keys. Some possible functions are:

- Change to insertion mode. This would involve a change to `UpdScreenData` or an alternate procedure.
- Delete character.
- Delete line.
- Search for a string.
- Search and replace.
- Move the cursor a page at a time.
- Move the cursor to a specified line number.

You don't need to control all of `ScratchPad`'s functions with keys. Menus are nice too. Maybe functions like searching and search-and-replace should be run from a menu.

`ScratchPad` could handle many more lines if it didn't have to use 80 bytes for each line regardless of its length. If you feel ambitious, you might look for a more efficient way to store the lines. This is a hard problem.

We used a trick we called "ugly" when we displayed the menu in `FileMenu`. There's an easy fix that involves one extra line of code. Hint: It's a `PRINT` statement.

CHAPTER 14

using library code

We want to print a calendar. We'll be happy with one month on the screen at a time, but we want to be able to select that month. The current month, and the months before and after it, are the most important, but we'd like to be able to see calendars for a wide range of dates.

If we knew where to put the dates, printing the calendar wouldn't be much harder than printing an ASCII table. Knowing where to put the dates is hard. Discovering, for instance, what day of the week April Fools' day fell on in the year 719 is a tricky business.

One of the most important rules for productive programming is "never reinvent the wheel." This means that you should not spend much time solving a problem that someone else has solved. Note carefully that this is a rule for *productive* programming. It doesn't always apply to things you may want to do.

It's fun to rework classic problems. You can look at it as a pointless but fun exercise like solving crossword puzzles. You can also try competitive wheel reinvention. Great fame (and much money) awaits anyone who can beat the world's best sort program (though to make your fortune, you'll have to adapt the program to mainframe computers).

Occasionally you'll be forced to re-solve a problem. You may be unable to afford the solution or unable to wait for it to arrive. That's life. Sometimes reality gets in the way of productive programming.

Programmers usually deal with three types of solutions: programs, subroutines and documents. A program is a complete, packaged solution and the clear productivity winner. The fastest way to produce a program is to pull out a disk with the finished product. A subroutine is a procedure that can't stand by itself. A programmer will have to invest at least a little work in building a program to run subroutines, but they are flexible tools. The least convenient medium for solutions is paper. You will find numerous good ideas in books and magazines.

In this chapter we'll use a subroutine to solve a problem. The subroutine is a procedure that will calculate a date from a year, month, week and weekday. It's a complicated procedure (actually a whole collection of procedures) that encapsulates knowledge about the calendar back to the year zero. Don't expect to understand the subroutine (though you might want to try. The calendar has gone through some interesting changes).

We will use a subroutine called `CalcDate`, which calculates the date of any reasonable day. You will find it at the end of this chapter. It should be called with a `RUN` statement like:

`RUN CalcDate(`*date*`,` *year*`,` *month*`,` *week*`,` *day*`)`

All the parameters are integers. The last four parameters choose a day between the first day in the year zero and the last day in the year 32767.

- Day is in the range 0 (for Sunday) through 6 (for Saturday)
- Week is in the range 0 to 5
- Month is in the range 1 (for January) through 12 (for December)
- Year is in the range 0 to 32766
- Date is returned from `CalcDate`

The `CalcDate` procedure will calculate the date (that is, the day in the month) of the day indicated by the other four parameters.

If `CalcDate` is given an impossible day, it will return a date less than one. Some impossible days are obvious: a month greater than 12 or less than 1, or a day greater than 6. Other impossible days are hard to avoid. How can we tell what day of the week a given month starts on? Is day 2 of week 0 of January 1989 possible, or does that year start on a Thursday?

OUTSIDE-IN DEVELOPMENT

Up to now we've been designing programs top down; that is, we've been starting with a main procedure, then writing the procedures it calls, then the procedures they call, and so forth. Now we are in an odd position. We'd like to design the program top down, but we already know one of the procedures that will be at the bottom.

We would probably have decided to print a calendar by going through the month from the first to the 31st discovering the day of the week that each date falls on. `CalcDate` doesn't fit into that design. It won't return a value for day of the week given a date. The limits of `CalcDate` push us strongly toward a design where we run through the month week by week and, within that, day by day.

GOALS

The calendar program should always start by printing the current calendar. If the user wants a calendar for some other month, the program should let him page though until the right month appears. The arrow keys seem the logical way to move through the calendar. We'll let the right and left arrows move forward and backward a single month. The up and down arrows will move forward and backward a year.

Reaching a calendar for some remote time will be difficult. A month in 1776 is over 200 key presses away. Keep that problem in mind. Later we will be looking for a good way to find calendars for distant times.

DESIGN

The calendar program will start by displaying this month's calendar, then let the user move to other months. We'll start the design by sketching the top level of a program with that function:

Get today's date into Year and Month
Until the user is done
Print a calendar for Year and Month
Let the user pick another Year and Month

In BASIC09 it doesn't look much different:

THE LISTING: `Calendar`

```
PROCEDURE Calender
 0000      DIM year,month:INTEGER
 000B      DIM Date_string:STRING[17]
 0017      DIM c:BYTE
 001E
 001F      Date_string=DATE$
 0025      year=VAL(LEFT$(Date_string,2))
 0032      year=year+1900
 003E      month=VAL(MID$(Date_string,4,2))
```

```
ØØ4D
ØØ4E       REPEAT
ØØ5Ø         RUN PrintMonth(year,month)
ØØ5F         RUN gfx2("curhome")
ØØ6E         GET #Ø,c
ØØ77         RUN NewMonth(c,year,month)
ØØ8B       UNTIL c=$B1
```

Calendar calls two procedures, PrintMonth and NewMonth. PrintMonth prints a month's calendar. NewMonth changes the values of month and year when the user presses an arrow key. PrintMonth deserves extra attention because it's influenced by outside-in design, so we'll save it for later.

THE LISTING: Arrows

```
PROCEDURE Arrows
 ØØØØ       PARAM c:BYTE
 ØØØ7       PARAM Month:INTEGER
 ØØØE       IF c=$Ø8 THEN  \REM left arrow
 ØØ28         Month:=Month-1
 ØØ33       ELSE IF c=$Ø9 THEN  \REM right arrow
 ØØ52           Month:=Month+1
 ØØ5D         ELSE IF c=$ØA THEN  \REM down arrow
 ØØ7A             Month:=Month-12
 ØØ85           ELSE IF c=$ØC THEN  \REM up arrow
 ØØAØ               Month:=Month+12
 ØØAB             ENDIF
 ØØAD           ENDIF
 ØØAF         ENDIF
 ØØB1       ENDIF
 ØØB3       END
```

Arrows has about the same job that ApplyArrow did in the ScratchPad program. It interprets arrow keys into motions. The job can be divided into two parts: understanding the arrow keys and finding the month we end up in.

It is good to limit a procedure's parameters as much as possible. We follow that principle carefully with the procedures Arrows and Correct.

The actions of the arrow keys can be stated in terms of months (a year is 12 months), so we will only pass the character from the keyboard, C, and the month to Arrows.

The Correct procedure expects dates that have impossible months. It adjusts the year and month to correct values reflecting the same month. For example, the month 20 in the year 1970 would turn out to be the month 8 in the year 1971, and the month -4 in the year 1982 would be the month 8 in the year 1981.

`Arrows` is a straightforward procedure (just lots of nested `IF` statements), but the arithmetic in `Correct` is tricky. The basic idea behind `Correct` is that it divides the `Month` variable by 12 to get a correction to the years' variable. Since there are 12 months in a year, `Month` divided by 12 is the number of years. Month 13 is one year and one extra month; month 3 is no years and three months. Those examples look good, but what about month 12? Our calculation would show that as one year and zero months. How about month -1?

The `Month` variable and the constant 12 are integers, so BASIC09 truncates the result of `Month` divided by 12. Truncation makes the fractions 0/12 through 11/12 come out to 0, so we can get the calculation of years to work well for all positive numbers of months by using `Month - 1` instead of `Month`. Unfortunately, truncation rounds up (toward zero) for negative numbers. We will have to use `Month - 12` in the calculation of years if `Month` is a negative number. Putting all this confusion into a procedure, we get:

THE LISTING: `Correct`

```
PROCEDURE Correct
 0000       PARAM Year,Month:INTEGER
 000B       DIM Shift:INTEGER
 0012       IF Month<1 THEN
 001E         Shift:=Month-12
 0029       ELSE
 002D         Shift:=Month-1
 0038       ENDIF
 003A       Shift:=Shift/12 \REM years of offset
 0057       Year:=Year+Shift
 0063       Month:=Month-12*Shift
 0072       END
```

WORKING TOWARD CALCDATE

In the `Calendar` procedure we called `PrintMonth` to print the calendar for a selected month. It is passed the year and month and should use `CalcDate` to generate the calendar. `CalcDate` takes year, month, week and day of week as parameters and returns a date. Year and month are fixed values from `PrintMonth`'s point of view; it changes the values of week and day of week. Eventually we will have to print a matrix of dates that will be seven days wide and might be as much as six weeks deep.

Nested `FOR` loops are the usual way of filling a matrix, and there is no reason not to use them here. We can nest the loops in either order:

```
FOR week:= 0 to 5
  FOR day := 0 to 6
```

or

```
FOR day := 0 to 6
  FOR week := 0 to 5
```

Printing the calendar week by week seems more natural, so we chose that way.

It turns out that the "natural way" was a good choice. `CalcDate` has strange rules about week 0 that make it possible for week 0 to have no days in it. If we had decided to print the calendar a column at a time, we might find the top row of the calendar empty. Since we are printing it a week at a time, we just keep track of whether there were any days in the week just printed and keep printing weeks on the same line until we find a week with days in it.

Printing a week might be a little complicated, so we use the usual trick and push the work off to another procedure.

THE LISTING: `PrintMonth`

```
PROCEDURE PrintMonth
 0000       PARAM year,month:INTEGER
 000B       DIM week,day,y_offset:INTEGER
 001A       DIM Month_Name:STRING[9]
 0026       DIM Anything:BOOLEAN
 002D
 002E       RUN gfx2("clear")
 003B       RUN Get_Month_Name(Month_Name,month)
 004A       PRINT USING "S27^",Month_Name+" "+STR$(year)
 0060       PRINT "Sun Mon Tue Wed Thu Fri Sat"
 007F
 0080       y_offset:=2
 0087       FOR week=0 TO 5
 0097         RUN PrintWeek(year,month,week,0,y_offset+week,Anything)
 00BB         IF NOT(Anything) THEN
 00C5           y_offset:=1
 00CC         ENDIF
 00CE       EXITIF NOT(Anything) AND week>0 THEN
 00DF       ENDEXIT
 00E3       NEXT week
 00EE       END
```

THE LISTING: `Get_Month_Name`

```
PROCEDURE Get_Month_Name
 0000         PARAM Name:STRING[9]
 000C         PARAM Month:INTEGER
 0013         ON Month GOSUB 1,2,3,4,5,6,7,8,9,10,11,12
 004A         READ Name
 004F         END
 0051 1       RESTORE 21
 0059         RETURN
 005B 2       RESTORE 22
 0063         RETURN
 0065 3       RESTORE 23
 006D         RETURN
 006F 4       RESTORE 24
 0077         RETURN
 0079 5       RESTORE 25
 0081         RETURN
 0083 6       RESTORE 26
 008B         RETURN
 008D 7       RESTORE 27
 0095         RETURN
 0097 8       RESTORE 28
 009F         RETURN
 00A1 9       RESTORE 29
 00A9         RETURN
 00AB 10      RESTORE 30
 00B3         RETURN
 00B5 11      RESTORE 31
 00BD         RETURN
 00BF 12      RESTORE 32
 00C7         RETURN
 00C9 21      DATA "January"
 00DA 22      DATA "February"
 00EC 23      DATA "March"
 00FB 24      DATA "April"
 010A 25      DATA "May"
 0117 26      DATA "June"
 0125 27      DATA "July"
 0133 28      DATA "August"
 0143 29      DATA "September"
 0156 30      DATA "October"
 0167 31      DATA "November"
 0179 32      DATA "December"
```

`PrintWeek` is passed the year, month and week that it should print. It also gets the x and y coordinates at which to print. It should set `Anything` to true if there are any days in the week, and false otherwise.

`PrintWeek` uses a `FOR` loop to count through the days in the week. This is where we will finally call CalcDate. Since we know the year, month, week and day of week, the call to CalcDate is simple. The procedure looks like this:

THE LISTING: PrintWeek

```
PROCEDURE PrintWeek
 0000       PARAM year,month,week,x,y:INTEGER
 0017       PARAM AnyThing:BOOLEAN
 001E       DIM day,date:INTEGER
 0029       AnyThing:=FALSE
 002F       FOR day:=0 TO 6
 003F         RUN CalcDate(date,year,month,week,day)
 005D         IF date>0 THEN
 0069           RUN gfx2("curxy",x,y)
 0080           PRINT USING "i3>",date;
 008D           AnyThing:=TRUE
 0093         ENDIF
 0095         x:=x+4
 00A0       NEXT day
 00AB       END
```

There is one small trick in PrintWeek. Remember that the first week in a month can start with days that were in the previous month. These days should show as blanks in the calendar. PrintWeek doesn't print blanks for empty spaces; it just keeps track of the right place to put each date and puts the cursor there before it prints.

THE LISTING: CalcDate

```
PROCEDURE CalcDate
 0000       REM given year, montht, week, and weekday return the day of the
 003E       REM month falling on the specified day.
 0064       PARAM Date,Year,Month,Week,Weekday:INTEGER
 007B       TYPE dateinfo=feb,sept,days_in_month,First_of_Month:INTEGER
 0092       DIM info:dateinfo
 009B       DIM DaysInMonth(12):INTEGER
 00A7       RUN DaysInMonths(DaysInMonth)
 00B1       RUN SetDateInfo(info,Year,Month,DaysInMonth)
 00CA       RUN WeekDayToDate(Date,Week,Weekday,info)
 00E3       END
```

THE LISTING: Jan1

```
PROCEDURE Jan1
 0000       REM Given a year return the day of the week of new years
 0037       REM day
 003D       PARAM year:INTEGER
 0044       PARAM day:INTEGER
```

```
004B      day=year+4+(year+3)/4 \REM Julian calender
0072      IF year>1800 THEN  \REM a recent year
008F        REM make the Clavian correction
00AD        day=day-(year-1701)/100
00C0        REM and the Gregorian correction
00DF        day=day+(year-1601)/400
00F3      ENDIF
00F5      IF year>1752 THEN  \REM Adjust for the Gregorian calendar
0126        day=day+3
0131      ENDIF
0133      day=MOD(day,7)
013E      END
```

THE LISTING: DaysInMonths

```
PROCEDURE DaysInMonths
0000      PARAM DaysInMonth(12):INTEGER
000C      DIM i
0011      DATA 31,28,31,30
0021      DATA 31,30,31,31
0031      DATA 30,31,30,31
0041      FOR i=1 TO 12
0053        READ DaysInMonth(i)
005D      NEXT i
0068      END
```

THE LISTING: SetDateInfo

```
PROCEDURE SetDateInfo
0000      REM This function updates info to reflect the given year and month.
0042      TYPE DateInfo=days_in_month,First_of_Month:INTEGER
0051      PARAM info:DateInfo
005A      PARAM Year,Month:INTEGER
0065      PARAM DaysInMonth(12):INTEGER
0071      DIM leap,work,i:INTEGER
0080      REM check the parameters
0097      IF Month<1 OR Month>12 THEN
00AA        info.days_in_month=0 \REM error flag
00C2      ELSE
00C6        RUN Jan1(Year,info.First_of_Month)
00D8        RUN Jan1(Year+1,work)
00E9        leap=MOD(work+7-info.First_of_Month,7)
00FE        IF leap=2 THEN
010A          DaysInMonth(2)=29
0114        ELSE IF leap<>1 THEN  \REM Adjustment
0130            DaysInMonth(9)=19
013A          ENDIF
013C        ENDIF
013E        info.days_in_month=DaysInMonth(Month)
014D        REM Now add up the days in all the months up to the current month
018D        FOR i=1 TO Month-1
```

```
Ø1A1           info.First_of_Month=info.First_of_Month+DaysInMonth(i)
Ø1B7         NEXT i
Ø1C2         info.First_of_Month=MOD(info.First_of_Month,7)
Ø1D4       ENDIF
```

THE LISTING: WeekDayToDate

```
PROCEDURE WeekDayToDate
 ØØØØ      PARAM Date,Week,Weekday:INTEGER
 ØØØF      TYPE dateinfo=days_in_month,First_of_Month:INTEGER
 ØØ1E      PARAM info:dateinfo
 ØØ27      Date=Week*7+Weekday-info.First_of_Month+1
 ØØ4Ø      IF Date<=Ø OR Date>info.days_in_month THEN
 ØØ57        Date=Ø
 ØØ5E      ELSE IF info.days_in_month=19 AND Date>=3 THEN
 ØØ77          REM The super-leap month
 ØØ8E          Date=Date+11
 ØØ99        ENDIF
 ØØ9B      ENDIF
 ØØ9D      END
```

THE LISTING: WeekInYear

```
PROCEDURE WeekInYear
 ØØØØ      PARAM Week,Year,Month,Date:INTEGER
 ØØ13      DIM DaysInMonth(12):INTEGER
 ØØ1F      DIM i,Day1,NextDay1:INTEGER
 ØØ2E      DIM Day:INTEGER
 ØØ35
 ØØ36      RUN DaysInMonths(DaysInMonth)
 ØØ4Ø      IF Month<1 OR Month>12 THEN
 ØØ53        PRINT "Impossible month "; Month; " in WeekInYear"
 ØØ7D        ERROR 1
 ØØ81      ENDIF
 ØØ83      RUN Jan1(Year,Day1)
 ØØ92      RUN Jan1(Year+1,NextDay1)
 ØØA3      IF MOD(NextDay1+7-Day1,7)<>1 THEN  \REM a leap year
 ØØC7        DaysInMonth(2)=29
 ØØD1      ENDIF
 ØØD3      Day=Day1
 ØØDB      FOR i=1 TO Month-1
 ØØEF        Day=Day+DaysInMonth(i)
 ØØFE      NEXT i
 Ø1Ø9      Day=Day+Date
 Ø115      Week=Day/7
 Ø12Ø      PRINT Week
 Ø125      END
```

THE LISTING: NewMonth

```
PROCEDURE NewMonth
 0000      PARAM c:BYTE
 0007      PARAM Year,Month:INTEGER
 0012      RUN Arrows(c,Month)
 0021      RUN Correct(Year,Month)
 0030      END
```

We have created a program that will print the calendar for almost any imaginable month. A subroutine from our libraries calculates the date of any day once given the day of the week, the week, the month and the year. That subroutine did most of the work in making the calendar. We just built enough of a program to call the subroutine and print the results.

PRINCIPLES

Building a calendar program from scratch would have been a big job. The research alone might have taken hours (check into the history of the calendar), and writing the code would have been plenty more work. Our goal was to print a calendar, not puzzle out a nice way to calculate dates, so it was fortunate that we had `CalcDate` in our library.

Programmers should be lazy, and one of the most productive ways to be lazy is to collect libraries of programs and fragments that you can hook together. You can build your own library by collecting fragments of code that look generally useful, buying subroutine libraries that look interesting, and looking for public domain code to add to your collection.

Think of the trouble writing CalcDate would have been, and start building your library.

There is another important principle that is closely related to "don't reinvent the wheel." It is "let the language work for you." You should let BASIC09 do as much work as possible. In general, this principle will reduce the number of statements in your programs, so you can tell which of several approaches is best by counting the statements in each.

POSSIBLE ENHANCEMENTS

This program badly needs a fast way to select a given month and year. The best method is to have a key bring up a window with prompts for the year and month. The user can select a month quickly and cleanly. Defining the shifted and controlled arrow keys to change the date by decades and centuries would be easy, but not as good as prompting for the date.

Even shuffling through a few months can be frustrating. You can press the arrow key much faster than the program can display months, and you may not be interested in seeing the months you are passing over. If you could read arrow keys until the user stops entering them, then make one big shift in the date, you could avoid the intermediate displays. You can do this with the InKey procedure. Before you call PrintMonth, call InKey a few hundred times to make sure that the user isn't about to type another key.

The display of the current month would be more useful if the current date were highlighted.

CHAPTER 15

living dangerously

Someday you may need to write a program without making a single error. Slow progress will be acceptable, but not errors. In this chapter we'll show you some tricks that will help.

The program for this chapter is intentionally difficult to debug. Our goal is to convince you that sometimes avoiding, or at least pinpointing, bugs is worth a heroic effort.

As you get more ambitious, you will want to open device windows from BASIC09. A program that modifies the attributes of a window has some trouble knowing what values will restore the window to its original state. Opening a new device window avoids this problem. The program simply DWENDs and closes the window when it is done. The use of device windows is also the only way to get OS-9 to put two or more active windows on a screen. This won't work with overlay windows. You can put any reasonable number of overlay windows on the screen, but only the top overlay in any device window will be active.

Device windows are useful, and they're easy to use from BASIC09. That is, they are easy to use, provided you never make an error. One serious error in a program with an extra device window selected and you've had it. The extra window will freeze up and you won't be able to get back to the BASIC09 window.

Let's see how this happens. OS-9 has a rule that says, "Every process will have one device window selected, and only selected windows can be reached with the CLEAR key."

When your BASIC09 program selects a window, that window replaces the window BASIC09 is talking to. A program error that throws you into the debugger or drops you out of your program without selecting the standard window will leave BASIC09 waiting for input from its window while you look at the selected window. If you could get to the other window, you could fix things up, but the select key won't take you there and you can't get the program to select the window until you unfreeze it. In short, you are stuck.

There are several ways to deal with the problem of frozen device windows. The obvious approach is to write correct programs. In the middle 1970s, top-down structured programming was an exciting idea. Some people thought that programmers trained in those methods would be able to remember every programming error they ever made. The idea was not that structured programming would lead to memorably hair-raising errors. Rather, they believed that programmers trained in structured programming would make only a few dozen errors in their careers. It hasn't worked out that way.

Testing programs carefully before enhancing them with new device windows is a good way to avoid problems. Adding support for special device windows when the rest of the program is working may introduce errors, but they should at least be easy to find.

Gritting your teeth and living with frozen windows is crude, but not foolish. You're almost certainly going to get caught with some frozen windows. Why not plan on it? Just make sure that you save everything in your BASIC09 workspace after every change. If you freeze that window, everything in the workspace will be unreachable, and you'll have to fall back on your latest save files.

We recommend a combination of all three approaches. Program carefully, leave device window support out as long as possible, and save often.

In this chapter we will develop a simple database program that runs in two device windows on one screen. We're going to start using windows quite early and try to build the program without errors that will drop us into the debugger.

SETTING OUT OUR GOALS

The model is simple. We want to build a program that will act something like a deck of index cards or a Rolodex. The user should be able to

- Add new cards
- Flip through the cards

- Search the cards
- Modify cards

We'll put a display of several cards at the top of the screen. The bottom of the screen will hold a command window. Commands from the bottom window will change the display in the top window.

We'll have the database run in text windows. They are not as powerful as graphics windows, but they respond faster than graphics windows and deserve at least one full-sized program.

THE TOP LEVEL

The top level of the database program is clear enough that we'll just write it down in BASIC09. Our procedure is called `Rolladex`.

THE LISTING: `Rolladex`

```
PROCEDURE rolladex
 0000       DIM DBPath:INTEGER
 0007       DIM DBWin1,DBWin2:INTEGER
 0012       TYPE record=start:INTEGER; key:STRING[32]; text(5):STRING[69
             ]
 0038       DIM subset(10):record
 0046
 0047       ON ERROR GOTO 100
 004D       RUN DBOpen(DBPath)
 0057       RUN DBStart(DBPath,subset)
 0066       RUN DBWindow(DBWin1,DBWin2)
 0075       RUN DBDisplay(subset,DBWin1)
 0084       RUN DBInteract(DBPath,DBWin1,DBWin2,subset)
 009D 100   REM in case of errors
 00B4       ON ERROR
 00B7       RUN DBClose(DBPath,DBWin1,DBWin2)
 00CB       END
```

What does this mean? We want the program to open the database file, select a handful of cards from it (called a subset), open two windows and display the cards in the top window, process commands (interact), and close the database file when it is done. If there are any errors, we'd like the program to close everything and stop.

The data structures at the top of the `Rolladex` procedure are part of the top-level design. There will be 10 cards in the subset, and each card will have the following fields:

Start:	The location of the card in the database file.
Key:	A special field that we'll use when we search the database.
Text:	Five lines of data.

The Rolladex procedure calls six other procedures. We have checked Rolladex carefully and believe that it will run without errors, but those other procedures are a problem. When we are testing a procedure, we don't want to worry about the procedures that it calls.

We will write the simplest procedures that Rolladex can call without failing. These substitute procedures are called stubs. Writing stubs to test Rolladex is easy; it doesn't depend on the behavior of the procedures it calls, so entirely empty procedures will suffice for all the stubs.

Empty procedures are enough to let us test the Rolladex procedure, but slightly more elaborate stubs make debugging easier. All the Rolladex procedure does is call a list of procedures in order. We can quickly verify that it is working if we make the stubs like:

```
PROCEDURE DBOpen
PRINT "In DBOpen"
END
```

Stubs aren't always this simple. Let's look at what happens when we go to the next level.

DBOpen is fairly simple. If it successfully opens the database file, it immediately returns. If there is no database file, it should create a new file. This is a bit more complicated, but not outrageous, and we don't have to worry about device windows because they haven't been opened yet. Here's the DBOpen procedure:

THE LISTING: DBOpen

```
PROCEDURE DBOpen
 0000         PARAM DBPath:INTEGER
 0007         DIM errno:INTEGER
 000E         DIM filesize:INTEGER
 0015
 0016         ON ERROR GOTO 100
 001C         OPEN #DBPath,"DBFile":READ
 002D         END
 002F
 0030 100     REM deal with open errors
 004B         errno=ERR
 0051         ON ERROR
 0054         IF errno=216 THEN  \REM No db file yet
 0071           CREATE #DBPath,"DBFile":WRITE
 0082           filesize:=SIZE(filesize)
 008C           PUT #DBPath,filesize
 0096           CLOSE #DBPath
 009C           OPEN #DBPath,"DBFile":READ
```

```
ØØAD      ELSE
ØØB1        ERROR errno \REM We can't handle the error. Pass it on
ØØDE      ENDIF
```

We can test DBOpen without changing any other procedures. We call it from Rolladex, which has been tested with six stubs. The only change we made was to replace the DBOpen stub with a real program, so any problems are almost certainly caused by DBOpen.

The next step is not so easy. We can't test DBStart until we have a procedure that prints the subset. DBWindow is going to open device windows (which sounds dangerous). DBDisplay needs subset from DBStart. DBInteract needs everything. Even DBClose can't be tested without open windows.

Just opening device windows isn't dangerous. It's selecting windows that can make debugging difficult. We can make the DBWindow stub open and initialize windows for DBWin1 and DBWin2 without any risk. This enhanced stub lets us test DBClose.

THE LISTING: DBWinStub

```
PROCEDURE DBWindow
 ØØØØ      PARAM DBWin1,DBWin2:INTEGER
 ØØØB
 ØØØC      OPEN #DBWin1,"/w":UPDATE
 ØØ19      OPEN #DBWin2,"/w":UPDATE
 ØØ26      RUN gfx2(DBWin1,"dwset",2,Ø,Ø,8Ø,18,1,2,3)
 ØØ5Ø      RUN gfx2(DBWin2,"dwset",Ø,Ø,18,8Ø,6,1,4)
 ØØ77      END
 ØØ79
```

DBClose comes out looking like:

THE LISTING: DBClose

```
PROCEDURE DBClose
 ØØØØ      PARAM DBPath,DBWin1,DBWin2:INTEGER
 ØØØF
 ØØ1Ø      RUN gfx2(DBWin1,"dwend")
 ØØ22      RUN gfx2(DBWin2,"dwend")
 ØØ34      RUN gfx2("select")
 ØØ42      CLOSE #DBWin1,#DBWin2
 ØØ4D      CLOSE #DBPath
 ØØ53      END
```

The stub for DBWindow is getting close to the real thing, but we don't know if it is working correctly, only that it isn't failing in a way that stops the program. We can't see the windows it is creating until we select them, which we are not doing yet!

If we write a stub for DBDisplay that ignores the window path that is passed to it and just dumps the contents of subset on the screen, we can use it to test `DBStart`. The stub for `DBDisplay` looks like this:

THE LISTING: `DBDisplay.stub`

```
PROCEDURE DBDisplay
 0000      TYPE record=start:INTEGER; key:STRING[32]; text(5):STRING[69
            ]
 0026      PARAM subset(10):record
 0034      PARAM DBWin1:INTEGER
 003B
 003C      DIM i:INTEGER
 0043
 0044      FOR i:=10 TO 1 STEP -1
 005A        RUN DBDispRec(subset(i))
 0067      NEXT i
 0072      END
```

In the spirit of keeping procedures so short that we can feel sure they will work, we made the stub for `DBDisplay` call another procedure:

THE LISTING: `DBDispRec.stub`

```
PROCEDURE DBDispRec
 0000      TYPE record=start:INTEGER; key:STRING[32]; text(5):STRING[69
            ]
 0026      PARAM subset:record
 002F
 0030      DIM i:INTEGER
 0037
 0038      PRINT "<"; subset.key; ">"
 0048      FOR j:=1 TO 4
 005A        PRINT subset.text(j)
 0066      NEXT j
 0071      PRINT subset.text(5);
 007C      END
```

Now we can replace the stub for `DBStart` with a real procedure:

THE LISTING: `DBStart`

```
PROCEDURE DBStart
 0000      TYPE record=start:INTEGER; key:STRING[32]; text(5):STRING[69
            ]
 0026      PARAM DBPath:INTEGER
 002D      PARAM subset(10):record
 003B
 003C      DIM i,j,errno:INTEGER
 004B      DIM filesize:INTEGER
```

```
0052        GET #DBPath,filesize
005C        RUN FillSet(DBPath,subset,10)
006E        SEEK #DBPath,0
0077        END
```

The main job of DBStart is to fill the subset array. The Seek statement at the end of the procedure ensures that every procedure that reads DBPath after DBStart will be able to assume that DBPath is rewound. It probably won't be important, but it is best to keep as many things known as possible.

Without FillSet, DBStart only reads filesize. You might wonder why it even does that. Reading filesize doesn't have anything to do with the operation of the program — it could be replaced with a Seek statement — but it helps with debugging. It's nice to know the value of filesize, and this Get is done before the device windows are opened so the value can be inspected with the debugger.

FillSet isn't the end of the line. Its job is to fill Subset with records from the database file. If there are fewer than 10 records in the file, FillSet should make up enough empty-looking values to fill the array.

THE LISTING: FillSet

```
PROCEDURE FillSet
 0000       TYPE record=Start:INTEGER; key:STRING[32]; text(5):STRING[69

             ]
 0026       PARAM Path:INTEGER
 002D       PARAM subset(10):record
 003B       PARAM Num:INTEGER
 0042
 0043       DIM i,Mark:INTEGER
 004E
 004F       IF Num=10 THEN
 005B         Mark:=1
 0062       ELSE
 0066         Mark:=subset(10-Num).Start+1
 007A       ENDIF
 007C       FOR i:=11-Num TO 10
 0090         RUN DBGetRec(Path,Mark,subset(i))
 00A7         Mark:=Mark+1
 00B2       NEXT i
 00BD       END
```

We suspected that other procedures would want to use FillSet, so we gave it some extra power. It need not always read 10 records into Subset. The Num parameter tells it how many records to read. This makes things a little complicated.

If Subset is partly full when FillSet is called, FillSet will be able to find a starting place in the file from the start values in

FillSet. When FillSet is called from DBStart, there is nothing in Subset, so FillSet has to assume that it should start from the beginning of the file. FillSet calls the DBGetRec procedure, which does a random read in the database file.

THE LISTING: DBGetRec

```
PROCEDURE DBGetRec
 ØØØØ      TYPE record=Start:INTEGER; key:STRING[32]; text(5):STRING[69
           ]
 ØØ26      PARAM Path:INTEGER
 ØØ2D      PARAM RecNo:INTEGER
 ØØ34      PARAM rec:record
 ØØ3D
 ØØ3E      DIM i:INTEGER
 ØØ45
 ØØ46      ON ERROR GOTO 1ØØ
 ØØ4C      SEEK #Path,SIZE(RecNo)+(RecNo-1)*SIZE(rec)
 ØØ65      GET #Path,rec
 ØØ6F      SEEK #Path,Ø
 ØØ78      END
 ØØ7A
 ØØ7B 1ØØ  REM No such record
 ØØ8F      ON ERROR
 ØØ92      rec.key:="_____"
 ØØA2      rec.Start:=RecNo
 ØØAE      FOR i:=1 TO 5
 ØØBE        rec.text(i):=""
 ØØCC      NEXT i
 ØØD7      SEEK #Path,Ø
 ØØEØ      END
```

Careful programming would require that we write DBStart, FillSet and DBGetRec one at a time, using stubs for the procedures that aren't yet finished. We haven't selected any windows yet so we are not on dangerous ground. Why don't you try writing the stubs?

We still have three stubs attached to Rolladex. Since DBDisplay and DBInteract both rely on windows, we will finish DBWindow. We need to have it select the window on the bottom of the screen. We also want it to change the color palette on the screen. The finished procedure looks like this:

THE LISTING: DBWindow

```
PROCEDURE DBWindow
 ØØØØ      PARAM DBWin1,DBWin2:INTEGER
 ØØØB      DIM i,color:INTEGER
 ØØ16
 ØØ17      OPEN #DBWin1,"/w":UPDATE
 ØØ24      OPEN #DBWin2,"/w":UPDATE
 ØØ31      RUN gfx2(DBWin1,"dwset",2,Ø,Ø,8Ø,18,1,2,3)
```

```
ØØ5B        RUN gfx2(DBWin1,"select")
ØØ6E
ØØ6F        FOR i:=Ø TO 15
ØØ7F          READ color
ØØ84          RUN gfx2(DBWin1,"palette",i,color)
ØØA2        NEXT i
ØØAD
ØØAE        RUN gfx2(DBWin2,"dwset",Ø,Ø,18,8Ø,6,1,4)
ØØD5        RUN gfx2(DBWin2,"select")
ØØE8        END
ØØEA
ØØEB        REM Colors for the palette registers in the new windows
Ø121        DATA $Ø5,Ø,$Ø7,$Ø1,$Ø2,$Ø4,$Ø3,$Ø6
Ø144        DATA Ø,$3F,$Ø9,$12,$24,$1B,$36,$2D
```

The stubs for DBDisplay and DBDispRec are already almost real procedures. We want each card to show up in an overlay window with different colors to set them apart, so we add overlays to DBDisplay. That, and directing the output to a device window, complete DBDisplay and DBDispRec.

THE LISTING: DBDisplay

```
PROCEDURE DBDisplay
 ØØØØ       TYPE record=start:INTEGER; key:STRING[32]; text(5):STRING[69

             ]
 ØØ26       PARAM subset(1Ø):record
 ØØ34       PARAM DBWin1:INTEGER
 ØØ3B
 ØØ3C       DIM i:INTEGER
 ØØ43
 ØØ44       FOR i:=1Ø TO 1 STEP -1
 ØØ5A         RUN gfx2(DBWin1,"owset",1,1Ø-i,1Ø-i,69,6,MOD(i,7)+1,MOD(i

               ,8))
 ØØ94         RUN DBDispRec(subset(i),DBWin1)
 ØØA6       NEXT i
 ØØB1       END
```

THE LISTING: DBDispRec

```
PROCEDURE DBDispRec
 ØØØØ       TYPE record=start:INTEGER; key:STRING[32]; text(5):STRING[69

             ]
 ØØ26       PARAM subset:record
 ØØ2F       PARAM DBWin1:INTEGER
 ØØ36
 ØØ37       DIM i:INTEGER
 ØØ3E
 ØØ3F       RUN gfx2(DBWin1,"clear")
 ØØ51       PRINT #DBWin1,"<"; subset.key; ">"
```

```
  FOR j:=1 TO 4
    PRINT #DBWin1,subset.text(j)
  NEXT j
  PRINT #DBWin1,subset.text(5);
  END
```

Now, of all the procedures called from the top level, only `DBInteract` is still a stub. We are ready to attack it. We know that the values it will be passed are good, and we have a working procedure that prints cards from the database.

The `DBInteract` procedure is just a big switch. It puts up a prompt in the command window and selects actions based on input from the user.

THE LISTING: `DBInteract`

```
PROCEDURE DBInteract
      TYPE record=start:INTEGER; key:STRING[32]; text(5):STRING[69]
      PARAM DBPath,DBWin1,DBWin2:INTEGER
      PARAM subset(10):record
      DIM c:STRING[1]
      DIM cmds:STRING[12]
      DIM CmdNum:INTEGER

      cmds:="FfBbSsUuAaQq"
      REPEAT
        RUN gfx2(DBWin2,"clear")
        PRINT #DBWin2,"Enter a command (Fwd,Back,Srch,Upd,Add,Quit): ";
        GET #DBWin2,c
        CmdNum:=(SUBSTR(c,cmds)+1)/2
        ON CmdNum+1 GOSUB 100,200,300,400,500,600,700
      UNTIL CmdNum=6
      END

100   REM No such command
      RETURN
200   REM Forward
      PRINT #DBWin2,"wd";
      RUN DBFwd(DBPath,subset)
      RUN DBReDisp(subset,DBWin1)
      RETURN
300   REM Backward
      PRINT #DBWin2,"ack";
      RUN DBBack(DBPath,subset)
      RUN DBReDisp(subset,DBWin1)
      RETURN
400   REM Search
      PRINT #DBWin2,"rch";
```

```
Ø1B6          RUN DBSrch(DBPath,DBWin2,subset)
Ø1CA          RUN DBReDisp(subset,DBWin1)
Ø1D9          RETURN
Ø1DB 5ØØ      REM Update
Ø1E7          PRINT #DBWin2,"pd";
Ø1F3          RUN DBUpd(DBWin2,subset)
Ø2Ø2          RUN DBDispRec(subset(1),DBWin1)
Ø213          RETURN
Ø215 6ØØ      REM Add
Ø21E          PRINT #DBWin2,"dd";
Ø22A          RUN DBAdd(DBPath,DBWin2,subset)
Ø23E          RUN DBReDisp(subset,DBWin1)
Ø24D          RETURN
Ø24F 7ØØ      REM Quit
Ø259          PRINT #DBWin2,"uit";
Ø266          RETURN
```

Study the trick in the line that has the SUBSTR function. This is a good technique to use when you have to select an action based on a character. The most general form of the trick uses a string and an array of integers. The code for this would go something like this:

```
x := SUBSTR(c,CMDS)
selection := array(x)
```

From Line 100 down, DBInteract is mostly calls to procedures we haven't written yet. We need to go through the same process with these that we did with the procedures called from Rolladex.

The DBReDisp procedure gets heavy use. It is the procedure that will update the top window, and it seems pretty easy. Maybe we can use a call to the DBDisplay procedure we have already written and tested.

It turns out that DBDisplay won't work. Simply rerunning DBDisplay puts a new batch of overlay windows on top of the old ones, and it turns out that OS-9 doesn't take kindly to this. It freezes the window so we can't even tell for sure what went wrong. Perhaps we ran out of memory for the overlays? In any case it's a good thing we were saving procedures after each change.

Maybe we can add a little code to DBDisplay that will OWend the overlay windows before it starts new ones. The problem here is that when DBDisplay is called from Rolladex, there are no overlay windows to OWend. Maybe we can try OWend anyway. Closing a window that isn't there might just return an error.

We don't suggest that you try it. It didn't just freeze our window; it crashed OS-9 so badly that we had to go back to RS-DOS before we could get OS-9 started again.

We know that when DBReDisp is called, there are 10 overlay

windows active. Trying to make DBDisplay serve two purposes turned out to be a bad idea. We'll have DBReDisp OWend the overlay windows and then call DBDisplay.

THE LISTING: DBReDisp

```
PROCEDURE DBReDisp
 ØØØØ       TYPE record=key:STRING[32]; text(5):STRING[69]
 ØØ2Ø       PARAM subset(1Ø):record
 ØØ2E       PARAM DBWin:INTEGER
 ØØ35
 ØØ36       DIM i:INTEGER
 ØØ3D
 ØØ3E       FOR i:=1 TO 1Ø
 ØØ4E         RUN gfx2(DBWin,"owend")
 ØØ6Ø       NEXT i
 ØØ6B       RUN DBDisplay(subset,DBWin)
 ØØ7A       END
```

Except that we haven't yet seen the data it displays change, DBReDisp seems to work fine.

Since we have an empty database, the DBAdd procedure would be a good place to start. It may be the most difficult procedure we could pick, but we need it now.

Four steps are required to add a record to the database file.

- Get the new record from the user
- Change filesize to reflect an additional record
- Append a new record to the file
- Update subset (if necessary)

They should probably be done in four separate procedures, but we're going to squash three of them together. The completed procedure looks like this:

THE LISTING: DBAdd

```
PROCEDURE DBAdd
 ØØØØ       TYPE record=Start:INTEGER; key:STRING[32]; text(5):STRING[69

             ]
 ØØ26       PARAM Path:INTEGER
 ØØ2D       PARAM Win:INTEGER
 ØØ34       PARAM subset(1Ø):record
 ØØ42
 ØØ43       DIM i:INTEGER
 ØØ4A       DIM rec:record
 ØØ53       DIM Path2:INTEGER
 ØØ5A       DIM filesize:INTEGER
 ØØ61
 ØØ62       RUN DBEditRec(Win,rec)
 ØØ71       GET #Path,filesize
```

```
007B      SEEK #Path,0
0084      OPEN #Path2,"DBFile":WRITE
0095      filesize:=filesize+SIZE(rec)
00A3      rec.Start:=(filesize-SIZE(filesize))/SIZE(rec)
00BB      PUT #Path2,filesize
00C5
00C6      SEEK #Path2,filesize-SIZE(rec)
00D6      PUT #Path2,rec
00E0      FOR i:=1 TO 10
00F0      EXITIF subset(i).Start=rec.Start THEN
0106        subset(i):=rec
0112      ENDEXIT
0116      NEXT i
0121      CLOSE #Path2
0127      END
```

You can see that acquiring the new record is the responsibility of DBEditRec. The rest of the work is all lined up after the call to DBEditRec. There's too much to do at once, but it can be divided into steps even though it is in one procedure.

Writing a new file size without adding data to the database file will corrupt the database, but that's fine. There's nothing in the database yet anyway. We can stub out DBEditRec and discard everything after

```
PUT #Path2,filesize
```

The test procedure is as follows:

Run Rolladex.
Select a for add a record.
Select q for quit.
Put a pause in DBStart.
Run Rolladex.
When it pauses, step along until we can inspect Filesize (remember that DBStart reads Filesize).
Continue with Rolladex (CONT).
Select a for add a record.

We continue until we are satisfied that the file size is being updated correctly. Now erase the database file before the incorrect value of Filesize causes trouble.

We can test the next part of DBAdd without corrupting the database. After we add the next two lines of code and make sure that the stub for DBEditRec is putting something recognizable into the records, we run Rolladex. Records won't show on the screen when we add them, so we have to quit Rolladex and start it again. The new records will be picked up by DBStart and appear on the screen.

We have to write the rest of the program in similar tiny steps. There are many more procedures, but the construction tricks are slight variations on the ones we have used already. See the end of the chapter for the result.

Selecting a device window from a BASIC09 program makes nearly error-free programming important enough to justify all possible care in program construction. Errors will freeze the window, leaving you with one piece of information: something's wrong. In the face of this problem, we built a database system that is about as useful as a Rolodex.

PRINCIPLES

When the debugging situation is bad, the best policy is to use tiny procedures and make small changes between tests. Stubs are an important tool for this approach.

Stubs are simple replacements for lower-level procedures. They are important in top-down programming, but useless in bottom-up programming. The analogous tool for a bottom-up programmer is the driver program. A driver program is a program that is designed to exercise the procedure that it calls. A careful bottom-up programmer writes a driver to test each significant procedure before he trusts it in combination with other real procedures.

POSSIBLE ENHANCEMENTS

The `Rolladex` database is limited to a maximum of about 80 records by file size. The maximum value for an integer is 32,767, and each record is about 400 bytes long. The limit could be greatly increased by changing `Filesize` to a real number. Do this carefully. When a procedure doesn't use `Filesize`, we often used `Size(i)` or any other integer variable to find the size of `Filesize`. Since real values are larger than integers, this calls for care.

The editor always requires complete replacement of a record. Can you adapt the `ScratchPad` editor to solve this problem?

A program that prints a formatted copy of the database, or a selection from it, would be useful.

The `DBAdd` procedure is a little ungainly. Can you divide it into one procedure for each of its parts?

Here is a complete set of the listings:

```
PROCEDURE rolladex
 0000       DIM DBPath:INTEGER
 0007       DIM DBWin1,DBWin2:INTEGER
 0012       TYPE record=start:INTEGER; key:STRING[32]; text(5):STRING[69
             ]
 0038       DIM subset(10):record
 0046
```

```
0047       ON ERROR GOTO 100
004D       RUN DBOpen(DBPath)
0057       RUN DBStart(DBPath,subset)
0066       RUN DBWindow(DBWin1,DBWin2)
0075       RUN DBDisplay(subset,DBWin1)
0084       RUN DBInteract(DBPath,DBWin1,DBWin2,subset)
009D 100   REM in case of errors
00B4       ON ERROR
00B7       RUN DBClose(DBPath,DBWin1,DBWin2)
00CB       END
PROCEDURE DBOpen
0000       PARAM DBPath:INTEGER
0007       DIM errno:INTEGER
000E       DIM filesize:INTEGER
0015
0016       ON ERROR GOTO 100
001C       OPEN #DBPath,"DBFile":READ
002D       END
002F
0030 100   REM deal with open errors
004B       errno=ERR
0051       ON ERROR
0054       IF errno=216 THEN  \REM No db file yet
0071         CREATE #DBPath,"DBFile":WRITE
0082         filesize:=SIZE(filesize)
008C         PUT #DBPath,filesize
0096         CLOSE #DBPath
009C         OPEN #DBPath,"DBFile":READ
00AD       ELSE
00B1         ERROR errno \REM We can't handle the error. Pass it on
00DE       ENDIF
PROCEDURE DBStart
0000       TYPE record=start:INTEGER; key:STRING[32]; text(5):STRING[69
            ]
0026       PARAM DBPath:INTEGER
002D       PARAM subset(10):record
003B
003C       DIM i,j,errno:INTEGER
004B       DIM filesize:INTEGER
0052       GET #DBPath,filesize
005C       RUN FillSet(DBPath,subset,10)
006E       SEEK #DBPath,0
0077       END
PROCEDURE DBWindow
0000       PARAM DBWin1,DBWin2:INTEGER
000B       DIM i,color:INTEGER
0016
0017       OPEN #DBWin1,"/w":UPDATE
0024       OPEN #DBWin2,"/w":UPDATE
0031       RUN gfx2(DBWin1,"dwset",2,0,0,80,18,1,2,3)
005B       RUN gfx2(DBWin1,"select")
006E
006F       FOR i:=0 TO 15
```

```
007F          READ color
0084          RUN gfx2(DBWin1,"palette",i,color)
00A2        NEXT i
00AD
00AE        RUN gfx2(DBWin2,"dwset",0,0,18,80,6,1,4)
00D5        RUN gfx2(DBWin2,"select")
00E8        END
00EA
00EB        REM Colors for the palette registers in the new windows
0121        DATA $05,0,$07,$01,$02,$04,$03,$06
0144        DATA 0,$3F,$09,$12,$24,$1B,$36,$2D
PROCEDURE DBInteract
0000        TYPE record=start:INTEGER; key:STRING[32]; text(5):STRING[69
             ]
0026        PARAM DBPath,DBWin1,DBWin2:INTEGER
0035        PARAM subset(10):record
0043        DIM c:STRING[1]
004F        DIM cmds:STRING[12]
005B        DIM CmdNum:INTEGER
0062
0063        cmds:="FfBbSsUuAaQq"
0076        REPEAT
0078          RUN gfx2(DBWin2,"clear")
008A          PRINT #DBWin2,"Enter a command (Fwd,Back,Srch,Upd,Add,Quit): "
               ;
00C2          GET #DBWin2,c
00CC          CmdNum:=(SUBSTR(c,cmds)+1)/2
00DE          ON CmdNum+1 GOSUB 100,200,300,400,500,600,700
0104        UNTIL CmdNum=6
010F        END
0111
0112 100    REM No such command
0127        RETURN
0129 200    REM Forward
0136        PRINT #DBWin2,"wd";
0142        RUN DBFwd(DBPath,subset)
0151        RUN DBReDisp(subset,DBWin1)
0160        RETURN
0162 300    REM Backward
0170        PRINT #DBWin2,"ack";
017D        RUN DBBack(DBPath,subset)
018C        RUN DBReDisp(subset,DBWin1)
019B        RETURN
019D 400    REM Search
01A9        PRINT #DBWin2,"rch";
01B6        RUN DBSrch(DBPath,DBWin2,subset)
01CA        RUN DBReDisp(subset,DBWin1)
01D9        RETURN
01DB 500    REM Update
01E7        PRINT #DBWin2,"pd";
01F3        RUN DBUpd(DBWin2,subset)
0202        RUN DBDispRec(subset(1),DBWin1)
0213        RETURN
```

```
Ø215 6ØØ   REM Add
Ø21E       PRINT #DBWin2,"dd";
Ø22A       RUN DBAdd(DBPath,DBWin2,subset)
Ø23E       RUN DBReDisp(subset,DBWin1)
Ø24D       RETURN
Ø24F 7ØØ   REM Quit
Ø259       PRINT #DBWin2,"uit";
Ø266       RETURN
PROCEDURE DBClose
ØØØØ       PARAM DBPath,DBWin1,DBWin2:INTEGER
ØØØF
ØØ1Ø       RUN gfx2(DBWin1,"dwend")
ØØ22       RUN gfx2(DBWin2,"dwend")
ØØ34       RUN gfx2("select")
ØØ42       CLOSE #DBWin1,#DBWin2
ØØ4D       CLOSE #DBPath
ØØ53       END
PROCEDURE DBDispRec
ØØØØ       TYPE record=start:INTEGER; key:STRING[32]; text(5):STRING[69
            ]
ØØ26       PARAM subset:record
ØØ2F       PARAM DBWin1:INTEGER
ØØ36
ØØ37       DIM i:INTEGER
ØØ3E
ØØ3F       RUN gfx2(DBWin1,"clear")
ØØ51       PRINT #DBWin1,"<"; subset.key; ">"
ØØ66       FOR j:=1 TO 4
ØØ78         PRINT #DBWin1,subset.text(j)
ØØ89       NEXT j
ØØ94       PRINT #DBWin1,subset.text(5);
ØØA4       END
PROCEDURE DBDisplay
ØØØØ       TYPE record=start:INTEGER; key:STRING[32]; text(5):STRING[69
            ]
ØØ26       PARAM subset(1Ø):record
ØØ34       PARAM DBWin1:INTEGER
ØØ3B
ØØ3C       DIM i:INTEGER
ØØ43
ØØ44       FOR i:=1Ø TO 1 STEP -1
ØØ5A         RUN gfx2(DBWin1,"owset",1,1Ø-i,1Ø-i,69,6,MOD(i,7)+1,MOD(i
               ,8))
ØØ94         RUN DBDispRec(subset(i),DBWin1)
ØØA6       NEXT i
ØØB1       END
PROCEDURE DBBack
ØØØØ       TYPE record=Start:INTEGER; key:STRING[32]; text(5):STRING[69
            ]
ØØ26       PARAM Path:INTEGER
ØØ2D       PARAM subset(1Ø):record
ØØ3B
ØØ3C       DIM i,errno:INTEGER
```

```
 0047
 0048      IF subset(1).Start>1 THEN
 0059        FOR i:=10 TO 2 STEP -1
 006F          subset(i):=subset(i-1)
 0081        NEXT i
 008C        RUN DBGetRec(Path,subset(1).Start-1,subset(1))
 00A9      ENDIF
 00AB      END
PROCEDURE DBSrch
 0000      TYPE record=Start:INTEGER; key:STRING[32]; text(5):STRING[69
            ]
 0026      PARAM Path:INTEGER
 002D      PARAM Win:INTEGER
 0034      PARAM subset(10):record
 0042
 0043      DIM SKey:STRING[32]
 004F      DIM keyloc:INTEGER
 0056      DIM c:STRING[1]
 0062
 0063      PRINT #Win
 0069      INPUT #Win,"Search key: ",SKey
 0082      RUN DBSrchSet(subset,SKey,keyloc)
 0096      IF keyloc<>0 THEN
 00A2        RUN LShiftSet(subset,keyloc-1)
 00B3        RUN FillSet(Path,subset,keyloc-1)
 00C9      ELSE
 00CD        RUN DBSrchFile(Path,SKey,keyloc)
 00E1        IF keyloc<>0 THEN
 00ED          RUN DBGetRec(Path,keyloc,subset(1))
 0103          RUN FillSet(Path,subset,9)
 0115        ELSE
 0119          PRINT #Win,"Key not found"
 012F          PRINT #Win,"Press any key to continue"
 0151          GET #Win,c
 015B        ENDIF
 015D      ENDIF
 015F      END
PROCEDURE DBUpd
 0000      TYPE record=Start:INTEGER; key:STRING[32]; text(5):STRING[69
            ]
 0026      PARAM Win:INTEGER
 002D      PARAM subset(10):record
 003B
 003C      DIM Path2:INTEGER
 0043
 0044      RUN DBEditRec(Win,subset(1))
 0055      OPEN #Path2,"DBFile":WRITE
 0066      SEEK #Path2,SIZE(Win)+SIZE(subset(1))*(subset(1).Start-1)
 0086      PUT #Path2,subset(1)
 0093      CLOSE #Path2
 0099      END
PROCEDURE DBFwd
 0000      TYPE record=Start:INTEGER; key:STRING[32]; text(5):STRING[69
```

```
            ]
ØØ26        PARAM Path:INTEGER
ØØ2D        PARAM subset(1Ø):record
ØØ3B
ØØ3C        RUN LShiftSet(subset,1)
ØØ49        RUN DBGetRec(Path,subset(1Ø).Start+1,subset(1Ø))
ØØ66        END
PROCEDURE DBReDisp
ØØØØ        TYPE record=key:STRING[32]; text(5):STRING[69]
ØØ2Ø        PARAM subset(1Ø):record
ØØ2E        PARAM DBWin:INTEGER
ØØ35
ØØ36        DIM i:INTEGER
ØØ3D
ØØ3E        FOR i:=1 TO 1Ø
ØØ4E          RUN gfx2(DBWin,"owend")
ØØ6Ø        NEXT i
ØØ6B        RUN DBDisplay(subset,DBWin)
ØØ7A        END
PROCEDURE DBAdd
ØØØØ        TYPE record=Start:INTEGER; key:STRING[32]; text(5):STRING[69
            ]
ØØ26        PARAM Path:INTEGER
ØØ2D        PARAM Win:INTEGER
ØØ34        PARAM subset(1Ø):record
ØØ42
ØØ43        DIM i:INTEGER
ØØ4A        DIM rec:record
ØØ53        DIM Path2:INTEGER
ØØ5A        DIM filesize:INTEGER
ØØ61
ØØ62        RUN DBEditRec(Win,rec)
ØØ71        GET #Path,filesize
ØØ7B        SEEK #Path,Ø
ØØ84        OPEN #Path2,"DBFile":WRITE
ØØ95        filesize:=filesize+SIZE(rec)
ØØA3        rec.Start:=(filesize-SIZE(filesize))/SIZE(rec)
ØØBB        PUT #Path2,filesize
ØØC5
ØØC6        SEEK #Path2,filesize-SIZE(rec)
ØØD6        PUT #Path2,rec
ØØEØ        FOR i:=1 TO 1Ø
ØØFØ        EXITIF subset(i).Start=rec.Start THEN
Ø1Ø6          subset(i):=rec
Ø112        ENDEXIT
Ø116        NEXT i
Ø121        CLOSE #Path2
Ø127        END
PROCEDURE LShiftSet
ØØØØ        TYPE record=Start:INTEGER; key:STRING[32]; text(5):STRING[69
            ]
ØØ26        PARAM subset(1Ø):record
ØØ34        PARAM Shift:INTEGER
ØØ3B
```

```
 003C       DIM i:INTEGER
 0043
 0044       FOR i:=1 TO 10-Shift
 0058         subset(i):=subset(i+Shift)
 006B       NEXT i
 0076       END
PROCEDURE FillSet
 0000       TYPE record=Start:INTEGER; key:STRING[32]; text(5):STRING[69
             ]
 0026       PARAM Path:INTEGER
 002D       PARAM subset(10):record
 003B       PARAM Num:INTEGER
 0042
 0043       DIM i,Mark:INTEGER
 004E
 004F       IF Num=10 THEN
 005B         Mark:=1
 0062       ELSE
 0066         Mark:=subset(10-Num).Start+1
 007A       ENDIF
 007C       FOR i:=11-Num TO 10
 0090         RUN DBGetRec(Path,Mark,subset(i))
 00A7         Mark:=Mark+1
 00B2       NEXT i
 00BD       END
PROCEDURE DBSrchSet
 0000       TYPE record=Start:INTEGER; key:STRING[32]; text(5):STRING[69
             ]
 0026       PARAM subset(10):record
 0034       PARAM SKey:STRING[32]
 0040       PARAM keyloc:INTEGER
 0047
 0048       DIM i:INTEGER
 004F
 0050       FOR i:=1 TO 10
 0060         keyloc:=SUBSTR(SKey,subset(i).key)
 0072       EXITIF keyloc<>0 THEN
 007E         keyloc:=i
 0086       ENDEXIT
 008A       NEXT i
 0095       END
PROCEDURE DBSrchFile
 0000       TYPE record=Start:INTEGER; key:STRING[32]; text(5):STRING[69
             ]
 0026       PARAM Path:INTEGER
 002D       PARAM SKey:STRING[32]
 0039       PARAM KeyLoc:INTEGER
 0040
 0041       DIM rec:record
 004A
 004B       KeyLoc:=0
 0052       SEEK #Path,SIZE(KeyLoc)
 005E       ON ERROR GOTO 100
```

```
0064       GET #Path,rec
006E       WHILE NOT(EOF(#Path)) DO
0079       EXITIF SUBSTR(SKey,rec.key)<>0 THEN
008C         KeyLoc:=rec.Start
0097       ENDEXIT
009B         GET #Path,rec
00A5       ENDWHILE
00A9 100   SEEK #Path,0
00B5       END
PROCEDURE DBGetRec
0000       TYPE record=Start:INTEGER; key:STRING[32]; text(5):STRING[69
            ]
0026       PARAM Path:INTEGER
002D       PARAM RecNo:INTEGER
0034       PARAM rec:record
003D
003E       DIM i:INTEGER
0045
0046       ON ERROR GOTO 100
004C       SEEK #Path,SIZE(RecNo)+(RecNo-1)*SIZE(rec)
0065       GET #Path,rec
006F       SEEK #Path,0
0078       END
007A
007B 100   REM No such record
008F       ON ERROR
0092       rec.key:="_____"
00A2       rec.Start:=RecNo
00AE       FOR i:=1 TO 5
00BE         rec.text(i):=""
00CC       NEXT i
00D7       SEEK #Path,0
00E0       END
PROCEDURE DBEditRec
0000       TYPE record=Start:INTEGER; Key:STRING[32]; text(5):STRING[69
            ]
0026       PARAM Win:INTEGER
002D       PARAM rec:record
0036
0037       DIM i:INTEGER
003E
003F       RUN gfx2(Win,"clear")
0051       INPUT #Win,"Key: ",rec.Key
0067       FOR i:=1 TO 5
0077         INPUT #Win,"Text line: ",rec.text(i)
0096       NEXT i
00A1       END
```

CHAPTER 16

let your coco twiddle its thumbs

Note: The programs in this chapter are designed for a full-sized, type 07 window. They can be modified for other window sizes and types, but as written, they will only work correctly for one window size and type.

Some people say that switching your computer on and off puts more wear on it than just constantly leaving it on. This could be an old wives' tale, or it could be a rumor started by cathode ray tube (the screen on your computer) manufacturers. If you leave your monitor on with your computer, you may find the phosphor (the stuff that makes the screen light up) burnt through in places where the same thing is displayed for long periods.

If you protect your phosphor by turning your monitor off or turning its brightness way down, you can't tell that your computer is on. You are likely to walk up to your machine and push its power switch to turn it on. We need a way for a Color Computer to show that it is alive and well (and on) without damaging its monitor. The CoCo should be able to sit around for days "twiddling its thumbs" in some noticeable way.

Some people whistle "tunelessly" when they have nothing to do. This sounds like a harmless way for a computer to spend idle time if you keep it in a private place. A quick listen will tell you if it is running. If you use an intercom as an electronic baby sitter, you can keep an ear on your machine from anywhere in your house. The noise of the computer whistling might keep you awake, but it certainly won't burn out the phosphor on the monitor.

If endearing little noises from your computer might disturb someone, we will have to invent another harmless trick. Perhaps a program that keeps something on the screen without damaging the phosphor. Our plan is to put a small image on the darkened screen and keep it moving around. No part of the screen will get abused because the image will never stay in one place for long, but the moving image will make it clear that the machine is running.

We are about to write two programs, one that makes little noises and one that keeps a nondamaging display on the monitor. For the suspenders-and-belt types, OS-9 would be happy to run both programs at the same time — the low-key equivalent of a siren and flashing lights.

SAVING THE OLD COLORS

Both programs will start by darkening the screen. Protecting the phosphor is their official reason for existence and the only way to meet that goal is to keep the screen black — mostly. Darkening the screen is not hard; putting the colors back afterward is another story. Letting the programs leave the screen dark when they finish would be a solution, but it would be seriously hostile behavior. That would be unacceptable. We want to create friendly programs.

Selecting a new device window with black borders and background would be a simple way to darken the screen, but we can't use any of the standard device windows by name. The "wild card" device window, /w, will give us an idle device window if there is one, but in a very busy system, all the device windows may be in use.

Overlay windows may offer a way out of our quandary. The windowing system creates new overlay windows whenever it needs them. They can preserve the screen that they cover; they can even select their own foreground and background colors from the underlying window's palette. They can't change the border color or use a color that isn't in the palette.

It won't be easy to use overlay windows. If black isn't in the palette, we will have to put black in a palette register. The color that was in that register will be gone. If the border isn't black, we'll have to change the border color. There's no direct way to save the old border color or palette, but we must save them if we mean to restore the screen to its original state.

Although there is no BASIC09 function or statement that will return the palette or border color to a program, there is a general-purpose function that we can appeal to when things look desperate. SysCall is the magic procedure. It gives BASIC09 programs direct access to OS-9. This direct access to OS-9 makes SysCall a powerful and dangerous tool.

OS-9 knows the palette and border color on a screen, and it will reveal them to any program that knows how to ask. The following BASIC09 procedure calls SysCall, which forwards two I$GetStat system calls to OS-9. The first GetStat gets the contents of the palette registers, and the second one gets the palette register numbers for the three standard screen colors: foreground, background and border.

THE LISTING: GetPalette

```
PROCEDURE GetPalette
 0000      PARAM Palette(16):BYTE
 000C      PARAM Selections(3):BYTE
 0018      TYPE registers=cc,a,b,dp:BYTE; x,y,u:INTEGER
 003D      DIM regs:registers
 0046      DIM code:BYTE
 004D      code:=$8D
 0055      regs.a:=1
 0060      regs.b:=$91
 006C      regs.x:=ADDR(Palette)
 007A      RUN syscall(code,regs)
 0089      regs.b:=$96
 0095      RUN syscall(code,regs)
 00A4      Selections(1):=regs.a \REM Forground palette register
 00CF      Selections(2):=regs.b \REM background palette register
 00FB      Selections(3):=LAND(regs.x,$FF) \REM border palette register
 0127      END
```

Once we have a copy of the palette and border color, we can change the screen colors as we see fit and restore the original values any time we like.

HUMMING TO ITSELF

We want to write a procedure that makes your computer darken the screen and make random quiet noises until the user presses a key. When a key is pressed, the procedure should restore the screen to its original state and return to its caller.

Let's start by outlining the procedure. We won't worry about details yet, just the high-level flow.

- Save the current colors
- Darken the screen
- Repeat
- Make a random noise
- Check for a key press
- Until a key is pressed
- Restore the original colors

Is that the whole thing? Probably. It contains the steps that generate the desired result: darken, generate noise, restore the screen.

The first step isn't as obvious as the other ones. It is implied by the last step. If we are going to restore the colors, we must have saved them.

Now let's look at the outline, line by line. We'll be ready to code the procedure when we're done.

We already talked about saving the current colors. Since we just wrote a procedure that gets the information from OS-9, all we need to do is call the procedure and save the values it returns.

If we planned to clear the screen or even write something on it, we would have to open an overlay window. We can ask OS-9 to save the data under an overlay window and restore it when the window is closed. In this case we don't need that kind of help. We're just going to make noises. We don't plan to write anything on the screen. Whatever is on the screen will disappear when we darken the screen, but we aren't going to erase it, just adjust the palette so all colors are displayed as black.

Since the colors on the screen are controlled by palette registers, we can turn them black by making all the palette registers code for black (the code for black is 0). There may be as many as 16 or as few as two palette registers in use, but we'll ignore that. We saved all 16, so we may as well zero them all. The `gfx2 palette` function is the tool we need. The code will look something like:

```
FOR i:=0 to 15
    RUN gfx2("palette",i,0)
NEXT i
```

The next step in the outline requires us to find a way to make a random noise (well, get the computer to make a random noise). Only one way to make noise is documented in the BASIC09 manual, the `bell` function of `gfx2`. The bell function makes a noise with a fixed pitch, volume and duration. Not enough for random noises. We are forced to use the `SysCall` procedure again.

Looking through the OS-9 technical manual we find `SS.Tone SetStat`. It gets OS-9 to make a noise and lets us specify pitch, volume and duration. It doesn't let us change the timbre (character) of the note, but it's the best we can find.

Random values to describe tones can be generated by the BASIC09 RND function. We'll use it three times for each sound to give a duration, volume and frequency. The technical manual gives the range of values it will accept for each parameter. These values should be:

Duration (length)	0 to 255
Amplitude (loudness)	0 to 63
Frequency (frequency)	1 to 4095

We want short, quiet beeps. You can modify the values to your taste, but the following ranges are a good starting point:

Duration	0 to 40
Amplitude	0 to 20
Frequency	1 to 4095

The description of `SS.Tone` tells us to squeeze duration and amplitude into one integer-sized register. To get a small number into the MSB (Most Significant Byte) of an integer, we multiply it by 256. We'll calculate the value for the X register like this:

```
regs.x := duration+volume*256
```

After the procedure makes a noise, it should check for a key press. We can't just read a character: That would make the procedure wait quietly for input. We have to use the `Inkey` procedure. It will return a character if there is any input. If there is no input, `Inkey` won't wait; it just returns an empty string.

The loop that keeps the procedure whistling will keep going until `Inkey` gets something other than an empty string.

When the loop exits, the procedure should restore the color information it changed. The procedure darkens the screen by zeroing all the palette registers, so we have to set all the palette registers back to their saved values.

Now that we understand the problem, it is easy to convert the solution into BASIC09. Here's what it looks like:

THE LISTING: `Hummer`

```
PROCEDURE Hummer
 0000      TYPE registers=cc,a,b,dp:BYTE; x,y,u:INTEGER
 0025      DIM key:STRING[1]
 0031      DIM regs:registers
 003A      DIM callcode:INTEGER
 0041      DIM note:INTEGER
 0048      DIM volume:INTEGER
 004F      DIM frequency:INTEGER
 0056      DIM duration:INTEGER
 005D      DIM Palette(16):BYTE
 0069      DIM Selections(3):BYTE
 0075      DIM i:INTEGER
 007C      BASE 0
 007E
 007F      (* Save the current palette and install a palette
 00B0      (* all full of black.
 00C5      RUN GetPalette(Palette,Selections)
```

```
00D4      FOR i:=0 TO 15
00E4        RUN gfx2("palette",i,0)
00FB      NEXT i
0106
0107      (* Set the values for syscall that
012A      (* won't change in the repeat loop
014C      callcode=$8E
0154      regs.b:=$98
0160      regs.a:=1
016B
016C      REPEAT
016E        (* Pick a random duration, volume, and pitch for the
01A2        (* next note.
01AF        duration:=RND(40)
01B9        volume:=RND(20)
01C3        frequency:=RND(4094)+1
01D2        regs.x:=duration+256*volume
01E6        regs.y:=frequency
01F2        RUN syscall(callcode,regs)
0201        (* Keep looping until the user hits a key
022A        RUN inkey(key)
0234      UNTIL key<>""
023F
0240      (* Restore the palette registers
0260      FOR i:=0 TO 15
0270        RUN gfx2("palette",i,Palette(i))
028C      NEXT i
0297      END
```

A TERMINAL ON A TERMINAL

You have to keep the same display on a screen for days before it will burn into the screen. Keeping a fixed image on the screen for seconds, or even for hours, will do no harm. We will write a program that shows the computer is running by displaying a small image moving around on the screen. The motion is good for the screen, and it makes it clear that the computer is running well.

We are not artists, so we will use a cartoon picture of what we see in front of us, a Color Computer, a monitor and a mouse.

There are two easy ways to draw a picture on the screen. We could use the drawing commands, mostly `Line` and `Fill`. It's easy to draw with these commands, but not fast. It is faster to load an image into an image buffer and `PUT` it on the screen. We'll do it the fast way.

An image has to be constructed before it can be put into an image buffer. We could construct the picture by drawing it with graphics functions (`Lines`, `Circles` and so forth) and copy it from the screen to a buffer. That is the easy and sensible way to do it, but just for fun, we'll do it another way. It is possible to define the picture in a buffer one dot at a time. That's what we'll do.

We have a picture something like this in mind: 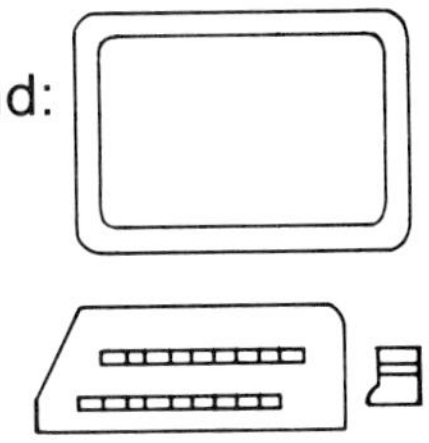

The first step in converting this into an image for the Color Computer is to draw the picture with X's.

```
________XXXXXXXXXXXXXXXXXXXXXXXXXXXXXX__
________XXXXXXXXXXXXXXXXXXXXXXXXXXXXXX__
________XXXXXXXXXXXXXXXXXXXXXXXXXXXXXX__
________XXXXXXXXXXXXXXXXXXXXXXXXXXXXXX__
________XXXXXXXXXXXXXXXXXXXXXXXXXXXXXX__
________XXXXXXXXXXXXXXXXXXXXXXXXXXXXXX__
________XXXXXXXXXXXXXXXXXXXXXXXXXXXXXX__
________XXXXXXXXXXXXXXXXXXXXXXXXXXXXXX__
________XXXXXXXXXXXXXXXXXXXXXXXXXXXXXX__
________XXXXXXXXXXXXXXXXXXXXXXXXXXXXXX__
________XXXXXXXXXXXXXXXXXXXXXXXXXXXXXX__
________________________________________
________________________________________
________XXXXXXXXXXXXXXXXXXXXXXX_________
_______XXXXXXXXXXXXXXXXXXXXXXXXX________
______XXXX__XX__XX__XX__XX__XXXX___XXXX_
_____XXXXXXXXXXXXXXXXXXXXXXXXXXX___XXXX_
____XXXX__XX__XX__XX__XX__XXXXXX__XXXXX_
____XXXXXXXXXXXXXXXXXXXXXXXXXXXX________
```

An icon of a Color Computer should be in color. Four colors should be enough: black, white, green and red. Now we need to redraw the picture with codes for the colors. The underscores and X's will serve for black and white. We'll add asterisks for green and dollar signs for red.

```
________XXXXXXXXXXXXXXXXXXXXXXXXXXXXXX__
________XXXXXXXXXXXXXXXXXXXXXXXXXXXXXX__
________XX**************************XX__
________XX**************************XX__
________XX**************************XX__
________XX**************************XX__
________XX**************************XX__
________XX**************************XX__
________XX**************************XX__
________XXXXXXXXXXXXXXXXXXXXXXXXXXXXXX__
________XXXXXXXXXXXXXXXXXXXXXXXXXXXXXX__
________________________________________
________________________________________
________XXXXXXXXXXXXXXXXXXXXXXX_________
_______XXXXXXXXXXXXXXXXXXXXXXXXX________
______XXXX__XX__XX__XX__XX__X$XX___$$$$_
_____XXXXXXXXXXXXXXXXXXXXXXXXXXX___XXXX_
____XXXX__XX__XX__XX__XX__XXXXXX__XXXXX_
____XXXXXXXXXXXXXXXXXXXXXXXXXXXX________
```

This picture has to be converted into numbers that the Color Computer can understand. Since we will be using four colors, each point (called a picture element or pixel) in the image will need two bits.

TABLE 16-A: Pixel Storage

2-color	1 bit per pixel	8 pixels per byte
4-color	2 bits per pixel	4 pixels per byte
16-color	4 bits per pixel	2 pixels per byte

The two-bit number for each pixel in a four-color image will hold the number of the palette register for that pixel's color.

The next step is to convert the picture to bits. For this we will need to know which palette register will go with which color. It's up to us, so let's assign them this way:

Register	Color
0	black
1	white
2	green
3	red

Now we have to recode the colors in the picture.

- Each _ will become 00 (binary 0)
- Each X will become 01 (binary 1)
- Each * will become 10 (binary 2)
- Each $ will become 11 (binary 3)

```
ØØØØØØØØØØØØØØØØØ1Ø1Ø1Ø1Ø1Ø1Ø1Ø1Ø1Ø1Ø1Ø1Ø1Ø1Ø1Ø1Ø1Ø1Ø1Ø1Ø1Ø1Ø1Ø1Ø1Ø1Ø1Ø1Ø1Ø1Ø1Ø1Ø1ØØØØ
ØØØØØØØØØØØØØØØØØ1Ø1Ø1Ø1Ø1Ø1Ø1Ø1Ø1Ø1Ø1Ø1Ø1Ø1Ø1Ø1Ø1Ø1Ø1Ø1Ø1Ø1Ø1Ø1Ø1Ø1Ø1Ø1Ø1Ø1Ø1Ø1Ø1ØØØØ
ØØØØØØØØØØØØØØØØØ1Ø11Ø1Ø1Ø1Ø1Ø1Ø1Ø1Ø1Ø1Ø1Ø1Ø1Ø1Ø1Ø1Ø1Ø1Ø1Ø1Ø1Ø1Ø1Ø1Ø1Ø1Ø1Ø1Ø1Ø1ØØ1Ø1ØØØØ
ØØØØØØØØØØØØØØØØØ1Ø11Ø1Ø1Ø1Ø1Ø1Ø1Ø1Ø1Ø1Ø1Ø1Ø1Ø1Ø1Ø1Ø1Ø1Ø1Ø1Ø1Ø1Ø1Ø1Ø1Ø1Ø1Ø1Ø1Ø1ØØ1Ø1ØØØØ
ØØØØØØØØØØØØØØØØØ1Ø11Ø1Ø1Ø1Ø1Ø1Ø1Ø1Ø1Ø1Ø1Ø1Ø1Ø1Ø1Ø1Ø1Ø1Ø1Ø1Ø1Ø1Ø1Ø1Ø1Ø1Ø1Ø1Ø1Ø1ØØ1Ø1ØØØØ
ØØØØØØØØØØØØØØØØØ1Ø11Ø1Ø1Ø1Ø1Ø1Ø1Ø1Ø1Ø1Ø1Ø1Ø1Ø1Ø1Ø1Ø1Ø1Ø1Ø1Ø1Ø1Ø1Ø1Ø1Ø1Ø1Ø1Ø1Ø1ØØ1Ø1ØØØØ
ØØØØØØØØØØØØØØØØØ1Ø11Ø1Ø1Ø1Ø1Ø1Ø1Ø1Ø1Ø1Ø1Ø1Ø1Ø1Ø1Ø1Ø1Ø1Ø1Ø1Ø1Ø1Ø1Ø1Ø1Ø1Ø1Ø1Ø1Ø1ØØ1Ø1ØØØØ
ØØØØØØØØØØØØØØØØØ1Ø11Ø1Ø1Ø1Ø1Ø1Ø1Ø1Ø1Ø1Ø1Ø1Ø1Ø1Ø1Ø1Ø1Ø1Ø1Ø1Ø1Ø1Ø1Ø1Ø1Ø1Ø1Ø1Ø1Ø1ØØ1Ø1ØØØØ
ØØØØØØØØØØØØØØØØØ1Ø11Ø1Ø1Ø1Ø1Ø1Ø1Ø1Ø1Ø1Ø1Ø1Ø1Ø1Ø1Ø1Ø1Ø1Ø1Ø1Ø1Ø1Ø1Ø1Ø1Ø1Ø1Ø1Ø1Ø1ØØ1Ø1ØØØØ
ØØØØØØØØØØØØØØØØØ1Ø1Ø1Ø1Ø1Ø1Ø1Ø1Ø1Ø1Ø1Ø1Ø1Ø1Ø1Ø1Ø1Ø1Ø1Ø1Ø1Ø1Ø1Ø1Ø1Ø1Ø1Ø1Ø1Ø1Ø1Ø1Ø1ØØØØ
ØØØØØØØØØØØØØØØØØ1Ø1Ø1Ø1Ø1Ø1Ø1Ø1Ø1Ø1Ø1Ø1Ø1Ø1Ø1Ø1Ø1Ø1Ø1Ø1Ø1Ø1Ø1Ø1Ø1Ø1Ø1Ø1Ø1Ø1Ø1Ø1Ø1ØØØØ
ØØØØØØØØØØØØØØØØØØØØØØØØØØØØØØØØØØØØØØØØØØØØØØØØØØØØØØØØØØØØØØØØØØØØØØØØØØØØØØØØØØØØØØ
ØØØØØØØØØØØØØØØØØØØØØØØØØØØØØØØØØØØØØØØØØØØØØØØØØØØØØØØØØØØØØØØØØØØØØØØØØØØØØØØØØØØØØØ
ØØØØØØØØØØØØØØØØØ1Ø1Ø1Ø1Ø1Ø1Ø1Ø1Ø1Ø1Ø1Ø1Ø1Ø1Ø1Ø1Ø1Ø1Ø1Ø1Ø1Ø1Ø1Ø1Ø1Ø1ØØØØØØØØØØØØØØØØØØ
ØØØØØØØØØØØØØØØ1Ø1Ø1Ø1Ø1Ø1Ø1Ø1Ø1Ø1Ø1Ø1Ø1Ø1Ø1Ø1Ø1Ø1Ø1Ø1Ø1Ø1Ø1Ø1Ø1Ø1Ø1Ø1Ø1ØØØØØØØØØØØØØØØØ
ØØØØØØØØØØØØØ1Ø1Ø1Ø1ØØØØØ1Ø1ØØØØØ1Ø1ØØØØØ1Ø1ØØØØØ1Ø1ØØØØØ1Ø1ØØØØØ111Ø1Ø1ØØØØØØ11111111ØØ
ØØØØØØØØØØØ1Ø1Ø1Ø1Ø1Ø1Ø1Ø1Ø1Ø1Ø1Ø1Ø1Ø1Ø1Ø1Ø1Ø1Ø1Ø1Ø1Ø1Ø1Ø1Ø1Ø1Ø1Ø1Ø1Ø1Ø1Ø1ØØØØØØØ1Ø1Ø1Ø1ØØ
ØØØØØØØØØ1Ø1Ø1Ø1ØØØØØ1Ø1ØØØØØ1Ø1ØØØØØ1Ø1ØØØØØ1Ø1ØØØØØ1Ø1ØØØØØ1Ø1Ø1Ø1Ø1Ø1ØØØØØ1Ø1Ø1Ø1Ø1ØØ
ØØØØØØØØØ1Ø1Ø1Ø1Ø1Ø1Ø1Ø1Ø1Ø1Ø1Ø1Ø1Ø1Ø1Ø1Ø1Ø1Ø1Ø1Ø1Ø1Ø1Ø1Ø1Ø1Ø1Ø1Ø1Ø1Ø1Ø1ØØØØØØØØØØØØØØØØ
```

Now we need to break all that binary data into byte-size chunks and convert the chunks out of binary. BASIC09 understands numbers in decimal or hexadecimal. It's easy to convert binary to hexadecimal, so we'll aim for that. A byte contains eight bits so we'll break the image into eight-bit columns:

```
ØØØØØØØØ ØØØØØØØØ Ø1Ø1Ø1Ø1 Ø1Ø1Ø1Ø1 Ø1Ø1Ø1Ø1 Ø1Ø1Ø1Ø1 Ø1Ø1Ø1Ø1 Ø1Ø1Ø1Ø1 Ø1Ø1Ø1Ø1 Ø1Ø1ØØØØ
ØØØØØØØØ ØØØØØØØØ Ø1Ø1Ø1Ø1 Ø1Ø1Ø1Ø1 Ø1Ø1Ø1Ø1 Ø1Ø1Ø1Ø1 Ø1Ø1Ø1Ø1 Ø1Ø1Ø1Ø1 Ø1Ø1Ø1Ø1 Ø1Ø1ØØØØ
ØØØØØØØØ ØØØØØØØØ Ø1Ø11Ø1Ø 1Ø1Ø1Ø1Ø 1Ø1Ø1Ø1Ø 1Ø1Ø1Ø1Ø 1Ø1Ø1Ø1Ø 1Ø1Ø1Ø1Ø 1Ø1Ø1Ø1Ø Ø1Ø1ØØØØ
ØØØØØØØØ ØØØØØØØØ Ø1Ø11Ø1Ø 1Ø1Ø1Ø1Ø 1Ø1Ø1Ø1Ø 1Ø1Ø1Ø1Ø 1Ø1Ø1Ø1Ø 1Ø1Ø1Ø1Ø 1Ø1Ø1Ø1Ø Ø1Ø1ØØØØ
ØØØØØØØØ ØØØØØØØØ Ø1Ø11Ø1Ø 1Ø1Ø1Ø1Ø 1Ø1Ø1Ø1Ø 1Ø1Ø1Ø1Ø 1Ø1Ø1Ø1Ø 1Ø1Ø1Ø1Ø 1Ø1Ø1Ø1Ø Ø1Ø1ØØØØ
ØØØØØØØØ ØØØØØØØØ Ø1Ø11Ø1Ø 1Ø1Ø1Ø1Ø 1Ø1Ø1Ø1Ø 1Ø1Ø1Ø1Ø 1Ø1Ø1Ø1Ø 1Ø1Ø1Ø1Ø 1Ø1Ø1Ø1Ø Ø1Ø1ØØØØ
ØØØØØØØØ ØØØØØØØØ Ø1Ø11Ø1Ø 1Ø1Ø1Ø1Ø 1Ø1Ø1Ø1Ø 1Ø1Ø1Ø1Ø 1Ø1Ø1Ø1Ø 1Ø1Ø1Ø1Ø 1Ø1Ø1Ø1Ø Ø1Ø1ØØØØ
ØØØØØØØØ ØØØØØØØØ Ø1Ø11Ø1Ø 1Ø1Ø1Ø1Ø 1Ø1Ø1Ø1Ø 1Ø1Ø1Ø1Ø 1Ø1Ø1Ø1Ø 1Ø1Ø1Ø1Ø 1Ø1Ø1Ø1Ø Ø1Ø1ØØØØ
ØØØØØØØØ ØØØØØØØØ Ø1Ø11Ø1Ø 1Ø1Ø1Ø1Ø 1Ø1Ø1Ø1Ø 1Ø1Ø1Ø1Ø 1Ø1Ø1Ø1Ø 1Ø1Ø1Ø1Ø 1Ø1Ø1Ø1Ø Ø1Ø1ØØØØ
ØØØØØØØØ ØØØØØØØØ Ø1Ø1Ø1Ø1 Ø1Ø1Ø1Ø1 Ø1Ø1Ø1Ø1 Ø1Ø1Ø1Ø1 Ø1Ø1Ø1Ø1 Ø1Ø1Ø1Ø1 Ø1Ø1Ø1Ø1 Ø1Ø1ØØØØ
ØØØØØØØØ ØØØØØØØØ Ø1Ø1Ø1Ø1 Ø1Ø1Ø1Ø1 Ø1Ø1Ø1Ø1 Ø1Ø1Ø1Ø1 Ø1Ø1Ø1Ø1 Ø1Ø1Ø1Ø1 Ø1Ø1Ø1Ø1 Ø1Ø1ØØØØ
ØØØØØØØØ ØØØØØØØØ ØØØØØØØØ ØØØØØØØØ ØØØØØØØØ ØØØØØØØØ ØØØØØØØØ ØØØØØØØØ ØØØØØØØØ ØØØØØØØØ
ØØØØØØØØ ØØØØØØØØ ØØØØØØØØ ØØØØØØØØ ØØØØØØØØ ØØØØØØØØ ØØØØØØØØ ØØØØØØØØ ØØØØØØØØ ØØØØØØØØ
ØØØØØØØØ ØØØØØØØØ Ø1Ø1Ø1Ø1 Ø1Ø1Ø1Ø1 Ø1Ø1Ø1Ø1 Ø1Ø1Ø1Ø1 Ø1Ø1Ø1Ø1 Ø1Ø1Ø1ØØ ØØØØØØØØ ØØØØØØØØ
ØØØØØØØØ ØØØØØØØ1 Ø1Ø1Ø1Ø1 Ø1Ø1Ø1Ø1 Ø1Ø1Ø1Ø1 Ø1Ø1Ø1Ø1 Ø1Ø1Ø1Ø1 Ø1Ø1Ø1Ø1 ØØØØØØØØ ØØØØØØØØ
ØØØØØØØØ ØØØØØ1Ø1 Ø1Ø1ØØØØ Ø1Ø1ØØØØ Ø1Ø1ØØØØ Ø1Ø1ØØØØ Ø1Ø1ØØØØ Ø111Ø1Ø1 ØØØØØØ11 111111ØØ
ØØØØØØØØ ØØØ1Ø1Ø1 Ø1Ø1Ø1Ø1 Ø1Ø1Ø1Ø1 Ø1Ø1Ø1Ø1 Ø1Ø1Ø1Ø1 Ø1Ø1Ø1Ø1 Ø1Ø1Ø1Ø1 ØØØØØØØ1 Ø1Ø1Ø1ØØ
ØØØØØØØØ Ø1Ø1Ø1Ø1 ØØØØØ1Ø1 ØØØØØ1Ø1 ØØØØØ1Ø1 ØØØØØ1Ø1 ØØØØØ1Ø1 Ø1Ø1Ø1Ø1 ØØØØØ1Ø1 Ø1Ø1Ø1ØØ
ØØØØØØØØ Ø1Ø1Ø1Ø1 Ø1Ø1Ø1Ø1 Ø1Ø1Ø1Ø1 Ø1Ø1Ø1Ø1 Ø1Ø1Ø1Ø1 Ø1Ø1Ø1Ø1 Ø1Ø1Ø1Ø1 ØØØØØØØØ ØØØØØØØØ
```

Look at each byte as two four-bit groups, and translate the groups according to the following table:

TABLE 16-B: Hex Translation Table

Bits	Hex Character	Bits	Hex Character
0000	0	1000	8
0001	1	1001	9
0010	2	1010	A
0011	3	1011	B
0100	4	1100	C
0101	5	1101	D
0110	6	1110	E
0111	7	1111	F

This gives us:

```
ØØ ØØ 55 55 55 55 55 55 55 5Ø
ØØ ØØ 55 55 55 55 55 55 55 5Ø
ØØ ØØ 5A AA AA AA AA AA AA 5Ø
ØØ ØØ 5A AA AA AA AA AA AA 5Ø
ØØ ØØ 5A AA AA AA AA AA AA 5Ø
ØØ ØØ 5A AA AA AA AA AA AA 5Ø
ØØ ØØ 5A AA AA AA AA AA AA 5Ø
ØØ ØØ 5A AA AA AA AA AA AA 5Ø
ØØ ØØ 5A AA AA AA AA AA AA 5Ø
ØØ ØØ 55 55 55 55 55 55 55 5Ø
ØØ ØØ 55 55 55 55 55 55 55 5Ø
ØØ ØØ ØØ ØØ ØØ ØØ ØØ ØØ ØØ ØØ
ØØ ØØ ØØ ØØ ØØ ØØ ØØ ØØ ØØ ØØ
ØØ ØØ 55 55 55 55 55 54 ØØ ØØ
ØØ Ø1 55 55 55 55 55 55 ØØ ØØ
ØØ Ø5 5Ø 5Ø 5Ø 5Ø 5Ø 75 Ø3 FC
ØØ 15 55 55 55 55 55 55 Ø1 54
ØØ 55 Ø5 Ø5 Ø5 Ø5 Ø5 55 Ø5 54
ØØ 55 55 55 55 55 55 55 ØØ ØØ
```

And that's the table ready to go into BASIC09 Data statements. See the end of the chapter for a BASIC09 program that does most of this conversion.

We will continue with the procedure by doing an outline:

Save the screen information
Adjust the screen colors as necessary
Set up an image buffer for the CoCo image
Set up another image buffer to erase the CoCo
Repeat until a key is pressed
  put the CoCo image at a random location
  wait a moment
  erase the CoCo image
  see if a key has been pressed
Restore the old colors
Kill the image buffer

Saving the screen colors is tricky, but it's a solved problem. Luckily we even put the operation in its own procedure so we can simply call the GetPalette procedure to save the color information. The Hummer procedure didn't have to worry about saving the contents of the screen. It could make every color in the palette black and know that the screen was dark. This program will display an image on the screen so we can't make all the colors black!

The OS-9 windowing package includes a tool for saving the contents of a screen. If you start an overlay window over another window, the contents of the bottom window can be saved. We'll let OS-9 help us out here. The procedure will start an overlay window with the save switch on, and OS-9 will cover the current screen with a new overlay window. When we are done, OS-9 will put the original screen back.

Now we have to prepare the screen for the image. We will put the four colors we need in the first four palette registers, darken the screen borders, turn off the cursor and turn off "logic." Remembering to turn "logic" off is tricky — especially since most of the time it's not an issue. Normally, OS-9 writes things on the screen by just drawing them in the right spot. When "logic" is turned on, OS-9 has other ways of putting things on the screen. Those other ways can really mess us up, so we are careful to turn "logic" off in case some other program left it on.

The cartoon of a Color Computer has to go into an image buffer before we can ask OS-9 to display it on the screen. We will tell OS-9 that we want to load an image with the GPLoad gfx2 function and then send the bytes that define the buffer. We'll have to do the GPLoad trick again for the blank image that we'll use to erase the computer image.

The GPLoad function needs several arguments. The graphics

type of the images is four-color, high resolution. The images are 40 pixels wide by 19 pixels high, and they use 190 bytes. The buffer group and buffer number are a problem. We can code a constant group and number into the procedure, but it's a bad idea. We'll do it anyway, but in Chapter 17 we'll show you a better way.

The loop that jumps the image around on the screen should be almost like the main loop in Hummer. We need one extra trick. We want the image to pause for a moment at each position. There is a pause command in BASIC09, but it is not the command we want now. The BASIC09 pause command puts BASIC09 into Debug mode.

One reliable way to make BASIC09 hesitate is to give it a bunch of work to do. Running around an empty FOR loop about 10,000 times should take a noticeable interval.

When the REPEAT loop ends, we are almost done. We'll have to put the screen back the way we found it. We'll restore three things:

- The palette registers
- The border color
- The original contents of the screen

We'll use the gfx2 Palette function to restore the colors, the gfx2 Border function to restore the border color, and the gfx2 OWend command to close the overlay window we've been using and restore the old screen.

We don't actually need to kill the image buffer. The program will work perfectly without this step. It's just good practice for a program to clean up after itself as much as possible. The gfx2 function KillBuff will remove a buffer from the system.

Remember, using buffer group one was a temporary shortcut. What if some other program also wanted to use group one? We need a standard way to choose group numbers so programs won't interfere with each other. In the next chapter we'll show you a procedure, GetPid, which will generate more useful group numbers.

Here's what the procedure that bounces the CoCo around on its own screen looks like when you put it all together.

THE LISTING: BUSY

```
PROCEDURE busy
 0000      (*
 0003      (* Image data that (roughly) describes a cartoon of
 0036      (* a Color Computer with a monitor and a mouse.
 0065      (*
 0068      DATA $00,$00,$55,$55,$55,$55,$55,$55,$55,$50
 0094      DATA $00,$00,$55,$55,$55,$55,$55,$55,$55,$50
 00C0      DATA $00,$00,$5A,$AA,$AA,$AA,$AA,$AA,$AA,$50
 00EC      DATA $00,$00,$5A,$AA,$AA,$AA,$AA,$AA,$AA,$50
```

```
0118        DATA $00,$00,$5A,$AA,$AA,$AA,$AA,$AA,$AA,$50
0144        DATA $00,$00,$5A,$AA,$AA,$AA,$AA,$AA,$AA,$50
0170        DATA $00,$00,$5A,$AA,$AA,$AA,$AA,$AA,$AA,$50
019C        DATA $00,$00,$5A,$AA,$AA,$AA,$AA,$AA,$AA,$50
01C8        DATA $00,$00,$5A,$AA,$AA,$AA,$AA,$AA,$AA,$50
01F4        DATA $00,$00,$55,$55,$55,$55,$55,$55,$55,$50
0220        DATA $00,$00,$55,$55,$55,$55,$55,$55,$55,$50
024C        DATA $00,$00,$00,$00,$00,$00,$00,$00,$00,$00
0278        DATA $00,$00,$00,$00,$00,$00,$00,$00,$00,$00
02A4        DATA $00,$00,$55,$55,$55,$55,$55,$54,$00,$00
02D0        DATA $00,$01,$55,$55,$55,$55,$55,$55,$00,$00
02FC        DATA $00,$05,$50,$50,$50,$50,$50,$75,$03,$FC
0328        DATA $00,$15,$55,$55,$55,$55,$55,$55,$01,$54
0354        DATA $00,$55,$05,$05,$05,$05,$05,$55,$05,$54
0380        DATA $00,$55,$55,$55,$55,$55,$55,$55,$00,$00
03AC        (* End of image data
03C0
03C1        (* Variables
03CD        DIM Buffer:BYTE
03D4        DIM palette(16):BYTE
03E0        DIM Selections(3):BYTE
03EC        DIM i:INTECER
03F3        DIM x,y:INTEGER
03FE        DIM key:STRING[1]
040A        BASE 0
040C
040D
040E        (* Save the current palette and put up an overlay screen
0446        (* with the right colors for the display we want
0476        RUN GetPalette(palette,Selections)
0485        RUN gfx2("owset",1,0,0,80,24,0,0)
04A7        RUN gfx2("palette",0,$00)
04BD        RUN gfx2("palette",1,$3F)
04D3        RUN gfx2("palette",2,$12)
04E9        RUN gfx2("palette",3,$24)
04FF        RUN gfx2("border",0)
0510        RUN gfx2("curoff")
051E        RUN gfx2("logic","off")
0531
0532        (* Load the CoCo image and the blank image into
0561        (* image buffers
0571        RUN gfx2("gpload",1,1,7,40,19,190)
0591        FOR i:=0 TO 189
05A1          READ Buffer
05A6          PUT #1,Buffer
05AF        NEXT i
05BA        RUN gfx2("gpload",1,2,7,40,19,190)
05DA        Buffer:=0
05E1        FOR i:=0 TO 189
05F1          PUT #1,Buffer
05FA        NEXT i
0605
0606        REPEAT
```

```
0608         x:=RND(639-40)
0616         y:=RND(191-19)
0623         RUN gfx2("put",1,1,x,y)
063E         FOR i:=1 TO 10000
064F         NEXT i
065A         RUN gfx2("put",1,2,x,y)
0675         RUN inkey(key)
067F       UNTIL key<>""
068A
068B       (* Restore the old palette and close the overlay window
06C2       FOR i:=0 TO 15
06D2         RUN gfx2("palette",i,palette(i))
06EE       NEXT i
06F9       RUN gfx2("border",Selections(2))
070E       RUN gfx2("owend")
071B       END
```

The image buffer is designed for a four-color screen, and the random screen locations are generated for a 640-by-192 screen. If you don't run this procedure on a type 07 graphics window, it won't work right.

If you leave your computer on all the time, you should either turn the monitor off or somehow arrange to dim the screen. Since we are programmers, we sneer at the idea of dimming the monitor with the front panel controls; we solve the problem with a program.

The first program was conservative. It turned the screen entirely black and indicated that it was running by making cute noises. Plain BASIC09 can change the screen to black and make a bell-like noise, but it can't restore the original colors or make any other noises. We got the extra power we needed with the SysCall procedure.

The second program was more adventurous than the first one. It bounces a small cartoon of a Color Computer around on the screen. The image doesn't stay anywhere long enough to damage the screen, but it quietly shows that the computer is running.

We spent lots of time building the image buffer for the computer cartoon. We started with a drawing on graph paper and gradually turned it into a list of codes that BASIC09 can send to gfx2. Perhaps we learned that we don't want to do that again! PicConvert can do most of the work automatically.

PRINCIPLES

The SysCall procedure is a BASIC09 programmer's secret weapon. It brings all the power and danger of assembly language programming to BASIC09. Look through the OS-9 technical reference for a list of the system calls. You can get at all the user-mode system calls with SysCall. Notice that it is easy to get into bad trouble.

If you feel like you should be able to do something, but you can't find any way to do it with BASIC09, check the technical reference. The `SysCall` procedure gives you access to the OS-9 system calls, and every OS-9 service is available through some system call.

POSSIBLE ENHANCEMENTS

The first possible enhancement is almost required. Use a `SysCall` to get the procedure's process number and use the process number as the buffer group for `Busy`'s image buffer.

Both `Hummer` and `Busy` require full-size screens. `Busy` requires a high resolution, four-color screen. If the screen attributes are wrong, the programs will malfunction. It would be better if they checked the screen attributes and returned a friendly message if the attributes were wrong. It would be best if they changed the screen attributes. Think about opening a device window with the correct attributes.

There's nothing sacred about the CoCo icon. Can you make a little picture of yourself or a friend?

THE LISTING: `PicConvert`

```
PROCEDURE PicConvert
 0000      REM Convert a picture from characters to hex codes for bytes
 003B      REM This program works for 4-color pictures with the colors
 0075      REM represented by:
 0087      REM _   Color 0
 0094      REM X   Color 1
 00A1      REM *   Color 2
 00AE      REM $   Color 3
 00BB      DIM Pixel:BYTE
 00C2      DIM Line:STRING[320]
 00CE      DIM ThisByte:STRING[1]
 00DA      DIM i,ByteVal:INTEGER
 00E5      DIM W1Path,W2Path:BYTE
 00F0      RUN gfx2("dwprotsw","off")
 0106      OPEN #W1Path,"/w":WRITE
 0113      OPEN #W2Path,"/w":UPDATE
 0120      RUN gfx2(W1Path,"dwset",0,0,12,80,12,1,0)
 0147      RUN gfx2(W2Path,"dwset",0,0,0,80,12,1,2)
 016E      RUN gfx2(W2Path,"select")
 0181      ON ERROR GOTO 200
 0187      PRINT #W2Path,TAB(15),"Enter Picture Description"
 01AD      PRINT #W2Ppath,TAB(10),"Encoded Picture Will Appear Below"
 01DC      LOOP
 01DE        INPUT #W2Path,Line
 01E8        WHILE Line<>"" DO
 01F4          ThisByte:=LEFT$(Line,1)
 01FF          Line:=RIGHT$(Line,LEN(Line)-1)
 020F          Pixel:=0
 0216          FOR i:=0 TO 3
```

```
Ø226 1ØØ        ThisByte:=LEFT$(Line,1)
Ø234            Line:=RIGHT$(Line,LEN(Line)-1)
Ø244          EXITIF ThisByte="" THEN
Ø25Ø            IF i=Ø THEN
Ø25C              GOTO 15Ø
Ø26Ø            ELSE
Ø264              WHILE i<=3 DO
Ø27Ø                Pixel:=Pixel*4
Ø27B                i:=i+1
Ø286              ENDWHILE
Ø28A            ENDIF
Ø28C          ENDEXIT
Ø29Ø            IF ThisByte="_" THEN
Ø29D              ByteVal:=Ø
Ø2A4            ELSE IF ThisByte="X" THEN
Ø2B4                ByteVal=1
Ø2BB              ELSE IF ThisByte="*" THEN
Ø2CB                  ByteVal=2
Ø2D2                ELSE IF ThisByte="$" THEN
Ø2E2                    ByteVal=3
Ø2E9                  ELSE
Ø2ED                    PRINT #W1Path,"Invalid character in picture."
Ø313                    GOTO 1ØØ
Ø317                  ENDIF
Ø319                ENDIF
Ø31B              ENDIF
Ø31D            ENDIF
Ø31F            Pixel:=Pixel*4+ByteVal
Ø32E          NEXT i
Ø339          PRINT #W1Path USING "H2",Pixel;
Ø349        ENDWHILE
Ø34D        PRINT #W1Path
Ø353 15Ø  ENDLOOP
Ø35A 2ØØ  PRINT "Done"
Ø365      RUN gfx2(W1Path,"dwend")
Ø377      RUN gfx2(W2Path,"dwend")
Ø389      RUN gfx2("select")
Ø397      CLOSE #W1Path,#W2Path
Ø3A2      END
```

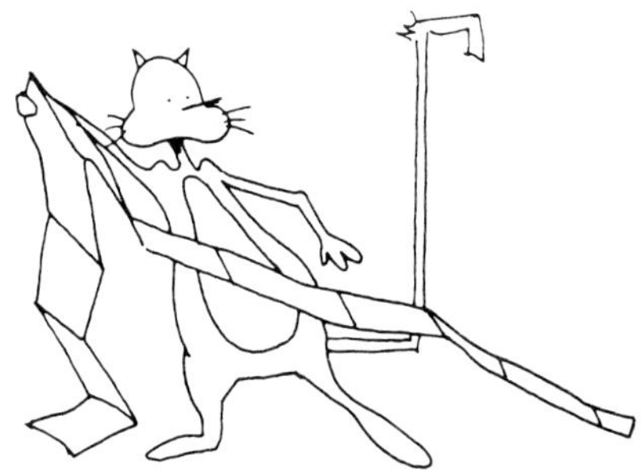

CHAPTER 17

putting it all together

We've created many useful programs. If we can hook them together they will make a nice package. A menu is called for.

There's nothing exciting about a menu. The procedure will be big, but much simpler than the programs we have been working with. Look for it at the end of this chapter. The trick is in assembling the parts after we have the menu.

PACKING AND COMBINING PROCEDURES

We have written a great deal of code. BASIC09 has to fit itself (about 24K), the program code, and the program data into 64K of memory. We have too much code for this.

BASIC09 lets us pack procedures. A packed procedure has the information that BASIC09 uses for debugging and editing removed. You don't want to pack a procedure until it is completely debugged. You particularly don't want to pack a procedure unless you have it saved to disk! Remember that a packed procedure can't be edited. If you pack a procedure without saving it first, you will have to type it in again (maybe recreate it) if you ever want to change it.

A packed procedure is smaller than the unpacked procedure it came from, but it takes a minimum of 8K of memory. Given that our procedures are mostly a few hundred bytes long, this doesn't sound like a good deal. At 8K per procedure and 24K for BASIC09, we could fit five packed procedures into BASIC09's workspace. Actually, we couldn't even fit five procedures; a program needs some space for variables.

If packed procedures take 8K each, what's the point in packing? For one thing packed procedures are a little faster than unpacked procedures. There is also a loophole in the 8K rule.

The version of OS-9 on the Color Computer allocates memory in 8K chunks. That's why packed procedures need a minimum of 8K each. The loophole is that it allocates memory to the file it is loading, not to the procedures. If we pack all our procedures into one big file, OS-9 will put them all into one chunk of memory. The combined length of the procedures we will combine is almost 16K, so 16K will be the size of their block of memory.

When you run a file containing many procedures, OS-9 will try to execute the first procedure in the file. It is happiest if the name of the first procedure is the same as the name of the file. We will put Menu at the beginning of the file and name the file Menu.

RUNB

Even with all our procedures packed into 16K, there isn't enough space for BASIC09, our procedures, and the memory they (particularly ScratchPad) need to run. RunB (at 12K) is about half the size of BASIC09. RunB and the procedures use 32K of memory, which leaves plenty for data.

OS-9 will use RunB automatically if you just type Menu. It will notice that the file, Menu, contains packed BASIC09 procedures and start RunB to interpret them. This is a good trick, but we can't use it. Without going into the details, when you use RunB this way, OS-9 gives it 4K of memory for variables. There is no easy way to get it to ask for more memory.

You will have to run RunB yourself. Start the program like this:

```
runb menu #24k
```

SOME OTHER WARNINGS

Remember that ScratchPad expects to find the standard pointers loaded. Before you run Menu, load the pointers:

```
merge /d0/sys/stdptrs
```

You should probably use the GetPid procedure at the end of

the chapter to get a buffer number for Busy. Choosing buffer number one was only acceptable as a temporary solution.

BUILDING THE MENU FILE

Basically, all we are going to do is pack all the procedures we have written into one file. In detail, there's a little more to it. It is easiest to build the menu file in pieces:

- Start a clean BASIC09 with plenty of memory (we use 32K).

- Load procedures for the ASCII programs:

```
ASCII_List
ASCII_Table
Control_Names
```

- Pack them into ASCII.chars:

```
pack* >ASCII.chars
```

- Kill the packed procedures:

```
kill*
```

- Load the procedures we used for ScratchPad: ScratchPad, Scroller, ScrollBottom, ScrollTop, ScrollXY, FileMenu, ScrollScreen, GetFName, UpdScreenData, ApplyArrow, PaintScreen, WritFile, ReadFile, QuitMenu and ClearBuf.

- Pack them into ScratchPad:

```
pack* >scratchpad
```

- Kill them:

```
kill*
```

- Load the procedures for Busy and Hummer:

```
busy
hummer
getpalette
```

- Pack them into ScreenSaver:

```
pack* >screensaver
```

- Kill them:

```
kill*
```

• Load the procedures for Calendar: Jan1, DaysInMonths, SetDateInfo, WeekDayToDate, Calendar, Get_Month_Name, PrintMonth, WeekInYear, CalcDate, PrintWeek and NewMonth.

• Pack them into Calendar:

```
pack* >calendar
```

• Kill them:

```
kill*
```

• Load the procedures for Rolladex: Rolladex, DBOpen, DBStart, DBWindow, DBInteract, DBClose, DBDispRec, DBDisplay, DBBack, DBSrch, DBUpd, DBFwd, DBReDisp, DBAdd, LShiftSet, FillSet, DBSrchSet, DBSrchFile, DBGetRec and DBEditRec.

• Pack them into Rolladex:

```
pack* >rolladex
```

• Kill them:

```
kill*
```

• Load the final version of Menu:

```
menu
```

• pack it into x:

```
pack* >x
```

• kill it:

```
kill*
```

• Change the data directory to the execution directory:

```
chd /d0/cmds
```

• Merge everything:

```
merge x ASCII_chars scratchpad screensaver calendar rolladex >menu
```

• Make Menu executable:

```
attr menu pe e
```

That's all. Now you can run Menu:

```
runb menu #24k
```

THE LISTING: GetPid

```
PROCEDURE GetPid
 0000      REM A Procedure to get a programs process id.
 002C      REM This can be used to get a graphics buffer that
 005D      REM won't get in any other program's way.
 0085      REM (Provided everyone uses their process id as their buffer
 00C0      REM number)
 00CA      TYPE registers=cc,a,b,dp:BYTE; x,y,u:INTEGER
 00EF      PARAM PId:INTEGER
 00F6      DIM regs:registers
 00FF      DIM callcode:BYTE
 0106      callcode:=$0C
 010E      RUN syscall(callcode,regs)
 011D      PId:=regs.a
 0128      END
```

THE LISTING: Menu

```
PROCEDURE Menu
 0000      DIM InputChr:STRING[1]
 000C      DIM WaitChr:STRING[1]
 0018      DIM low,high:INTEGER
 0023      DIM Keys:STRING[18]
 002F      DIM KeyNum:INTEGER
 0036
 0037      Keys:="lLaApPcCsSnNdDqQ"
 004E      REPEAT
 0050        RUN gfx2("owset",1,0,0,30,10,1,2)
 0072        PRINT "            Menu  "
 0087        PRINT " a:   Display ASCII Table"
 00A4        PRINT " l:   Display ASCII List"
 00C0        PRINT " p:   ScratchPad"
 00D4        PRINT " c:   Calender"
 00E6        PRINT " s:   Screensaver1"
 00FC        PRINT " n:   Noisy saver"
 0111        PRINT " d:   Database"
 0123        PRINT " q:   Quit"
 0131        PRINT "           Selection:  ";
 014C        GET #0,InputChr
 0155        KeyNum:=(SUBSTR(InputChr,Keys)+3)/2
 0167        RUN gfx2("owend")
 0174        ON KeyNum GOSUB 100,200,300,400,500,600,700,800,900
 019F      UNTIL KeyNum=9
 01AA      END
 01AC 100  REM Invalid selection
 01C3      RETURN
 01C5 200  REM ASCII List
 01D5      RUN gfx2("owset",1,5,3,15,2,1,3)
 01F7      INPUT "Lowbound:",low
 0208      INPUT "Highbound:",high
 021A      RUN gfx2("owend")
```

```
Ø227        RUN ASCII_List(low,high)
Ø236        GET #Ø,WaitChr
Ø23F        RETURN
Ø241  3ØØ   REM ASCII Table
Ø252        RUN ASCII_Table
Ø256        GET #Ø,WaitChr
Ø25F        RETURN
Ø261  4ØØ   REM Scratchpad
Ø271        RUN ScratchPad(ScratchState)
Ø27B        RETURN
Ø27D  5ØØ   REM Calender
Ø28B        RUN Calender
Ø28F        RETURN
Ø291  6ØØ   REM Run screensaver
Ø2A6        RUN busy
Ø2AA        RETURN
Ø2AC  7ØØ   REM run noisy screensaver
Ø2C7        RUN hummer
Ø2CB        RETURN
Ø2CD  8ØØ   REM run database
Ø2DF        RUN rolladex
Ø2E3        RETURN
Ø2E5  9ØØ   REM quit
Ø2EF        RETURN
```

POSSIBLE ENHANCEMENTS

The Menu procedure would work much better if it opened overlay windows for some of the other procedures to run in.

special items index

general index